THE
Vanguard
ARTIST

THE Vanguard ARTIST

PORTRAIT and SELF-PORTRAIT

BY

BERNARD ROSENBERG
and NORRIS FLIEGEL

CHICAGO / 1965

Quadrangle Books

Library of Congress Catalog Card Number:
65-18244
FIRST PRINTING

Designed by Vincent Torre

For REBECCA, MARION *and* WILLIAM

ACKNOWLEDGMENTS

WE ARE DEEPLY indebted to our friends, Joseph Bensman and Irving Howe, for their careful reading of this book in manuscript. Their attentiveness to infelicities of style and inconsistencies of content—which, at our own risk, we did not always revise—were coupled with understanding and encouragement from first to last. Our wives, Sarah Rosenberg and Zenia Fliegel, were as helpful—in wifely ways, and hardly less so by their scrupulous professional attention to detail and organization.

Others read parts of the manuscript, and we thank them for their unfailingly intelligent suggestions: Emanuel Geltman, editor at The Free Press; our colleagues, Melvin M. Tumin of Princeton, Lewis Coser of Brandeis, and Israel Gerver, an art expert and practitioner of parts in the U.S. Department of Health, Education and Welfare; and Ben Seligman, educational director of the Retail Clerks International Union.

We wish to thank very warmly our publishers and editors, Ivan Dee and Melvin Brisk, for the confidence they have shown in us. Their moral and financial support has been of inestimable value.

But their best intentions and ours would have been unavailing without the superb cooperation of those painters and sculptors we approached "out of the blue." Regrettably, they must remain anonymous to the reader, although anything but anonymous to the authors. If this book gives these men and women a forum, it will have served its major purpose.

Contents

INTRODUCTION   I

1 *The New York School: Emergence and Triumph*   I I
   THE MAGNETISM OF NEW YORK / THE REVOLUTION IN
   AMERICAN ART / THE BREAKTHROUGH TO INDE-
   PENDENCE

2 *Generational Conflict*   39
   THE ISOLATION OF AGE GROUPS / RESENTMENTS OF
   YOUNGER ARTISTS BY THEIR ELDERS / THE RESENT-
   MENT OF "EASY SUCCESS" / RESENTMENT OF CYNICISM
   IN THE YOUNGER GENERATION / THE DISENCHANT-
   MENT WITH POLITICS / THE EXHAUSTION OF TALENT
   AND THE FAILURE OF YOUTHFUL PROMISE / RESENT-
   MENT OF THE MARKET MENTALITY OF YOUNGER
   ARTISTS

3 *Social and Psychological Characteristics*   65
   THE ARTIST'S SELF-IMAGE / THE PERSONAL QUALITIES
   NECESSARY FOR THE TRUE ARTIST / SENSE OF RESPON-
   SIBILITY AND CAPACITY FOR WORK / INTELLIGENCE /
   SUFFERING / SENSITIVITY / FREEDOM AND INDEPEND-
   ENCE / SOLITUDE AND PRIVACY / DISCIPLINE AND
   DEDICATION / COURAGE / "EGO" / INNOCENCE / THE
   COMPOSITE SELF-PORTRAIT / TALENT, CREATIVITY AND
   "GENIUS"

4 *Origins: Familial and Cultural*   IOI

THE EARLY APPEARANCE OF TALENT / PARENTAL REC-
OGNITION AND ACCEPTANCE / PARENTAL OPPOSITION
/ EARLY EXPOSURE TO "CULTURE" / ENVIRONMENT
AND EDUCATION / SOCIO-ECONOMIC BACKGROUNDS /
EARLY FREEDOM AND THE MODEL STIMULUS / THE
ABSTRACTED MODEL AND THE OFFER OF WORK

5 *Alienation and Integration*   I43

THE ARTIST AND THE ARTISAN / ALIENATION FROM SO-
CIETY / THE DISENGAGEMENT OF THE ARTIST / THE
AFFIRMATION OF WORK / THE REJECTION OF "APPLIED
ART" / THE NEW SUCCESS AND ITS DANGERS / ARTISTIC
AUTONOMY AND PERCEPTION / REJECTION OF THE
MIDDLE CLASS LIFE / THE ARTIST AS PROPHET

6 *The Artist and His Publics: The Ambiguity of
Success*   I79

CONFRONTING SUCCESS / CONFRONTING THE "PUBLIC"
/ FRIENDS / BUYERS AND COLLECTORS / VIEWERS /
CRITICS

7 *Museums and Dealers*   2I5

THE GROWTH OF THE MARKET / THE MARKET INFLU-
ENCE ON ART STYLES / THE MUSEUM AS A PURVEYOR
OF "NOVELTY" / THE IRRELEVANCY OF TASTE IN THE
MUSEUM / ANOMIE IN STYLES OF ART / ACCEPTANCE
OF THE ART DEALER / SOCIAL AND ECONOMIC NECES-
SITY OF THE DEALER / RESENTMENT OF DEALERS

8 *Women Artists: A New Force*   25I

THE REASONS FOR FEMALE "INFERIORITY" / MALE
CHAUVINISM / PREJUDICE AGAINST FEMALE ARTISTS /
THE ROLE CONFLICT OF THE FEMALE ARTIST / THE
COSTS OF ROLE CONFLICTS

9 *The Negro Artist*   279
       THE NEGRO'S DILEMMA / ECONOMIC AND SOCIO-CUL-
       TURAL POVERTY / THE INFLUENCE OF HISTORY /
       PSYCHOLOGICAL PROBLEMS / THE BURDEN OF PERSON-
       ALITY / ADDENDUM

10 *The Artist: Inside or Outside?*   305
       MAKING DO / THE PERILS OF SUBSIDIZED ART

Appendix—   329
Creative Energy: Sexuality and Sublimation
       PSYCHOANALYTIC THEORIES OF ART / "OVERT" SEXU-
       ALITY IN ART / THE LACK OF SUBLIMATION / ENERGY,
       CREATIVITY AND QUALITY / CREATIVITY AND SEXUAL
       INDULGENCE

       NOTES   355

       INDEX   361

xi

Introduction

Why do you paint?
For exactly the same reason I breathe.
That's not an answer.
There isn't any answer.
How long hasn't there been any answer?
As long as I can remember.
I mean poetry.
So do I.
Tell me, doesn't your painting interfere with your writing?
Quite the contrary; they love each other dearly.
They're very different.
Very: one is painting and one is writing.
But your poems are rather hard to understand, whereas your paintings are so easy.
Easy?
Of course—you paint flowers and girls and sunsets, things that everybody understands.
I never met him.
Who?
Everybody.
Did you ever hear of nonrepresentational painting?
I am.
Pardon me?
I am a painter, and painting is nonrepresentational.
Not all painting.
No: housepainting is representational.
And what does a housepainter represent?
Ten dollars an hour.
In other words, you don't want to be serious.
It takes two to be serious.
Well, let's see . . . Oh, yes, one more question: where will you live after this war is over?
In China; as usual.
China?
Of course.
Whereabouts in China?
Where a painter is a poet.

—Quoted in Charles Norman, *The Magic Maker: E. E. Cummings*, New York, 1958, pp. 257-258; taken from an imaginary interview in the foreword to the catalogue of Cummings' 1945 show of paintings at the Rochester Memorial Art Gallery.

T HESE PITHY and not so whimsical lines carry much of the message we wish to convey in this book. In confronting a number of artists with questions similar to those posed by Cummings' imaginary interviewer, we received equally poetic replies.

Certain questions, notably those that have to do with the nature and causes of creativity, seem to us to be unanswerable. While skirting these questions, we attempt, extensively in one chapter and obliquely in others, to specify some of the characteristics of artistically creative people, a subject which it is always possible to embellish and embroider. In several other chapters we attempt to sketch in some of the topographical features of the "country" the artist inhabits. It should be clear that in describing the shared characteristics of creative artists, we do not imply a causal relationship between them and artistic talent and creativity.

Three years ago we set out to study the vanguard painter and sculptor in his natural American habitat, that is to say, in certain parts of New York City. We thought it important, even urgent, to enlarge our understanding of the social and psychological situation of artists at a critical moment in their history and our own. We agreed with Cummings, and with another poet, Randall Jarrell, that:

> Art matters not only because it is the most magnificent ornament and the most nearly unfailing occupation of our lives, but because it is life itself. From Christ to Freud we have believed that, if we know the truth, the truth will set us free; art is indispensable because so much of this truth can be learned through works of art and through works of art alone. . . . If, knowing all this, we say: Art has always been for the few, *we are using a truism to hide a disaster. One of the earliest, deepest, and most nearly conclusive attractions of democracy is manifested in our feeling that through it not only material but spiritual goods can be shared; that in a democracy bread and justice, education and art, will be accessible to everybody. If a democracy should offer its citizens a show of education, a sham art, a literacy more*

3

> *dangerous than their old illiteracy, then we should have to
> say that it is not a democracy at all, but one more variant of
> those "People's Democracies" which share with any true
> democracy little more than the name.*[1]

In many premodern societies, aesthetic expression was much more
widely dispersed than it now is, and as Robert N. Wilson recently
observed: "It has been hypothesized by aesthetic and literary scholars that in some era of prehistory all men were artists, or perhaps
better that each member of society had skills which permitted him
to assume the creative role at some time. The seemingly spontaneous
elaboration of the primitive dance would lend credence to this
view."[2]

For such a society, art in all its forms was an organic part of a
unified culture, utilizing symbols which by virtue of a coherent set
of common experiences were naturally meaningful to everyone. By
contrast, in modern society *art* has become the special preserve of
increasingly esoteric practitioners, created for a small audience of
aficionados who constitute their primary public. For the remaining
large majority of the public, the mass media have supplied a steady
flow of "sham" art, in which the calculated manipulation of symbols evokes pseudo-aesthetic responses. The numbing effect of this
barrage of stimulation has been much discussed, as have the resistance
and suspicion which develop in persons subjected to it. Those over-
exposed to mass culture are either completely deadened by it or,
being suspicious of all messages, finally respond to *no* message. Thus
the artist who wishes to reach a wider public meets with attitudes
appropriate to viewing television commercials, but not for appre-
hending his message. Yet as work declines everywhere in the
Western world, especially in the United States, it is replaced by
more mass culture; if physical labor exhausts fewer people, television stupefies more of them. Finding an alternative to work is the
need that presses in upon us. We believe that art could be such an
alternative. As we enter a new post-industrial age, with more and
more "leisure" time, the possibility of restoring art to its old centrality—but this time on entirely different foundations—offers itself
as a hope. If every man cannot be an artist, the contemplation of
art may still be available to every man.

To us art has this potential to be a critically important force in our social reality. It is not indispensable to life (only food, drink, and shelter are); the individual can survive without it, but only by diminishing himself so that ultimately he is less than a full man. This diminution is the dreadful prospect that confronts us at just that point in history when growth and transcendence may be within man's reach.

We believe that art enhances man, that it is life-giving, and that the artist, while less than a paragon, is something of an exemplar— from whom we have much to learn. There is no better way of learning from him than by going directly to him, a task we jointly decided to undertake. For us the experience was pleasant and edifying; our findings are offered to readers because we want to share that experience. Our objective can be attained only if we give the artist the spotlight, permitting him to speak as much as possible for himself. The body of this book is therefore made up of straight quotations, of artists speaking to us; what they have to say is surrounded by our own sociological and psychological analysis. If the latter is subordinate to the former, it is above all because we do not wish to replace the picture with the frame. What follows, then, is the beginning of a beginning of what might be learned through our methods from and about the contemporary artist.

Our data derive from unstructured, informal, depth or focused interviews. We mapped out certain themes whose exploration was designed to test a number of hypotheses implicitly and explicitly formulated in the literature about artists. Following no particular sequence, we took care to cover the same topics in each interview, hoping by indirection to elicit spontaneous responses, asking direct questions only when necessary, letting the discussion flow freely wherever it promised to be revealing. In every case we encountered an initial awkwardness—but this was quickly overcome, and with our tape recorder on, we three chatted for at least two hours. Afterwards there was invariably more talk, much of it as fascinating as the interview proper. At no point was it terribly formal, a fact we ascribe to the presence of three people. A tandem interview, in which one man spells another, picking up leads his colleague may miss, turned out to be ideal for our purposes. Indeed, after this experience we would not dream of doing an interview for research purposes in any other way. The air of informality produces something, happily, much more like conversation than interrogation.

We can say for our part that the conversation was good. The artists were guaranteed anonymity; there was no question of our quarreling with them; we were engaged in a common quest for knowledge. We got on swimmingly. There was none of the friction that exists in an academic setting where "humanists" are pitted against "scientists" in a mutual and irrational state of hostility. We anticipated that some of our respondents would protest against outsiders encroaching on their domain. None did. Apparently, interpreters, more than creators, worry about the likes of us laying hands on their subject matter. Actually, those who have ventured into the sociology or the social psychology of art and artists know that they endear themselves to nobody in Academia: if the humanist regards them as trespassers, the social scientist regards (and dismisses) them as humanists. To our delight, this problem never arose among the artists we spoke to—perhaps because they are not academicians in any sense of the word.

Who are they, and what are they? And how many of them did we reach? They are, in the first instance, successful painters and sculptors, men and women who enjoy a full measure of acceptance from their most respected peers and critics. Starting from a master list of fifty, we contacted and interviewed twenty-nine artists, of whom seven were women. Five of the twenty-nine were primarily sculptors (including two who specialized in "junk"), five were more or less realistic painters, and the rest were abstract expressionists. The study, begun late in 1961 and completed in 1962, took place before the full surge toward Pop Art. A year or two later we should certainly have sought out such painters as Jasper Johns and Robert Rauschenberg, for our intention was to report on the New York School. That school in 1961-62 spelled abstract expressionism more than it does today. Rapid shifts are part and parcel of the contemporary art scene, and they are dealt with as we go along.

We made no attempt to secure a representative cross section of American artists. To do so would be indispensable to survey research, a technique which has its uses—but they are not ours. We do not envy the statistician who seeks to quantify, with immaculate validity and reliability, a unit of study as amorphous as that of "artists." The insuperable barrier to that enterprise might well be definition. Is every man who so designates himself an artist? Should the Sunday painter be included? Is the sculptor who never had a show, but may be a genius working away in obscurity, to be excluded? A random sample is impossible precisely because no faithful census could ever be made of artists. There was no point, we thought, in trying to cut through this definitional and statistical thicket.

Yet we may lay claim to a certain kind of sample, one sometimes called a *purposive sample.* We had heard much about alienation and the artist and suspected that that dreary topic would almost certainly have a bearing on our study. If so, and no matter what alienation might mean, we wanted to control for its presence among artists embittered by failure. If successful artists were alienated, their condition could not be a by-product of sour grapes. Therefore we decided to include only successful artists, those held in high esteem by their peers and by "men of good taste" in the art world. We consulted a great art historian and a fine arts critic, and they gave us guidance. Consequently, while we did not interview "all the best artists in New York," none we did interview are unfamiliar to those who take an interest in contemporary art, most are prospering financially, and all are "established." If we discovered that any of them were unhappy, uneasy, uncomfortable, or worse, it could not be for the usual reasons—those that stem from resentment based on grinding poverty and gross neglect.

These artists are alike in many ways. For the most part they eloquently affirm one creed, some so eloquently that we often felt they could as easily be poets as painters or sculptors. Their responses were varied but patterned—along sexual, generational, sociological, and other lines. And yet it is possible to speak of a composite portrait that we have striven to create in this book. Readers should not be put out by the underrepresentation of old-fashioned social realists. We know that in certain predictable reactions they differ from the majority of our artists. They would look back with more nostalgia on WPA, and they would be more favorably disposed to government support of the creative arts in our time. They dislike the work of their successors and would in all probability denounce it as fraudulent. With all that, we are confident that their social situation and the feelings it arouses, their problems, attitudes, and impulses are much the same as those of the artists they despise. The fraternity is divided, but it is a fraternity.

And what of alienation? The word appears as part of a chapter title, but scarcely anywhere in the text do we refer directly to the phenomenon. It does, however, deserve some discussion.

Alienation has by now come to mean both too much and too little. It is threadbare from overuse by those who have shorn the idea of all conceptual clarity. We nevertheless find it valuable to distinguish three of the innumerable meanings currently attached to alienation:

1. Alienation in the Marxist sense—which means alienation from, and detestation of, one's work.

2. Alienation in the sense of powerlessness, a feeling that neither one's destiny nor that of the world can be controlled.

3. Alienation as a repudiation of dominant values; in our case, values associated with money and the "good things that money will buy" in a pecuniary civilization.

If we limit ourselves to these three meanings, how does the kind of artist we have studied shape up on the first score, alienation from work? We may say that he does not qualify at all. No one is less alienated than a painter at work in his studio. More than the rest of us he derives satisfaction and fulfillment from his work. Marx thought that under the capitalist organization of production, industrial operatives became alienated; that with the complex division of labor, a proletariat emerged and exhausted itself in monotonous and meaningless labor. In our time, most of us have been proletarianized: clerical workers now outnumber factory workers, and they have no more love for their work than any other interchangeable part in the vast impersonal machine which modern society has become. Marx himself, in his early manuscripts, always made an exception of the artist as "unalienated man" *par excellence*. He is more than ever that exception, and Marx's youthful vision of the good society as a community of artists, of free men autonomously going about their business of self-actualization, is more than ever the appropriate vision.

What of alienation as a sense of powerlessness? Here there is a mixed picture: the artist, on our evidence, would have to be rated plus and minus, yes and no. He feels as impotent as most men to determine the course of world-historical events, to share significantly in decisions that others will make about war and peace, nuclear weapons, or other less weighty political affairs quite beyond his control. On the other hand, as we try to show in the chapter titled "Alienation and Integration," the artist is a man convinced that through his art he achieves much mastery over himself, and by touching the consciousness of others changes the world.

The ideal typical artist is fully alienated in the third sense: he repudiates those values which exalt money, fiercely denying that beyond a necessary minimum of creature comforts it can be used to buy good things.

We would argue that the artist, in order not to be alienated from his work, must be alienated from the dominant commercial values of his civilization. For as long as American artists knew that financial success was unattainable, the issue was clear-cut. Now such success is attainable, a change which disrupts everything that appeared to be settled for so long. We have chosen to make this change a major pivot of our study, and it hovers over every line in the book. Other things, for another book, have had to be slighted or omitted.

This, therefore, is not a total picture of living artists. We should like to have dealt more with their styles of life, their peer-group associations, their movement uptown and subsequent spatial distribution. But first things first. The new climate, the new avidity for new art, the new success, its threats and temptations: these struck us as of the first importance.

We confess to a bias in favor of these artists who made our work a delight. At best, with their full complement of human faults, they embody man as a free, spontaneous, and ungovernable spirit. There is nothing more precious than that spirit, nor more in danger of extinction in this age of the locusts.

1

The New York School: Emergence and Triumph

Though painting power, along with so much other power, came to America in the Forties, there was still no money. But a painter like Willem de Kooning, America's most famous and most highly rewarded *avant-garde* painter, looks back regretfully to the period. He appreciates his greater current success and his money, but he felt more reality then, more security, more exuberance.

—MARVIN ELKOFF, 1965

To CONDUCT our interviews we never left the city of New York, or for that matter the island of Manhattan. Within its confines most American art takes shape, and there that art comes to be known or not—as the case may be. It has always been a center for painters and sculptors, but no one foresaw twenty years ago that New York would become *the* world art center. Of course, young artists of an earlier day flocked to the big city from their homes in the hinterlands. Yet, for those who were truly ambitious, New York was merely a way station en route to Paris, the city where talent was appreciated, wholesomely fed, nourished, brought to a fine bloom, and appropriately rewarded. But by the 1960's, as for some little while before, we feel no great shock when a painter living in New York dismisses Paris as an artistic suburb of his city. One could scarcely have found an American artist, no matter how patriotic, ethnocentric, and arrogant, who until recently would have made such a claim. There is now nothing outlandish about it. What Paris, London, Rome, and Athens were, New York is.

For better or worse this radical, and perhaps momentary, change has taken place in the years following World War II. Ironically enough, these were the same years in which New York lost large parts of its upper and lower middle class who fell over themselves in a headlong flight to suburbia. True, the very wealthy—among them many patrons—remained in force, side by side with the poor but employed working class and an increasingly sullen and resentful *lumpenproletariat*. As the landscape was defaced by barbarous architecture, while solid citizens departed, marginal wage earners seethed in rotting ghettos, and interracial tension reached an all-time peak— art came into its own, labeled FOB New York. The new mood is expressed as follows: "I'm absolutely appalled at how little innate French art there is. Wherever you go, you see the American influence. Why, even in Japan they imitate Franz Kline." New York art may be said to have swept the civilized world. It has penetrated the Iron Curtain, thriving openly if permitted, going underground only when necessary, flourishing with every thaw. Lately, international prize-winning work tends either to be made in or derived

13

from the New York School. At least for the historical moment, a traditional *arrière-garde,* which timidly followed its European betters, has been transformed into the *avant-garde* that confidently leads all others. So great is this dominance that it can apparently cause Pop Art no less than Action Painting to prosper abroad.

THE MAGNETISM OF NEW YORK

Everyone knows that the Armory Show of 1913 was a major turning point for the American sensibility. However, there was a later, more thoroughgoing change, deemed by those who participated in it to be nothing less than a revolution. Before this revolution of abstract expressionism, or action painting, New York was artistically insignificant; since the revolution it is pre-eminent. We will presently deal with this phenomenon as living artists recollect it. The question remains: why New York? Why the artist's present preference for that churning metropolis? Let us consider one or two reasons. Elsewhere we explore some more.

A distinguished foreign-born artist says:

> *This question came up a few days ago at Harvard where I gave a couple lectures. People got up and asked me why I liked New York. They said, "Look at us. We have caves, we have grounds, we have woods, we have fields. Isn't it wonderful! Why the hell do you live in New York?" So, I said, "Well, to be quite frank, I think you're sick. More than any city I know, New York is human. Absolutely! You know why? Because, it's dirty, it's cut up, it's rough, it stinks. You couldn't really put anything into New York. All our human qualities are there already. So New York is utterly chaotic and neurotic, and I personally cannot imagine living anywhere else. I'm happy here. I wouldn't leave for anything in the world. If you offered me, say, a supervisory position or whatever, maybe a chance to settle down in Europe, I would refuse it. And I know most of my colleagues would.*

Having learned English abroad by reading American literature and viewing Hollywood films, he set out, upon reaching these shores, to see the whole country, crossing it ten times by car: "I was very curious about America. I passionately wanted to know what made it tick. Oh, I traveled a lot, with all sorts of sidesteppings and side-trackings." But he always came back to New York. There, amid all the clangor and excitement, he found the greatest peace, and as he also puts it, "the maximum possibility of projecting oneself." "An insufferable month" in San Antonio was too much for him:

> *When I came back, I said to my lawyer, "I have just re-turned from a village of cannibals, nice sweet cannibals." Now, I don't want to be rude, but the experience was really horrifying. I couldn't spit without hitting a retired military man. I realize Texas isn't the United States, but I don't be-lieve it's possible to match New York anywhere else, the special atmosphere, with all the chaos and madness—where an artist can discover himself, become himself, and remain himself.*

"Chaotic" and "neurotic" as positive terms applied to the (like-wise positive) "madness" of New York City do not occur with great frequency in artists' dialogue. They do, however, convey much the same meaning as "ferment," "effervescence," and "stimulation" —code words to be taken in the most complimentary sense. The hurly-burly that drives others out of New York is precisely what attracts artists to it, the more so as proper middle class people evacuate the premises, leaving a tiny minority of wealthy families and an army of the poor. The more urban life crackles with for-bidding electric currents which frighten a timid bourgeoisie into the outskirts of town, the more artists are at home. With formal re-spectability so far removed, "out there" somewhere, the great city becomes a better place in which to make aesthetic revolutions. The middle class exodus was an invitation to painters and sculptors who could now breathe more freely among their own kind in an environ-ment which, though filled with latent and actual violence, was yet more tranquil than one dominated by middle class virtue.

If it is comforting to have fellow artists nearby and to have cultural resources at hand, it is also of the utmost importance that in New York an artist can make himself into an anchorite. The city provides exposure, "maximum projectability"—and an available cur-tain of concealment. In the forties and fifties, but less so today in the backwash of revolution, an artist could plunge into the social maelstrom or escape from it with equal ease:

> *It's not hard to be a hermit in New York, and there were times when we all became hermits. I mean I have a telephone. I use it to call out. I also have signals so that friends can get through, but not just casual callers. Getting away from the kooks, and at times from everyone, is a big thing. It's tougher now than ten years ago, but some of us are pretty resourceful.*

A painter contends that, "You have to *drench* yourself in the current scene, and *then* get away," and that neither immersion nor escape is easily achieved outside New York. Like most, she has tried other places to see if they would do, and visited many more, but all were wanting in what New York alone seemed to provide. Speaking respectfully of a town with 200,000 inhabitants in which, to her surprise, she met twelve good painters, the urban artist praises her provincial acquaintances by conceding that they were very intense while complaining that "they all had certain peculiar characteristics." Such as? "Well, you could see they were all influenced by reproductions, not by originals. Every bit of their work had a greyish look, like reproductions. I just told these artists that they would have to come to New York and actually go to shows."

The ahistorical cast and the contemporaneity of New York fascinate some of its most faithful artistic denizens. Thus: "I like New York because it's abstract and not bogged down with history or a lot of old ruins. The artist comes here and feels free. I think the main reason is that he isn't pulled back. He can go on." Another painter, whose origins were in the Midwest, speaks of the "terrible attachment" he once had to the life of his home town, and that for a long time he remembered only its poetic aspects. While still nostalgic for the old and familiar, highly romanticized surroundings of his childhood, he resisted "big city life" and then found himself falling under its spell. He now holds that: "In New York we artists become part of the landscape, part of all the problems that plague everyone, really part of our time, the essential part." Yet another artist, a New Yorker since 1936 when he left his birthplace in the Southwest, elaborates a common theme:

Visually, New York has almost no history. It has lots of old buildings, but you see them abstractly, color against color, sizes and forms against sizes and forms. I accepted all this in New York from the very beginning, much as one accepts mountains and canyons and cliffs in the country I came from. The buildings and the narrow streets never bothered me. I loved New York from the time I arrived, and I've never even liked any other city I've ever been in.

In addition to the contemporaneity of New York, there is its intellectuality. Even a landscape painter, for whom nature is of the first importance, spends only his summers in wide open spaces, getting his fill, drinking it all in, and then coming back home to New York for ten months of every year:

Here in the city I work on my ideas. I see what other people are doing, and I sort of work myself up into a frenzy in order to bring my painting to its full potential. At a certain point I have to become very reflective, very quiet, very contemplative about something so that it can become subject matter for painting. I'm no action painter. I can't generate paintings out of art history the way some artists can. I feel very dependent on visual stimulus.

There are, then, emotional, perceptual, and intellectual needs which a little bit of the country and a great deal of the city most satisfactorily gratify. They constitute the magnet that draws artists irresistibly to New York and holds most of them in that city. Few Americans are as rooted as they. A glance at census data on mobility from city to city and state to state within the United States is enough to convince any detached observer that, as a people, we suffer from St. Vitus's dance. Artists, in this sense, are more stable than most of their countrymen. Their restlessness seldom takes them for long (or very far) outside the city. Other places, on their collective testimony, bore, depress, and disorient them. There are defectors who leave for good and others who never arrive. They are the rare birds who do not flock together, unlike most of the best of them who do.

It is the proximity or availability of fellow artists, not constant association with them, that makes New York different. The company is potentially congenial; the right people are not far off; but they can always be kept at arm's length. One chooses to be sociable or not. In smaller, less cosmopolitan cities, there is no such option, and men tend to suffer from enforced isolation or enforced and artificial gregariousness. Most of America outside New York—except for summer colonies established by artists, and abandoned by them as tourists follow—is understood to be *Winesburg, Ohio* and *Middletown*, writ large:

> *Well, I can't concentrate in the country. I'm so easily bored with the people who live out there. I can't relate to them or something. There aren't many artists around, and those who are have to live a pretty bourgeois life. You have to call people up, you know, stay in constant communication. Here in New York you just step out on the street, and you can either take it or leave it, go visit people or stay home. The freedom's fantastic . . . I left Illinois in 1940, and I've never been back. You can judge from that . . .*

The contemporary artist is characteristically more conscious of history, at least art history, than any of his Western predecessors. It is therefore no surprise that he should so often couch his preference for New York in historical terms. Hence:

> *It's clear from the whole history of our civilization that you need a metropolitan environment to create art, or anyway, to create a* school *of art. There are exceptions like present-day Italy where you have a bit of art activity in Milano, a bit in Venice, a bit of it in Rome, even a very little bit in Bologna. But certainly in France, in England, and in America, and in Germany, too, it's all centered in one big city.*

And there is this afterthought: "New York is chaotic, and artists are attracted to chaotic places. The country is very unchaotic." Do artists absolutely need a place like New York? "Well,, it hasn't happened for a long, long time that some guy came out of the woods with a full-blown body of important works."

If we mull over the claim that an urban environment is necessary to the creation of *schools* of art, we are better able to understand the celebration of New York as an art center and to apprehend a

18

significant undercurrent of dissatisfaction with what is happening now in this city. For the excitement and vitality of New York are connected with a revolution, the creation of a new school which took place rather quietly in the forties and more spectacularly in the fifties.

European capitals are said to have languished just as New York enjoyed its greatest spurt of creative energy:

> *I visited Paris, London, Rome, Madrid, southern Spain. Paris was typical. I found that it was like the fatigued people. Artists painted, of course—they don't stop that even if there's a revolt next door—but they were tired, running out of proper ideas. You still see a kind of professionalism. That's what remains at the fingertips when everything else goes.*

A new note is sounded by those who say that such invidious comparisons are no longer valid. They agree that fatigue has overcome other cities, that New York was wonderfully immune to it "while things were happening," when it was "exciting and provided real incentive," well before this decade which "has made the city sort of static and dead." Consequently, the artist once stimulated by New York may remain within its environs only out of inertia: "I'm used to it and entrenched in it. We own a house. My friends are here." But the old magic is gone: "Ten years ago it was essential, if you wanted to be an abstract painter, not to go to Paris but to be in New York and see what was going on and go to the bars and hear the talk, and go to the studios and to all the shows. I don't feel that way anymore." What has changed, and why is it bad? "Well, I think that now New York is full of duties and manners. And instead of seeing twenty artists, we see hundreds. Instead of a few too many relationships that are meaningless, there is a potential for thousands."

So quantity takes its toll, falsifying some and diluting other personal relationships. To have very many relationships is necessarily to attenuate them all. Only limited segments of personality ever touch each other. Depth is sacrificed to partial contact; responses become mechanical. In short (and at worst), an artist's life among innumerable artists gets to be as impersonal as that of any other city man.

If a swarm of artists produces impersonality, so of course does the marketplace which relentlessly displaces people as it swells and expands. New York is not what it used to be in the glory days for artists who object to a speculative, exploitative, investment-minded orientation which causes "a Rembrandt to bring $2,300,000—and that doesn't mean a bloody thing except a kind of commercial madness."

Meanwhile, the New York School of art keeps going triumphantly around the world, making conquests for the art and for the city which those closer to both may view with more misgivings. The spirit abroad is clearly expressed by two Englishmen, Andrew Forge and David Sylvester, in a discussion prompted by an exhibition of American art at the Tate Gallery in London: *54/64—Painting and Sculpture of a Decade*.[1] Forge remarks:

> *The overriding impression was of the enormous variety and also the enormous compactness of the American situation— the feeling one has that everybody knows about everybody else's painting and that there is a kind of running commentary going on within each work. This creates a very concentrated and electric ambience: the least inflection that an individual artist puts into it counts and has repercussions and echoes which other people can pick up and use. And that's exactly what now seems to have evaporated from the Parisian scene. . . .*
>
> *The interesting thing about the way in which England comes out of this confrontation is that one feels (perhaps over-optimistically, perhaps prematurely) that this kind of concentration of atmosphere is just beginning to build up here.*

Artists on the scene in New York confirm this impression, but they change the tense: "Just ten years ago most of the painters around here *were* very very close. Not that they were all painting alike or in the same way. They were quite diverse in every sense of the word. Now, the work has scattered, become international, moved out." And the old intimacy is gone, replaced by "publicity and promotion." The compactness and variety that provoke admiration and a touch of envy in London may already be on their way out in

New York. But whatever the time-lag in perceiving a reality that changes even as one observes it, something perfectly extraordinary, unheralded, and unprecedented did take place in New York. What happened, in a nutshell, as an old hand suggested to us, is that: "Finally, we had a milieu, with all its ramifications, all its complexities." And what did that mean? His answer is explosive: "Why, it meant that there was money to be made, there was love to be distributed, there was rejection to anticipate. There were all these things, and out of them came something challenging and marvelous. I mean, you couldn't sit still. You couldn't go to sleep. They wouldn't let you."

THE REVOLUTION IN AMERICAN ART

After WPA came the war, and with it a new style, indeed a new school whose exponents and avatars created the full artistic milieu America had never known before. It is not easy to reconstruct the events which led to this notable development. Every narrative account we have studied is flawed by tendentiousness: in evaluating current and recent art, the historian tends to be either selectively attentive or harshly inattentive. No doubt we are still too close to these events to form a disinterested view of them. Nevertheless, objective data do emerge from a brief chronicle like that of the art critic Hilton Kramer, who has mixed feelings about his subject:

> *Abstract Expressionism came out of the war years of the forties when the energies and ideas of the thirties were turned to other purposes. An impulse that derived from a sense of community enterprise was now focused entirely on the preoccupations of the self adrift in its own consciousness. What remained of the thirties ideology was the Marxian sense of history now perversely transmuted into an aesthetic teleology that could only be realized by the individual artist pressing some tiny fragment of his education and disappointed hope—to the brink of dissolution, and thereby vindicating his separate identity as a creative force. The crucial shift was from an impulse more or less socialist in spirit to one that fell back on the resources of the self with an exis-*

tential dolor and intensity. The war dissipated not only the optimism of the thirties but any usable sense of connection with society at large. The presence in New York during the war of a large number of European modernists (Léger, Miró, Mondrian, Lipchitz, Ernst, Breton, and others), themselves cut off from their native milieux and abstracted from everything but their styles and careers, created a synthetic art-centered culture that isolated many American artists from the social expectations of the thirties, forcing each man to become the lonely agent of his own development. Many of the artists who started out in the thirties feeling they were on the side of history discovered in the forties that it was enough, if it was not indeed preferable, to be on the side of art history, even if that seemed to be leading into an ever narrower corridor of the mind.[2]

Whether the corridor was narrower or broader is an open question, a matter of taste, which requires us at least in these pages to weasel a bit and invoke the questionable maxim: *de gustibus non disputandum est.* That the corridor was new is more generally accepted, but it too may be challenged. There are those who stoutly maintain that everything of value in Abstract Expressionism and its many variations can be found in the earlier work of Kandinsky, Braque, Klee, Mondrian, and half a dozen other modernists. It is always thus with "revolutions": some unfailingly see them as total changes, others as mere manifestations of the same old thing, *corsi, ricorsi.* It is always possible to demonstrate that much can be said for both sides, that here as elsewhere there are elements of continuity and of discontinuity. Nothing exemplifies this dualism better than the presence and influence of great European artists who left Europe for awhile and found temporary refuge in New York City. American artists learned something from them, but the lesson is far from simple. We can say, for instance, that a truly native but non-regional art arose hereabouts just as contact with Europe was cut off. Yet, at the same time, contact came to be closer than ever because important European artists abruptly appeared in our midst. And the impact they made derived no less from their physical presence than from the work they did. The man Léger set one kind of example, his paintings another. Both were suddenly available on one's doorstep for the first time—and not only to emulate but to reject as well. The artistic results may be judged good, bad, or indifferent, but to American artists of the time the net effect was one of bracing liberation.

The war produced a great dislocation which by itself—according to more than one older artist—helped to free the whole American psyche. Artists in this country felt greater confidence in their own work as they rubbed shoulders with some of Europe's most gifted painters and sculptors:

> *It wasn't so much their work, because the European artists came to America and continued to do what they had done in Europe. It was their way of life that influenced us. You see, they were professional artists. Most of us were not. We earned our living a dozen different ways. They were well-known artists who came here and lived on their success—which gave us the idea—we really hadn't thought of it before—that one could be an artist and nothing else.*

Here was something to think about: the idea of being a full-time artist. American painters, once they were surrounded with men who embodied the idea, were quick to learn it. Startled at first, they presently began to ask, "Why not?" (Just so, European and Latin American academics have learned from Fulbright scholars that there can be such a thing as "the full-time professor." Many and mysterious are the ways of acculturation.)

The refugee artists personified independence, an attractive trait which Americans set out to imitate. At the same time, these "great personages" from abroad turned out to be human—all too human:

> *As the war began, New York City filled up with European artists. Most of them had fled from Hitler. It was rather disillusioning to meet them, or rather, it cut them off their pedestal. For example, X.Y. told me that he and Gorky and a whole group of abstract painters were awed by Léger, you know, from a distance, in 1938. Then Léger came to America, and X.Y. said everyone stood around with bated breath. Léger had this palette, and he picked up a brush, and stuck*

it into red paint and put some on the canvas. They all looked at each other and said, "But, that's just like us." The same thing happened when Max Ernst was here. These men were myths to us as long as they were in Paris, and the myths were overpowering. Once they got here, we could really take their measure.

Cutting the European myths down to size, seeing their human dimensions, dispelling the aura, made the task American artists were about to undertake seem less incredible. About this, too, they were emboldened to ask, "Why not?" and furthermore, "Why not now? We can tackle the problem ourselves. You don't have to be superhuman. They're not, and look how far they've gone." Their disillusionment gave New York artists a kind of perspective by incongruity. It was an eye-opening experience which motivated and invigorated.

There is more to the story. For one thing, these Europeans descended upon the American scene just as WPA art trailed off and terminated. A vacuum existed with the removal of government subsidy, and no one knew exactly what would replace it. Neither the Great Art Public nor the Affluent Society nor the Cold War, which would soon transform everything, had yet been clearly foreshadowed. So:

The war did bring all those Paris painters, and some from Rome and Berlin. We saw that they were men. They had problems not terribly different from ours. But the big thing was that they were involved in daring to live their own lives. They weren't waiting for any government to solve their problems, and there was no reason—or we began to feel there was none—for us to wait.

Having French artists in America helped to liberate New York artists from that "previous state of dependency" on French art of which they were so acutely aware. By the same token, it helped to liberate them from a previous, if short-lived, state of dependency on the United States government. In just a few years, for as long as the WPA Arts Project lasted, they had become habituated to a barely adequate form of support—and its loss left them somewhat bewildered. Unexpectedly joined by exemplary Frenchmen, American painters and sculptors decided to strike out on their own. Even the Surrealists had done it; in fact, they were right here doing it now! Again, the Surrealist influence was twofold: in art style, of course, but quite as much in life style:

> *Although we knew something about Surrealism, we didn't really understand the life of the Surrealist. When Ernst and Breton and some of the others came to this country, they established a relationship to society, to the* petit bourgeois *world, which we had never really seen before. A lot that has come to life in American art over the last twenty years was strongly influenced by Surrealism. I know Clement Greenberg and some other critics think Cubism was more important, but I don't think so, and neither do most of my friends. Surrealism was a very big element, both in a technical sense and I would say even more so in the attitude that Surrealists had toward life around them.*

The question of influence is enormously complex, as any art historian would be the first to tell us, for who, if not he, scours the source material and cudgels his brain over this question? Yet probably we could agree that for influence to work smoothly and directly, a favorable climate, one hospitable to innovation, must first exist. There was such a climate in the 1940's, and it had been emerging for some time.

One respondent, who lived through it all, goes so far as to argue that Léger, Miró, Mondrian, and Hofmann (the only one to stay) were more at home in the United States than they had been in Europe. He tells the story of Mondrian, who when he saw his first specimens of New York art soon after coming to America, exclaimed, "But this is exactly like me, as if I had done it!" He doubts that these artists were then as fully accepted in Paris as they were in New York. The mutual shock of recognition that took place can be explained historically, but in economic terms one may say that French art production eclipsed the American by far, while American art consumption had for some time exceeded that of France. Long before the climactic confrontation, says a knowledgeable respondent:

> *We were buying and showing French art more than they*

> *were in Paris. When I went to Paris in the forties, you
> couldn't even see a Picasso. You couldn't see a Matisse. You
> came and saw them here. The truth is that we have in
> America today the wealth of all the painting that was pro-
> duced from 1840 on up. That's what has made the differ-
> ence.* We actually transported the culture to this country. *The
> Louvre couldn't find a good example of Seurat when they
> needed one. A Chicago collector had to give it to them. The
> Barnes Foundation has seventy-six of the finest Cézannes,
> 126 Renoirs that Barnes started buying in 1902. Every other
> collector in America was buying up the Impressionists. It
> actually began with Mary Cassatt. Anyway, young American
> painters came in contact with the contemporary scene.*

With such extended preparation yielding a total state of receptivity, American art could assimilate an influence at first hand that
had, after all, never been terribly remote. And the propitiousness
of it! Many American artists, recalling how they felt then, speak of
a halt that had just been called, a stoppage and a re-examination,
an interregnum spanning the time it took for a collective sensibility
to move toward new aesthetic statements. There was much talking
and writing and a virtual suspension of painting, the reflective period
immediately antecedent to starting afresh. In pooh-poohing the
chauvinism characteristic of people who belatedly celebrate contemporary American art, a painter unintentionally casts a bit of light on
the origins of that art. He asserts that "there was a great will to
achieve autonomy for American painting. It lasted and grew after
the war. I mean, it was related to the post-war American feeling of
power. It had to do with winning the war and becoming the dominant country. It seeped down to the artists, and I think they decided
it was the American Century for them, too." Whether they see the
change as a complete rupture with the past, or nothing more than
the fruition of tendencies long aborning, everyone feels that the
times provided a mighty upsurge. American art made its breakthrough to a new perception of reality, and soon after, American
artists came into their own as world figures.

Many things had to simmer before they came to a boil in New
York. Arshile Gorky, accurately identified by one post-Revolutionary

painter as "the daddy of that group," is said to have had to re-capitulate the whole history of modern art before he became his own master: "He started with Cézanne and worked his way through early Picasso, Cubism, later Picasso, synthetic Cubism, and then Miró. Finally, he painted in his own abstract manner." Similarly, Jackson Pollock, another "daddy of that whole group," who is credited by an older painter with having "really put our art on the scale that we now know it," is also classified as "a direct descendant of Mondrian. In other words, Mondrian provided reason—to the point of being unreasonable about it. That's the paradox about Mondrian, that he had a madness about reason. What Pollock did was acquire that reason straight from Mondrian. So he could go directly to the madness. It was the other side of Mondrian. His colors and everything else, all over, are the pattern of Mondrian." Despite the allegedly clear lineage, there is in this observation no intention to detract from Pollock's achievement: a descendant is after all not a twin. Non-objective art surely antedates Abstract Ex-pressionism by several decades. There is abundant reason to view the latter as a variant of the former. All the same, our informant thinks that Pollock made a tremendous difference. He gives the American innovators their due, modestly omitting himself. ("De Kooning, too. He's a terrific craftsman. The way that man handles a brush, it looks as if it got there by some force other than his hands.") Speaking of the European forerunners:

> *They didn't give automatism the importance Pollock ulti-mately gave it. In terms of actual technique, of spontaneity, or urgency, of the livingness that finally came about, you can hardly exaggerate the role our group played.*

No one could have anticipated how successfully that role would be played. It had to be acted out against the backdrop of regional and provincial art, art whose narrow social content hardly allowed for the universalism that abstractionists began to seek. They not only had to reverse their own field, which must have been the most difficult wrench of all, they had to defy the gods of American artistic taste—all the while absorbing and recasting the European influence, now not from afar but up close. They thereby created the New York School—and out of it came the whole distinctively American scene. A sculptor who looks with satisfaction on what he and his confrères helped to bring forth, tells us:

> I suppose we were the originators, or maybe I should say the developers, the men with the ideas that began to make us different from the European artists—and different from the American artists who were more provincial. It really all came out of that group in the early forties: Motherwell, De Kooning, Rothko, Gottlieb, and some sculptors like Lassau and Hare and myself.

At the time this movement was born, its midwives felt that something uncanny and almost miraculous had happened. Now they can look back upon it as necessary, predetermined, perhaps inevitable. According to one theory, whatever its genesis:

> An art movement is like a picture: at a certain point the parts fall into place, and then it's all right. The picture is there. It's done. The picture will succeed if certain psychological and social conditions are just right for that specific thing. Or you may get an anticipation of that psychological moment within which the picture will fit. And that's exactly what happens in art history. It has nothing so much to do with momentary opposition as it has to do with a specific need at a given time.

Many artists, then, who made a revolution which once seemed to them to be fantastic, now relive it or review it as if they were determinists: the times called for their art—and they responded in full vigor. There was nothing conscious or deliberate about it: "The paintings we did fulfilled a social need, but we never had to consider that need, because, you see, it corresponded to our inner need."

Recapturing the excitement of "this American Revolution in painting" that he observed at close quarters, an artist otherwise parsimonious in his praise exults, "These people were big and strong and intelligent enough to find themselves, to make their break and stick with it." He notes that:

> They had to paint, and they painted, moving gradually from one bad picture to a better picture, and so on. Finally, they

resolved certain philosophical, I should say moral and ethical, problems—and achieved one glorious moment of discovery. They found little truths, their own personal truths. That's what made them continue to do things that were called ridiculous. They were not appreciated—and it didn't matter any more than success and fame do now. All that's peripheral; it's society's, not theirs.

Who were these men, bent so strenuously on furthering their vision? "Well, the Impressionists were young guys. The Cubists were young. We were almost all old guys." If not really old guys neither were they very young. The best of them had created a comfortable niche for their work, which they need not have abandoned. The decision to start all over, at or near middle age, had its harrowing side. It went beyond the kind of questioning and self-criticism every creative artist must constantly maintain. For the move they made, conviction and motivation had to be inordinately powerful:

My friends and I had achieved some excellence and recognition by the tail end of the thirties. If we had continued doing what we were doing, we would have had a fairly ready market. If we had kept on with it, we certainly would have profited from the growing awareness of art in the New York audience, its growing acceptance. But we chose to start off on a new path. When we began to do non-representational art, we were really undertaking a tremendous adventure. There were some advantages that the feeling of adventure gives you. We also had the advantage of a kind of élan and comradeship that came from talking with other artists who were interested in the same thing. But we were all completely excluded from our society, the society around us, particularly because we were dropping the work whose content was felt to be so important at that time. I mean, content which had to do with political and economic problems. We dropped all that, and alienated ourselves even further from those patrons, those museums, those institutions which might have begun to be interested in us. Can you imagine what psychological hazards there were in this kind of independent thinking? It required a certain amount of courage. It required, above all, the ability to scorn heaps of adverse criticism, in the newspapers, the periodicals, everywhere. We were attacked unmercifully . . .

Breaking through to a radically different perception, restlessly experimenting and defiantly exhibiting, provoked colossal ridicule. Jackson Pollock was dubbed "Jack the Dripper." For the better part of a decade, abstract artists were the butt of jokes according to which small children or chimpanzees were as gifted as they. Inured to the ridicule—which was a sustained cry of the Yahoo—they could scarcely thrill to the subsequent, equally facile but bathetic praise emanating from those who only recently had nothing but dispraise for all abstract or "modern type" art. By now, "They [the very same people] are very snooty about realistic painting, and profess to see no virtue in it," an attitude vanguard artists disdain. For them, style as such does not determine quality, and quality, while always rare, may occur in any style or school.

THE BREAKTHROUGH TO INDEPENDENCE

No aspect of our problem is more fascinating than that of men and women, well past the first blush of youth, who already had a foothold in the world and spurned it in favor of a course that could only isolate them. Never were they thrown more fully onto their own resources. Many speak of having been captivated by the idea of scale (knowing but not caring that it made their work even less marketable), even as the French had been taken by the idea of craftsmanship. Economic impoverishment and its sudden abatement went hand in hand with the idea:

> *I think the big painting a curious phenomenon. It had something to do with the fact that when we were all broke we had to work on small canvases, we had to work on paintings for months at a time because otherwise we wouldn't have had any material to work with. And then when artists began to get a little money, I think there was such a desire to buy a roll of canvas, like the one I have there is twelve feet high . . . I know when I got hold of some money, I bought enough material to supply an art store. But of course the*

large canvas would not sell. I mean, we knew they were white elephants, but we just had to make some. For me, the height of it was to make a painting twenty feet wide by ten feet high, which in other periods an artist would only make on the basis of a commission. He'd never dream of doing it for himself. It's only now that artists commission themselves. But, you know, I had the feeling even fifteen years ago that the artist was his own patron.

This is the artist's ultimate expression of self-sufficiency. Painters and sculptors like to think that they create and re-create themselves, as well as their work. We shall see that to the question, "Whose opinion matters to you?" they first indicate a narrow circle of peers and then, when pressed, admit that no one else's opinion really matters. But to become one's own patron, to do just what one likes, unconcerned about buying and selling, about pleasing or shocking, about what's new and what the critics will say, is a rare and wonderful thing. In New York at the inception of their movement, about twenty-five years ago and for some years thereafter, a band of painters and sculptors seceded from the conventional art world. The independence they secured for themselves has not been matched before or since—and they took full advantage of it. For just then, with the heat off, they made their big breakthrough. It came under fortuitous conditions that many observers would regard as ideal. If the creative act in all ages, and most especially in ours, requires a certain detachment—whether voluntary or involuntary—New York in the forties provided a perfect setting for the consummation of that act. Consider the remarks of Lewis Mumford, who, after declaring that in "their high moments of creativity there is no inner difference" between the scientist, the technician, and the artist, goes on as follows:

> *Yet those who use the term "creative arts" are not altogether on a false scent, when they single out a special group of activities as being committed, with a certain intensity of purpose and singleness of goal, to the creative act as such. For what we mean here by "creative" is that these arts have no other reason for existence than to draw forth from human experience new values and to embody those values in forms*

*to which the artist has given an independent and self-sus-
taining life, which may long outlast the occasion that brought
them into being. This is a special kind of creativity. Though
the creative arts have always occupied a secure and even
generous place in the human economy, it is only now that we
begin to suspect what an important part they play in molding the human personality; and how much that part may be
fortified by a* certain withdrawal from practical duties and
environmental pressures. *(Our emphasis.)*

Elsewhere in the same article, Mumford writes:

*To say of one of those arts that it has a certain practical use
—that a novel serves as a bandage for the eyes on a dull rail-
road journey, or that music may take the place of a sleeping
pill before going to bed—is not to say anything in favor
of its essential nature. For the only true use of the creative
arts is creation itself. Their function is to engender creativity
in the observer and participant, releasing him from habit
and routine, deepening his feelings and emotions, focusing
more sharply his perceptions, clarifying his inner nature,
bringing into existence a meaningful unity out of what
seemed in the act of living a contradictory or a bafflingly
incomplete experience, lacking in value or significance.*[3]

However they weather the test of time, America's best abstract
artists of the forties and fifties feel in their bones that they reached
such a peak as Mumford describes, fulfilling their true mission,
thereby allowing art to serve its own most authentic function. When
art emanated more or less exclusively from European centers, our
artists envied Europeans for whom they eventually felt sorry. Good
fortune for an artist came to mean—being an American! "Poor
Berlioz was a French composer in a German era of music. That was
his tragedy. It doomed him to an unsuccessful career. There was no
way for a French composer to overcome German dominance. And
there's no way today for a European painter to overshadow an
American!" In place of the old inferiority complex, we see a new,
more typically American brashness bordering on cockiness, something
which, with greater seemliness, simply gives rise to the kind of con-

fidence a man feels when the world thinks that he has earned it. Even an artist for whom "the New York School is just the greatest, most direct, logical, sequential development. It was an outgrowth of Cubism which was a direct outgrowth of Cézanne's planes which were a direct outgrowth . . ." and we cut her off before she took us back to the Lascaux cave drawings—or beyond, into an infinite regress—even this artist grants that a new conception, a new perception, usually called a real breakthrough, actually developed.

Now and then, a painter with all the dubiety and contrariety of his reaction to success and the younger generation, invidiously contrasting the golden past and the corrupt present, will still make a clear-cut claim of moral superiority over affluent European artists:

> *None of us has a million dollars in the bank—like some of them. All that money offends and embarrasses me. Of course we want to live and live well. But I don't think any American artist wants the obligation of big wealth and all the attention it requires. Most European artists don't understand that about us. They can't figure out why De Kooning doesn't produce more and set higher prices. Now, a man like Picasso, my God! He's got a factory. His things go all over the world, making five times more than De Kooning makes. Some of our young people are pretty bad, but it's the Europeans who are really avaricious.*

The great days preceded success, which proved to be so ambiguous, as well as wealth, whose magnitude had to be minimized lest it become too great an embarrassment. In glorifying those days the artist cannot be charged with idealization of his youth, a relatively drab and sterile period as he sees it now. The marvels came later, and they were subjectively experienced as a kind of rebirth or regeneration:

> *In the thirties, when many of us were in our thirties or a little older, we were doing work imposed upon us by different disciplines, by a certain political and economic milieu. Artists who worked on the WPA—and that means practically all of them—and who got involved in the Artist's Union and communism, were trying to submerge their personalities—although they didn't use that language. The sense of rebirth*

came when we felt we were really artists and nothing else. Which doesn't mean we weren't moved any more with compassion for suffering and disaster, and all that. We just didn't feel we had to use it in our work.

To be reborn this way required withdrawal from society—and a closing of ranks outside its stricter precincts. Fraternity was essential for the twice born, who lost it with the deepest regrets as they re-entered society. "It was our community that helped us break through to a world of marvelous possibilities." This community was composed of men and women who had already been through the mill and who were not too tired to go through it all over again.

There is a close, if less than perfect parallel between this American group of the 1940's and a celebrated French group of the 1870's. We know of no such specific moment for the Americans as existed for those Impressionists in France who selected the spring of 1874 to defy the Salon and organize an exhibition of their own. All the same, in many ways we can, *pari passu,* nearly substitute one set of names for the other—so much alike was the basic social experience of both schools. Take John Rewald's monumental study of Impressionism, start with the little band of rebels, including Monet, Renoir, Pissaro, Cézanne, and Berthe Morisot, and see how remarkable the correspondence is. Rewald begins his monograph with the exhibition of 1874, itself a breach of established custom, but, he points out, the works on display seemed at first glance to be even more revolutionary:

> *The reaction of visitors and critics was by no means friendly; they accused the artists of painting differently from the accepted methods simply to gain attention or pull the legs of honest folk. . . .*
>
> *When the Impressionists organized their first group exhibition, they were no longer awkward beginners; all of them were over thirty and had been working ardently for fifteen years and more. They had studied—or tried to study—at the École des Beaux-Arts, gone to the older generation for advice, discussed and absorbed the various currents in the arts of their time. Some even had obtained a certain success at different Salons before the Franco-Prussian War. But they had declined to follow blindly the methods of the acclaimed*

masters and pseudo-masters of the day. Instead, they had derived new concepts from the lessons of the past and the present, developing an art all their own. . . .

Although their canvases shocked their contemporaries as being brazen, they represented in fact the true continuation of the endeavors and theories of their predecessors.[4]

History never repeats itself—and never fails to repeat itself. To stress the similarities is not to deny the differences. Both are important, but the mere fact that one can legitimately compare any group of painters in the United States with a legendary group in France is a matter of some wonderment. At no other time would it have been possible to make such a comparison without also making laughable or presumptuous claims for American art.

A heightened tempo of change is the most marked sociological characteristic of the past century. Like scientific theories and intellectual currents, art movements run their course more rapidly than ever. These days their dissolution is heralded in their appearance. The original New York School, insofar as it was a school, may be said to have come and gone more rapidly than Impressionism, and yet without the vertiginous speed of whole schools which passed beyond our vision in this decade before we could more than catch a glimpse of them.

I would say that someone like Jackson Pollock went through a long, long formative period before he evolved the style by which he came to be known. When Pollock arrived he knew he was there; he had spent a lifetime getting there; and he knew why he was there.

Today everything moves faster, slips through the artist's fingers, and gets communicated the world over. Color reproductions provide instant stimulus and ready-made influence. Rapid visual communication discourages slow growth toward an unknown end; our painter, reflecting on Pollock's typically long apprenticeship, puts himself in the same company:

I feel I know why I am here, but in many countries, in many parts of Europe, in Latin America and Asia, there's no opportunity for solid grounding in the arts. Nevertheless, every-

one sees Paris Match, *and there are the international editions of* Life. *Their pages are full of the latest* ism, *the latest* cachet *in art—which can be a hundred years ahead of what they have in their local museums, schools, or libraries. They try to be part of the present without any real understanding of why they do it, and the work they do reflects all this. I've seen the same thing right here, in our colleges and high schools. It's a lot less excusable in the U.S., but just as big a danger.*

There is a genuine afterglow, but the brief bright golden moment has ended, all but extinguished by too much success too easily attained by a generation awash in publicity. "Artists can't come together and retain the close relationship they had before." The lament is common to young and old, even to an artist in his twenties who says, "I can still sense the thrill they must have felt ten or fifteen years ago. I was just a kid, but I grew up on the stuff they did." It was, paradoxically, the collectivity of artists as a band of brothers that generated individuality, and when the collectivity collapsed, individuality suffered grievous losses. The unique aesthetic vision stands in some sort of organic relationship to a communion, or at least to a community of artists.

A major contributor to the New York School remembers how he and his friends, who had converted a neighborhood cafeteria into a coffee house, used to discuss the American landscape. They thought that "only boobs tried to paint it, and *they* fell on their backsides." Local color regionalists were too literal and superficial:

> *In America we had a clashing form that surprised us out of our elemental feelings, and we couldn't have that in Europe. I knew the difference. For me that European landscape was saturated by one symbol—a grey, silvery envelopment. We were developing a personal landscape. Anyhow, that's the metaphor I like best. The American landscape is the environment you live in, its tension. When you make it your inner concept, when you can't run away from it, then it becomes real. I think that's roughly what happened to us as we talked and read and worked.*

Each artist had to internalize the "landscape" in his own manner, but all of them retreated from American society, the more profoundly to establish their identity as Americans. Just as cliques produced individuation, so an atomized art world produced standardization. By the same token, cosmopolitanism led to native art: Europeans in Paris and New York helped Americans find themselves. An early admirer of Klee reports that he loved texture, until in the forties:

> *I realized that to use texture as a crutch was wrong. Following Klee, or my understanding of Klee, if a composition or a painting didn't work, I'd use a little texture, and that easily made the whole thing right. So I decided to do away with texture. I suppose, in a sense, I was looking for the hard way. I didn't want it to be easy, and I eliminated texture for that reason. Finally, I eliminated tonality for the same reason. I wanted to work with the basic things that were so right in themselves that you couldn't doctor them up.*

The contrast comes to light in a story (whose details we omit) with which an older artist regaled us during one of our interviews:

> *We lived in a brownstone, and there was a composer in the same building. I was going downstairs one night, and he opened the door and said, "Why don't you come in? There are some young painters here who would like to talk to you." . . . Anyway, I had to mail a letter. Later, I returned and asked what they wanted to talk to me about. He said, "I don't know. They're with you, avant-garde and all that. They admire you, but they also feel that you're their enemy." I said, "What do you mean?" He said, "Well, they don't get shows—and like that." They were in their twenties! Well, I ran down the whole list: I was forty-five when I had my first show. Dali was forty-two. De Kooning was forty-three or forty-six. Hofmann was sixty-eight. Pollock was in his thirties, but I never thought of him as a young guy. Motherwell was young. Those were the two exceptions. But they weren't so young. They were older than these fel-*

lows. And I told them, if they had ability, all they had to do was show me. We'd go down and see their work. If it looked as if there were real potential, we'd all break our necks to get them a show. I just don't understand this insidious, cynical way of looking at art as if there's a career in it. We weren't worried about showing then: we were worried about being able to make a painting.

What artists worry about, their anguish as bearers of special goods in a society undergoing total change: this is basically the subject matter of our book.

2

Generational
Conflict

What's more enchanting than the voices of young people, when you can't hear what they say?
—LOGAN PEARSALL SMITH, 1934

LIFE, both mutable and immutable, is as variable as it is constant; while all is flux, everything remains the same; each of us has a unique biography, and all men are alike. For our species and for nature at large: *plus ça change, plus c'est la même chose.* It is with a lively sense of this paradox that we have set down the words of living artists, for who knows better than they that a single well-wrought concrete image contains the world? Joseph Conrad, who enfolded his moral system in beautifully constructed tales, once took umbrage when a critic attacked him for his prolixity. The novel *Chance* was said to be too long. In petulant self-defense Conrad replied that he could have written the whole story on a cigarette wrapper, indeed that he could capture the whole human condition simply by saying that man is born, he suffers and dies. Endlessly to elaborate and illuminate this condition, by concretely symbolizing it, is quite possibly the artist's highest mission. He immerses himself in the multifariousness and the consistency of life, and—more to our point—cannot help exemplifying both tendencies in his own person.

Great art, at the level of universality, reaches across space and time. It is also rooted in a given place, a specific period, the here-and-now of a changing society. And so are its creators. For them, as for the less possessed, there are existential, situational, psychological, and historical determinants of behavior. Whether firmly or loosely stitched into the social fabric, men cannot wholly escape it—any more than they can disentangle themselves from the space-time continuum. Artists, more than most of us, are outside yet still inside society, focused on the timeless yet still bound by time—no less than they are international in outlook yet tied to national character.

We feel obliged to make this rather banal and portentous statement, which one way or another we will be making throughout the book. It applies particularly to the content of this chapter. Anyone who talks intensively and extensively to creative artists is bound to be struck by the generational factor which differentiates them. This factor operates on every level of consciousness. It is manifest in deliberately formulated opinions and in a variety of attitudes that are often less intentionally revealed.

How could it be otherwise? To come within hailing distance of contemporary society is to come near a whirlpool that sucks men in or ejects them altogether. The process is endlessly repetitive, encompassing one generation after another, spanning a vague but ever smaller period to which we are all bound hand and foot. Nowadays the rapidity of social change is such that "generation" signifies but a few years, and each generation is made up of people with incommunicable experience which they vainly try to convey to their juniors and seniors. No doubt human beings always derived special comfort from association with their age mates who, having seen similar things, eventually "spoke the same language." But in more serene and stable times, the life-cycle meant that everyone could look forward to (or back upon) a common progression from one stage to the next. To be young was a condition intelligible to all those who, after all, had once been young themselves.

Today, and not just because we are all somewhat amnesiac, the young tend to baffle the old or, often enough, the just slightly older—and vice versa. Decades ago, it was already apparent that a father could not assume his son was having much the same encounter with life that he had had as a boy. With the acceleration of social change to an unheard-of velocity, parents and their offspring suffered a new strain. Frequently there was a complete breakdown in communication. The behavior of teen-agers became incomprehensible to their elders, who were swiftly defined as old-fashioned. Talking to one's own kind (and not to do so was to risk talking in a void) more and more involved talking to one's own generation. By now, siblings, if they are spaced over several years, will be raised in radically different environments and on possibly divergent pediatric principles that may make them strangers to each other. Never were men and women more fully the prisoners of their generation than they are at this moment in world history.

THE ISOLATION OF AGE GROUPS

Most of these sociological observations were made twenty-five years ago in a prophetic essay by Kingsley Davis on parent-youth conflict.[1] Davis also noted an extraordinary amount of intergenerational rivalry in the United States as contrasted with other countries and cultures where age-grading obviated or mitigated it. Such rivalry is markedly present among artists, and much of it is publicly expressed in resentment, bewilderment, spite, scorn, and impatience. To begin with, there is simple social distance that grows out of one's having been around when certain events took place. These events, though formative for one generation, are scarcely understood by another:

> *Look here, now I'm sixty years old. I have lived this way since 1914. My attitude toward world affairs is different from that of, let us say, any generation since the Second World War or since Korea. It so happens that they don't even know what the word "Guernica" means. They know the picture: every little goddam detail is analyzed. They know all about it, but they don't know anything about its origins. This came to me two years ago, right here, with twenty-year-old people. . . . That's one difference between us, but there's something else, more profound. You see, I cannot conceive of going through life without deep engagements. Where are theirs? I think it is not a question of beatniks, of a lost generation—which is nonsense in my eyes. It's a question of lacking values. That's what bothers me about them, their lack of values.*

Some artists face up to the problem quite objectively; more of them denigrate the other generation even as they suppose themselves to be denigrated by it:

> *When we get old, as I think I am, we become more isolated. It's hard to associate with young artists because their aims are so different. Some of them very frankly say when we're not present that they wish we would drop dead and make room for them. They'd like to dispose of us. We're in their way, and that makes it rather difficult to fraternize with them.*

It is symptomatic that, at sixty or thereabouts and in the full flow of creative production, this renowned painter accepts his "old age."

43

And, if the father must be slain symbolically by children who feel more than before an importunate urge to establish the succession, there is no reason why he should not regard himself as aged before his time. But he misperceives the degree of murderous hostility directed at him. For there is no doubt that he does exaggerate: the condition is real, but whatever its subliminal substance, not so overtly extreme. Also, this artist, like many of his fellows, reciprocates the real and imagined hostility. Lamely and defensively, if more or less accurately, he puts it to us: "Well, the thing is, you really can't have the same sort of respect for a young artist that you might have for an artist of your own age who's gone through the same battles that you have." Behind this assertion there lie a number of more defensible value judgments—to which we shall presently refer.

In part, chronological stratification is artificially induced by historians. They are professionally disposed to make useful but arbitrary divisions, for instance, by subdividing the twentieth century into decades, so that artists of the twenties emerge as distinct from artists of the thirties, forties, and fifties. Exhibitors who show "Art of the Sixties," created perhaps by "Artists Under Thirty-Five," also contribute their share to the generational illusion. Yet, of course, it is not all illusion. A perceptive painter observes:

> *It's almost as though they stratified themselves. You seem to get a batch of artists all born in the year 1904. That's very curious, you know. . . . And then there seems to be a jump of another ten years. . . . In 1950, Bill and Arshile Gorky and Franz Kline and Motherwell and Barney Newman, oh, a whole group, used to hang out together and go to the Cedar Tavern and sit around a table and chew the fat. And then, after all of them became famous, they all went their separate ways, and each of them seems to have an entourage, a circle which more or less revolves around them. . . . After that, there was another group: Grace Hartigan and me, Joan Mitchell, Larry Rivers, Jane Freulicher, Ray Parker—a whole new lineup. We used to meet, about five years later, at the Cedar and chew the fat. Now we've all grown apart, and there is a new group there. It's not far*

different from what happened in Paris in the twenties. Picasso and Matisse and Braque and the rest were very close when they were younger, and then as they got older they all spread apart. It's a general phenomenon. I think what happens is that you know everything that everyone is going to say. There's nothing left for Franz Kline to say to me now except possibly to make a joke. I know his whole kick.

There is much meat in such testimony which bears on generational separation and generational nucleation. Many young people with a common calling grow up together, get to be known, and ultimately exhaust their interest in each other. They form new circles which may include the young and admiring who attach themselves as satellites to their stars. Fresh forms of interaction do take place, new faces replace the old, a successful artist moves up and out of his youthful surroundings. Yet, with age and fame, he is also likely to be more isolated, and therefore prone to fewer—and not just different—forms of interaction. His life becomes more privatized, a function of age, and not necessarily *old* age:

Social life is amongst people more your own age: they invite you and you invite them. But I don't socialize much any more. I used to a lot, even ten years ago. But the very fact of a family keeps you more restricted. You have a child, and you can't get out without a baby sitter. I mean, things move in a pattern that isolates you.

I lived in the Village, and they tore the building down. The only place I could get an apartment this big was uptown on the West Side. I'm a long way from the Village. I don't go to the Cedar Bar. I don't know when parties are going on. So I stay away from them. It doesn't matter.

RESENTMENTS OF YOUNGER ARTISTS BY THEIR ELDERS

Socializing less, and when at all mostly with people he has known for a long time, the older artist seldom affects indifference toward those he scarcely knows, i.e., younger painters and sculptors on their way up. When feeling hurt by their hostility, he lashes back at them. The relationship, or its absence, is obviously important, always producing an emotional reaction of some strength. One painter, when he lowers his guard, provides us with an insight into this love-hate syndrome:

> *The only public that means anything to you, the one from which you most want recognition, when all's said and done, is the coming generation. If some young artist takes off from a picture on this wall, if he comes here to this studio of mine and looks at something, and three years later I see he's done a picture like that, I know that he's found something, and he's put his life on it. I have touched him.*

Here, through deeply tangled emotions, we cut close to the bone, and raw psychic needs are revealed. If youth "naturally" rebels against the antecedent generation of forebears and progenitors, how much more "naturally" and inevitably will it do so in the visual arts where a deliberate rupture with the past is constantly demanded. Without making that rupture there can be no originality, and originality is widely taken to be a synonym for creativity. There are other compelling reasons, but this one by itself assures that the aspiring artist will seek to disencumber himself of his immediate predecessors and their influence. At the same time, notwithstanding an identical experience of their own, the older artists wish to please and impress those who follow them; to do so is to attain a kind of Platonic immortality, not, says one painter, "in the way my son makes me immortal, that kind of physical continuity, but as a sign of the significance of my work, how much of an imprint or impact it has made."

There is thus an inherent tension: the young wishing to earn their spurs by emancipating themselves from the old, who want to leave a mark (and indeed, to perpetuate it) through the young. Allowing for those who remain on the sidelines, a group of sympathetic observers and noncombatants, and for various degrees of fierceness, the battle rages. Few are far above it. One, describing himself as a member of "the second generation," points out that he always felt reverent toward the older men who nevertheless seem to be bitter about younger ones coming up and making good. With much reflection, he takes an understanding and indulgent view, dismissing their querulousness as a foible: "After all, they had a long hard struggle. They didn't make it as easily as we did." Another representative of the intermediary generation tries to see it as his elders do:

> *Even artists my age painted abstractly and got to be known in a hurry. Now these kids suddenly come up with a machine gun, or Coca-Cola bottles, you know. I can show you catalogues of the stuff. I mean, I used to think myself all I had to do was put a little red over there and a little blue over here. Well, I'm sure that anybody who painted in the social realist way like Jack Levine, and then watched these kids come up and go baaaaang!—would wonder: "What the hell are they doing? That isn't painting. What does it have to do with painting?"*

Some venom is directed at newcomers by older artists "who are out of date, out of fashion, and very angry." But for these elders, whether they are showing and selling or not, all is gall in any case, and they are as vehement in denouncing any of their contemporaries who have "gone abstract." Competitiveness is another non-generational factor making for personal embitterment that culminates in a war of all against all: "Unless you get to the very top, there's always somebody doing better, no matter what, always somebody." The plastic and pictorial artist of today reminds one respondent of "a North Carolina mountain man with a gun in front of the door. He has his own stake, and anyone who gets a little more is in for trouble. I think you find this attitude among artists because their work is so hard to judge . . ." If his analysis is at all sound, if militant proprietary guardianship of one's own problematic stake is widespread, we should expect to find most of it in our newest crop of artists, which is exactly where older artists locate the problem. Yet, insofar as the attitude is compounded of pride, vanity, and a measure of uncertainty, it is less a matter of age than of individual differences which exist in every age.

Furthermore, the rare spirit rises above any such conflict. Our *rara avis* was a woman whose career-line is altogether extraordinary: in her twenties (the century's early thirties) she won some acclaim as a painter, then married an artist and for years neglected her own work; a divorce ensued, and with it a most energetic resumption of painting. In her own words, "When I left X, I immediately

47

worked like a madwoman, day and night for twelve years. I had enough acceptance to make me feel very fulfilled and good about the world. I thought: how wonderful, in middle age to have this marvelous thing." Starting out anew after a long lapse, and more successfully than ever, offered her a point of vantage much like that of young artists, but it also convinced her that she and they should be grateful to the old-timers who had "hacked out the way" and "broken the ground" for them. A show of hers had just been very well received, and that event prompts her to say: "I bet a dollar, no, I bet anything, that if I had had that show sixty years before, nobody would have looked at it. A lot of other people had to come first and go hungry for a long time before I could have this easy success." The credo she affirms is, "Let there be art, and let it keep coming up with the generations." Then, with considerable warmth, "I don't want this to stop, for God's sake. Because if Max Weber felt like that, if Stuart Davis felt like that, think how hard it would have been for all of us."

THE RESENTMENT OF "EASY SUCCESS"

That the trailblazers suffered severe economic hardship to make their breakthrough, and thereby lessened the hardship for their successors, is something they know best of all. Those a bit younger also know, and they realize that the up-and-coming artist owes more than just an aesthetic debt to his dedicated predecessors:

> *It used to be that art was hopeless as an economic activity . . . Now, there's one of the things I really hate about that jerk Canaday who writes for the* Times. *He's so insidious about this, and middle-aged women gobble up everything he writes. Well, I never knew Kline and De Kooning very well, but back in the late forties they were around and I would speak to them. They were trying to make out somehow, to stay alive and do their painting. And they were having a goddam tough time getting the groceries. They couldn't get exhibitions uptown. The best they could do was maybe a little reproduction and a little magazine art once in a while.*

48

They really had it hard. And those great big canvases—why, it used to be that if you made a canvas six feet long and four feet high, you were accused of showing off. Nowadays you can make a canvas ten feet high and fifteen wide, and nobody says anything. Well, they began to work on these wild, what they call abstract expressionist canvases—which were enormous for that day. I heard people say, "Well, why not? Nobody's going to exhibit them anyway, and nobody's going to buy them. So why not make a great big picture instead of ten little ones? It costs me just as much and it's just as hopeless. Meantime, I can see what happens." It was a gesture of despair and it was a sort of liberation. Well, they did great things. Now, the reason I bring Canaday up is a column he wrote—I can't quote it exactly, but he slammed all the last twenty years of American painting, and he said, "Now that everybody is running after modern American art, Kline and De Kooning have jumped on the bandwagon." Hell, if there was a bandwagon, they built it from the wheels up.

As a rebellious child begins to appreciate his father only when he too becomes a father, so an artist of the middle generation may empathize with older artists only when he too is cast off by the young. One painter in his thirties, but recently a scornful rebel striking out on his own, finds the latest fashion in art repellent. He reports: "I was talking to B. L. about my reaction to the new Pop Art, and he said, 'Now you know how I felt all these years.' It was very touching. He's in his late fifties, I guess, and he's been through it a few times. I had never had it before."

If he lives out a normal life span, the number of times a modern man, regardless of his occupation, will have this experience is greater than ever before. He will be hit harder and sooner by wave after wave of youthful pretenders. A fairly recent arrival to the world of well-known artists recalls that at first, "I never dreamed I'd have my pictures shown in my twenties or that they'd appear in a mass circulation magazine. The Ninth Street Show in 1950 made my heart turn to be in it." His rapid ascent in the fifties was considered amazing, and he rightly experienced it as such. "But today, it would be regarded as a slow crawl. There's something wrong with you if you're not shown at a dealer's by the time you're twenty-one!"

It is within this framework of struggle for one generation and relative ease for another (with the second largely a product of the first), that veterans criticize novices. Partly because they made life easier for those who followed, it sometimes seems to older men that the easier life—not art—has begun to attract young people. Such a development produces mixed motives whose impurity is regarded as an abomination, a profanation comparable to that of a theological student bent on entering the ministry to guarantee his financial security. The analogy is a common one, for the clergyman's calling is often likened to the artist's. Some respondents go further in this key:

> *The best art is done for itself and not for what it can produce in the way of living. But that's true for whatever you do that's well done. If you find a cabinetmaker who can make you beautiful furniture today—but I mean good furniture— you'll discover, even if he charges you for his work, that he has another job which supports him—so that he can make furniture for its own sake . . . which is not at all like being in the furniture business.*

Youngsters for whom the possibility of making a fast buck is something new, as it is for their elders, may nevertheless miscalculate by seeking big money in art. Admittedly, the contrast between "then" and "now," even if "then" was only yesterday, is very great. A woman artist, still young and rather famous when not much beyond girlhood, sees herself as a bridge between the generations, and reminds us that, "When I first showed pictures, if you got two hundred dollars for one, that was a lot. Maybe a few of the older painters were getting $1,000, and that was an awful lot. But now anything under $4,000 is sort of unknown." All the same, she sounds a warning: "Too many of these kids, hundreds of them, just framing things, can't expect to sell them at such prices. If they do, they're in for a big surprise!"

RESENTMENT OF CYNICISM IN THE
YOUNGER GENERATION

This same woman tends to be rather censorious of the kids who are not so many years removed from herself. She finds those "on the beat side" depressed, angry, hopeless, and, finally, just lazy. Her group, as she remembers it, may also have felt that way, but not as much so. Why not? "Because I don't think the world came that close that horribly in the forties as it does now." She understands but deeply deplores the cynicism, indolence, demoralization, and anomie of "beat kids." Their art, removed by no great temporal gap, still does not speak to her:

> *I guess I sound old-fashioned, but the whole thing has gotten very mushy and very infantile and very uninteresting. Most of the work is not valuable to me. It gives me no new insights. If it shocks me, I get the feeling that I've been déjà-shocked. When it's amusing, it borders on hysteria. I find all this quite destructive, like pot-smoking. It doesn't interest me . . . I often get the feeling at a show of younger people that somehow or other the idea is: nothing's sacred, what the hell, it's all a great mess anyway, so take this, too. You know.*

Finally, it is the artificiality of their behavior and of their work that troubles her most. Whatever root-identity there may be is overlaid with "so many poses and roles with so much makeup" that the "real thing" gets lost for good.

Affluent or poor, the older artist considers himself a champion of total involvement in art. The presentation of self in everyday life, as Erving Goffman calls it,[2] the assemblage of "poses and roles and makeup" may be necessary in all other sectors of social life. But they have no place in art where, to those who uphold this tradition, spontaneity means much more than socially acceptable role-playing. The mercenary impulse, combined with a craving for fame or notoriety, is ruinous in proportion, as it causes the artist to be like other people at just those points where he must differ from them. "Young painters," says an expatriate of the twenties, "are far less adventurous than we were in my generation. None of them would go to Paris with three hundred dollars—and stay ten years, as I did." Nor need they. Conformity and time-serving timidity may simply occur as a result of greater economic security, premature recognition, and stepped-up publicity in whose glare the beginner is mistaken for a full-blown genius.

Is this attitude a kind of nit-picking by the aged who are crotchety and who become splenetic when they contemplate their replacement by a new crop of upstarts? Probably, along with the substance, there is an element of bad faith. But that the substance is there was recently affirmed (chiefly for fiction in America, but it fits fine art as well) by John W. Aldridge, a literary critic writing in the *New York Times Book Review*.[3] Aldridge declared:

> *I suppose there has never before been a time when the rewards for being merely promising in the arts have been so large or instantaneously bestowed, when the chief threat to new talent has so patently been not neglect but recognition gained when there is too little to recognize, a debt to fortune contracted too far in advance of possible repayment. In no field does this seem truer at the moment than in the field of the novel, where we seem to suffer from a special anxiety for distinction, and where our anxiety has caused us to act as though distinction could be wished or propagandized into being.*

The highly charged, competitive atmosphere to which Aldridge refers is as palpable for painting and sculpture as for literature. It is, as he notes, "an atmosphere which has conditioned us to the idea that our productive power in the arts should be at least equal to our huge industrial and scientific potential, and that on all fronts we ought to be moving ahead with vigor."

A large part, then, of what the elderly artist-as-critic sees is no mirage. Museums *have* progressed rapidly from the exhibition of work by living artists, which in itself was an abrupt change, to *first shows* for certain young and untried artists. One might suppose that, with such tokens of public acceptance, the artist would feel better about himself and his work. But no. When in previous decades he was most likely to be ignored and neglected, the American artist (as his memory brings it back to him now) felt boundless confidence. On the other hand, to be noticed, accepted, rewarded, and celebrated today has caused much of his self-confidence, and with it the élan and the exuberance of an earlier day, to ooze away:

> *I don't know anybody in my period who committed himself to being an artist and who had all these reservations about how good he might be. We were very innocent. We thought well of ourselves, and we sort of thought everybody we knew was going to be very special, too. You never heard the idea that's going around now, that "I'm not good enough. I'm getting into the wrong crowd, and they're pulling me down into a ditch." It's new. Well, America is different. The world is different. In the twenties, you could really think you were going to be great, and everybody was thinking the same thing, oh, on all sides. It was, if you know what I mean, the normal, legitimate attitude, and you started with it.*

We were very innocent is the operative phrase in this quotation. It stops just short of rhapsodizing a decade. Hemingway's beautiful evocation of his creative and carefree youth as an artist among artists in Paris between the wars, his "Moveable Feast," is especially poignant because it turned out not to be movable. An older, not wiser, but now worldly wise and corrupt spirit broods over the irrecoverable days of joy and naiveté. It is not simply the case that someone like Hemingway aged, but that *youth* may be robbed of its innocence— even as some old men preserve theirs.

To take the artistic trail blazers and use their lives as models for one's own is to opt for inauthentic experience. Those who judge young artists harshly find them learning from gossip about a trio like Kline, De Kooning, and Pollock how to get ahead in the world:

> *Everybody knows the story of that group, its struggle, their relations with various people. So, you're young and you have this thing about making it. Well, now you have a primer, a copybook, or maybe it's a road map. The myth of these people is around for everyone to examine. You can almost turn to the page that tells you how to make it now. Over at the Cedar Bar, where people listen very willingly to one*

> *another, there's a callow painter who's already the younger De Kooning. He knows De Kooning and Pollock had to do certain things and he'll do them too, not because he has a big struggle but just to get attention. It's conniving. It stinks things up.*

There are artists who bend over backwards to be fair, who strenuously avoid glorifying their own generation and vilifying another. They observe, for instance, that there have always been cynical artists:

> *When I was a younger guy, we could all have been successful. We could have done Negroes with ropes around their necks forever. We could have claimed that we were involved in the American Image, that it wasn't really Jack Levine's fire escape in Boston but the pushcarts on Orchard Street, and it wasn't the one-horse shay in Kansas either. A lot of guys did that in my time.*

And then there were others like himself, who did not. He refuses to speculate about a possible increase in the proportion of cynics but admits that, for young people, "whether they should ride a tide or create a so-called aesthetic polarity to that tide" is a bigger problem than it used to be. And by way of explanation he points out that: "It's easier for a talented person to show, but it's also easier for an untalented person to show, and for the difference between them to be blurred." In his zeal to be fair, he refuses to slander artists, telling us—since we chatted with him as academic men —that the university is no better: "Guys sell out everywhere," which is to shift the blame from artists onto society. Social scientists would be inclined to do the same thing, but doing it dishonors artists who prefer their peculiar status and a set of standards different from those by which other men are measured.

THE DISENCHANTMENT WITH POLITICS

No artist ever escaped from society, but for some time during the period of Romanticism and its aftermath, the artist saw himself as a rebel within society. Any older artist continues to see himself as a person who systematically subverts society. He does this in his work by a process which we will try to suggest (in Chapter Five), and he does it in his capacity as a citizen of the republic. If he is better than average today, the young artist will still subvert aesthetically, but not politically. No contrast is drawn more sharply than this one between the political oldsters and the apolitical youngsters:

> *Older artists who came up during the Depression see things quite differently, but then, in those days everyone, not only artists, spoke more freely and considerately of his fellow man. Everyone was more concerned about the needs of mankind. That isn't the case so much today in any group. It's less common with the public in general—or among artists.*

This is to say that times have changed, that ideologies once warmly embraced no longer attract many men, that they are disenchanted with politics, that the artist as a creature of his age expresses this state of affairs, and that he could hardly do otherwise. Older painters and sculptors carry a residual commitment to political radicalism which stamps them as the anachronisms they really are. Young artists, more attuned to their times, recognize the ideological exhaustion (about which so much as been written for fifteen or twenty years), and they withdraw from politics. No one claims a perfect correlation between political attitude and age, and no one doubts its approximate accuracy: the majority of young artists are in this sphere like the majority of young Americans. Where others are over-involved (in the rat race), so are they, and where others are under-involved (in politics), so are they. Engagement in status-striving and disengagement from politics, when both are widely fashionable, appear to long-time practitioners of art as a single act of conformity and of betrayal. They are apprehensive (although never just that, for fear is mingled with faith in another turn of the wheel) that the difference between artists and non-artists will become entirely exiguous. And many think that when this difference narrows, so does the difference between art and non-art, a second, more serious, and complicated matter related to—if not simply stemming from—the first. There is no ready explanation for the phenomenon. Who merely fans and what really fuels it, we cannot say. But none of our artists old enough to feel pressure from their juniors would question the validity of Leo Tolstoy's prescient assertion that:

> *In our society art has become so much corrupted that not only has bad art come to be regarded as good, but there has even been lost the very conception of what art is, so that, in order to speak of the art of our society, it is necessary first of all to segregate true art from the adulterations.*[4]

THE EXHAUSTION OF TALENT AND THE FAILURE OF YOUTHFUL PROMISE

The task which Tolstoy enjoined us to undertake (but for which he did not provide suitable criteria) is more formidable at present than it was half a century ago, and much more formidable for Americans than it was a decade ago. This too sets the age groups apart. How frequently do our more mature artists remark upon the slow, cumulative quality of their education: "Art wasn't available in New York the way it is now. We saw shows and things at that time. But how much of it was there in the early thirties or the late thirties? Damn little. Today conditions are phenomenal, especially with all those little cooperative galleries and all." The scarcity of art that could be directly experienced slowed down educational processes which have since been speeded up—at what cost, a thoughtful and observant artist recounts. After noting that there is a tremendous amount of talent in our schools, that work done now "is far superior to any done before in schools," that quality is a dime a dozen, and failure almost inevitable because youth does not fulfill its promise, talent or no talent, he goes on:

> *Maybe art is such today that it requires something else. After all, talent comes from what's available—and everything is available to these students. They look around and the whole world of art is right there in front of them. In no time at all they go through the history of contemporary painting. They'll do this and that and that and that, and do it all well and understand it completely. Yet after they leave school most of them fall apart.*

The surfeit of art available to art students helps to account for their feverish experimentation and ultimate exhaustion: they try everything and they tire of everything. Enhanced and very nearly unlimited opportunity leads to a stumbling block on which artistic promise falls, splinters, and breaks. At its worst, the enormously expanded universe of art turns out actually to have contracted. In such a universe we can segregate true from adulterated art only with the greatest difficulty, and much true art will be suffocated while its opposite is applauded. The informant most scandalized by aborted or deformed talent blames much of it on publicity:

> Harper's *magazine devotes a whole issue to art. Life maga-*
> *zine comes out with a whole issue on art. The glamour of*
> *it is getting worse than Hollywood. These publicists seem*
> *to be saying: "Go into Art. You'll find a gold mine." They*
> *even have a stock market. Now you may say this tends to*
> *rush things. With this possibility of mass success, a lot of*
> *young people bypass certain experiences in their art which*
> *would make it possible to survive or endure what they will*
> *have to face. Do you realize that there are kids on the scene*
> *now who were selling as students—and selling on a big*
> *scale? In other words, it didn't pay to learn . . . Well, in*
> *the last ten years we've had a tremendous number of young*
> *painters come into New York. Lots of them are given a*
> *great deal of attention. If you look at their work you feel*
> *that now's the time when they've got to sit down and really*
> *paint. Of course, this is true not only for them but for*
> *mature painters, too. But what chance will they have after*
> *their so-called success? That's the question . . .*

There is a persuasive theory embedded in these ruminations, according to which experience can insulate an artist (though it may not suffice even for him), but that, by becoming celebrities too soon, many of the young are deprived of experience. The quiet novitiate, an extended period of steady work without public celebration, toughens and inures a man to success. With adequate preconditioning and time to grow he can take it in stride. Young men in a hurry, overambitious to start with, who "click" on the marketplace find it difficult to resist the ballyhoo which envelops them.

57

If anyone has enough ballast to keep from soaring into the Cloud Cuckoo Land of mass communications, it is the older artist. He is likely to have acquired ballast in the form of a wry and skeptical attitude: "Someone recently said to me, 'Oh, you're successful now.' So, I looked at him and I said, 'All I can see that's different is that when I was not successful, I went around telling everybody how good I was. Now that I am successful, everybody is trying to tell me how much better I am than I think I am." Wanting in perspective, which comes experientially if at all, the young man runs a greater risk of being unbalanced by publicly fostered fantasies of success, and, too often, that Bitch Goddess will emasculate him.

RESENTMENT OF THE MARKET MENTALITY OF YOUNGER ARTISTS

Naturally, the case is different if his sights are set not on art but on money, or rather on the art of imitation as a vehicle to pecuniary success. "A great example" is offered by one youngish artist, already well known in his own right to readers of *Time* and *Life:*

> *This guy's only twenty-five years old. He comes from the Midwest. He's been in New York just three years, left college without finishing. J.F. is his name. He was formerly associated with me at the XYZ Gallery, but now he does this other stuff, painting somewhat in the area of Jasper Johns, objects . . . objects in paintings. Recently he made a big splash. And all this was ignited by his reading very carefully every single copy of* Arts, Art News, *and any other art magazine that came his way, reading between the lines, reading on the lines—and he had a marvelous eye. He caught everything that was catchable in those pages. And then: mad travel all night on a weekend to come to New York. He was still on his comet; he saw every noteworthy gallery in New York. He would go back home and make a big show there. . . . This is happening all over America. Contrasted to the older fellows who passed through a long period of fairly unimportant work on their part in a milieu that was* dry dust, *these kids—even ten years younger than*

*I am, for heaven's sake, can make it, but fast. And they're
very hip people, very knowledgeable in the best sense. They
know everything that's going on. And how aware they are
that they can just come to town—and take over. . . . J.F. says,
"Look, I come from a good upper middle class family in
Akron, and I'm very fashion-conscious." He wears the best
clothes, custom-made now. The man's charming and an
absolute wonder to behold as he operates. He doesn't see
artists anymore; he only sees collectors. None of his old
friends are good enough any more. I'm sort of amazed at
the audacity of it. Here's a guy who gets the message that
you can storm New York and make it as an artist. J.F. said,
"I want to make money." And by God, he's doing it! He's
riding high on the crest of fashion, rubbing his gimmick art
in our faces, but who knows where he'll be in a few more
years?*

There is nothing terribly unusual about this case—except perhaps
its blatancy. Many others "operate" as cynically as J.F., but less
openly, more deviously. Everything we were able to learn at first
and second hand supports the generalization made by Mark Harris,
a novelist no longer young but not yet old:

*With assistance and subsidies commonplace now, hustlers
and imitators have got the hang of things. More and more
they fabricate projects they would never have undertaken
without the prospect of aid, which they will never complete,
and which they now promote in the morally flexible language of public relations, showing off those newspaper
notices which pass in the public mind as the equivalent of
labor itself—Name and Fame in the gossip columns, four
appearances on "Open End," Well Known, Best Selling. (A
Santa Fe painter, superior and little known, recently observed
of one of her townsmen that, though he had done little
work for years, he had a reputation for quality and industry.
How was such a thing possible? "He telephones the newspaper every time he thinks about creating a painting," she
said.)* [5]

The Santa Fe artist—and he has his counterpart in every section of the land—can spin myths about himself through skillful use of the communications industry. Whether planting messages in that industry or extracting them in the manner of J.F., everyone acknowledges communications' pivotal position. This fact as much as any other helps us to understand why, in or out of the arts, today's child cannot be quite like yesterday's. Thus, for the man who looks back to Paris in the twenties, when "it was really revolutionary," to a time when, he fondly recollects, "new things were happening to everybody," it is important to note that: "In those days we didn't have the communications channels that you have now." What bearing does this have on the creative effervescence of Paris forty years ago?

> *Well, if somebody had a French magazine with a picture of Picasso's in it, that was news. It was big stuff. The picture would be brought around and discussed. It was a subject of great interest.*

As recently as the twenties, artists were accustomed to receiving intellectual and aesthetic stimuli directly from other artists. After the Natives returned to America, their cultural conviviality persisted for some time. Now it is on the wane. Our returnee continues his reminiscence:

> *There was the poet, Kenneth Rexroth. Have you ever heard of him? We grew up together in Paris in the same house. Rexroth was a high-powered young intellectual straight out of Chicago, and he knew a lot of Chicago people when they were just coming into their own as literary artists. He was also very widely read. I remember reading T. S. Eliot and Dante through his prodding at that time when I was still in my teens. There was always that kind of stimulus and a sense of curiosity, of wonder and excitement that's lacking now. We were aware of a more mysterious world out there, but with all this new communication, if you say something at a café table in Rome, it's known the next day in Paris and New York. We had nothing like that. I mean, Picasso was a mysterious genius way off somewhere. And we all had this unappeasable curiosity about things.*

A sense of mystery and of wonder is hard to preserve when so much comes to be revealed so soon to those whose curiosity cannot outlast their disenchantment. The inside dopester makes his wares into public property, and he peddles them everywhere. News travels fast; people do the same; the velocity of their movement matches the speed with which messages are communicated—and all this in a general setting that makes for steeply accelerated social change. Artists probably lagged behind most others in adjusting to the present tempo. There are many far from decrepitude today for whom the measured pace, the slow and gradual "ripening" they were taught to favor, still makes sense. A painter in his thirties speaks of the customary idea conveyed by any teacher of consequence to his art student, that: "It will take you twenty years to be a painter." Even he was exposed to that dictum. However, "Nobody talks that way today. No teacher would dare to say it without feeling that the young man or young woman would have a baleful gleam in his eye."

Young men and women "on the make" are necessarily in a hurry —and their elders of every generation impeach them for pursuing careers just like those that dehumanize most of us, and for being dishonest to boot: they have taken the low and easy road but (with exceptions like J.F.) still lay claim to higher goods. The claim is illegitimate. The claimants have overdrawn their account. They have invited spiritual bankruptcy and artistic ruin—and all disingenuously—by playing a double game. The seasoned artist, worried about any sign of dissimulation in himself but well fortified against it, sees an army of poseurs shoot up in his old haunts: "Why, I don't know the old place any more. It's so full of false moustaches and false beards. The phony atmosphere drives me wild."

And this from an artist further along in years:

> *The older generations were more honest. They were interested in being artists, and the new generation, I think, is more interested in money, success, finding the easy way. The older artists were willful and determined. They lived by a tradition the young ones don't have. Young ones pay lip service to a few artists they feel are important, but it's only lip service—for ulterior purposes. They'll do like J.S., move themselves this way and that way—as long as there's a tangible advantage in it. . . . Those who came in with me,*

*like Jackson Pollock, had a basic honesty. After that, some
other guy discovered he could paint, too, but his attitude
isn't the same as Pollock's any more. Pollock really believed;
this other fellow doesn't, but he gets attention, too. It's all
art, and the public doesn't understand it. So who cares what
you're really thinking? . . . Now, I'm not saying that such
people have no talent. I'm just saying that the chance of
their things having some sort of survival becomes less and less
and less. It's like a contemporaneous thing that happens right
now—and it's over with. What's sad is that there are very
talented guys who, I think, pervert their talent to fit in
with some mass production of work—which might be what
it really is.*

Whatever "it really is," the older artist fancies that his principles
are being cynically forsaken by young people who will not admit
what they are doing. The cost of this betrayal is inferior art. Once
again ethics shades off into aesthetics. The ethical bias is pragmatic.
Hence, from this point of view, to be morally reprehensible does
not pay, or does not pay off in artistic dividends. He who compromises himself by being fashionably rebellious, by switching styles
for the sake of financial gain, may walk off with a larger purse,
but his consciousness will have shriveled.

It is against the background of this stern pragmatic philosophy
that an Action Painter admits, "Abstract art may have run its
course." If so, he feels, further advance is now in order; the times
call for it, but no one seems to be answering. Instead, he dubs
the neo-realism of our time "reactionary," a return rather than
another step forward: "Perhaps I'm prejudiced, but I haven't seen
a figure painting or a landscape painting or a sculpture that represents a major breakthrough." Is the recrudescence of figurative art
a mistake? He denies it, contending that: "In art, the only mistakes
are things that don't work." Nor does he see anything inherent in
representational forms which prevents artists who have taken them
up again from succeeding. In sum, "It's just that in all this representational work there are no major inventions or procedures such
as we developed when we began to do non-representational paintings
and sculptures."

If older artists have any message at all for their juniors, it boils down to this: "Don't jump on the bandwagon. Build it yourself." Failure to heed this admonition drains too many young painters and sculptors of self-reliance—without which militancy and defiance disappear, and individuality dissolves. Cocking an ear to the market not only produces a weird posture in the artist, it makes his tools that much harder to wield, twists his hands, and distorts his vision —while smoothing his path to full social integration.

3

Social and Psychological Characteristics

. . . And a pleasant lot they are too, cheerful and healthy and leading regular lives. . . . His besetting maladies are digestive, due to poverty, undernourishment, and irregular meals. He needs lots of food. In middle and later life he sometimes has rheumatism. But he is seldom too ill to paint.

As soon as the light goes bad his painting day is over. He thereupon refreshes his mind by making love to his model or by quarreling with his wife, and goes out. From four till midnight he is gay and companionable. After midnight he is disagreeable because he knows he should be in bed. It is chiefly after midnight that he takes to alcohol, when he takes to it at all. He is a man of moderate habits, abundant physical energy, and a lively though not scholarly mind. . . .

They keep a cleaner separation than any other kind of man I know between their lives and their work, even, in their work, between vision and execution. Their vision is personal and subjective, their rendering of it precise, objective, non-emotional. All the emotional things like sexuality, politics, elegance, family life, and religion are kept strictly in the background of their lives as private games, subjects for talk, indulgences for the darker hours of the day.

Mark you, my portrait of the Painter is of the ideal, or rather average painter, the easel-painter as he exists among his sixty thousand brethren in Paris or New York. . . .

—VIRGIL THOMSON, 1939

THERE ARE both subtle and obvious social pressures operating to absorb the artist and to render his likeness into that of Everyman. Whether these pressures simply reflect society's unconscious jealousy and collective resentment of the artist's freedom and gratifications, or whether they represent a reaction to the anxiety which his art engenders, or any number of other motivations, informed and lay people increasingly tend to label him as "no different from the ordinary person." These "assimilationists" recognize that in the past an artist was often viewed negatively—someone different and separate. He was "less than a man," a common judgment with direct sexual connotations of effeminacy and possible homosexuality, which in its mildest form put the artist down as a dandy.

He or his "image" also existed in an equally unfavorable, but somewhat romanticized, version. He was seen as spectacularly successful with women, really "too much" of a man, irresistible in his allure for the female, and therefore an object of ferocious envy and hostility for the male. Where there were no allusions to sexuality, economics became important. The artist was an inadequate male for failing to support his spouse, for permitting her to support him while he engaged in non-productive work. Alternatively, he was shallow, cynical, and concerned only about advancement and success —when not dismissed as an idealist, completely "out of this world." At all times he was a caricature of a man who, if he did not fit these molds, was widely expected to be dirty, bedraggled, starving, or in some inevitable way bizarre.

THE ARTIST'S SELF-IMAGE

We find little feeling among artists that these old stereotypes of the "wild man," the dissolute wastrel, the somewhat effeminate creature inclined toward all kinds of unmanliness, persist to any great extent in the public mind. Although many are uncertain about how they are actually perceived, most artists feel that their status has risen as they have become more successful economically. Further, there is a "normalizing" movement afoot whose spokesmen dissent from such moderate studies as those by Miguel Prados [1] and Anne Roe,[2] because they "have unwittingly served to reinforce some of the stereotypes about artists: that they are persons apart from other persons, that their very separateness and uniqueness are in some way essential ingredients for their productivity and the contributions that they make," and that they are "activated by 'pure' motivations, by the desire to create, and not by material gain or the desire to please a superior." [3] This move to reduce the artist to typicality is sometimes countered by an equally uncritical attempt to romanticize him. He is elevated and rhapsodized to the point where he is no longer merely respected as an extraordinary man but becomes a kind of superman: "The truth is that great artists in particular are healthier, more at peace, and wiser than the run of men. Their cup runneth over; hence their art." [4]

In our study, the artists' self-image diverges from either extreme. Their statements show a much greater objectivity, an unexpected willingness to try to see themselves realistically, without recourse to traditional stereotypes. Yet delineation of "his kind" remains a complex task for the artist. It is exceedingly difficult for the insider (as for the outsider) to maintain objectivity. There are no definitive standards against which artists' views can be matched, for while several attempts have been made to appraise artists objectively, the results are at best suggestive, at worst misleading.

The two extreme and generally uncritical attitudes, those that disparage and those that idealize, have no real interest or meaning. Both seriously distort the truth by truncating it, by dealing primarily with the artist's behavior as a social being or a psychological entity while ignoring his true functions as a painter. Their accuracy or inaccuracy is of no immediate concern to him; the artist maintains that there is a sharp dichotomy between two of his roles, those of citizen and of painter, and that the former is mostly irrelevant to the latter. Self-appraisals are more likely to be consonant with comments such as this one by a philosophical critic:

> *Here are men—modern painters—who take art seriously. Perhaps they take life seriously too, but if so, that is only because there are things in life—aesthetic ecstasy, for instance —worth taking seriously. In life, they can distinguish be-*

tween the wood and the few fine trees. As for art, they know that it is something more important than a criticism of life; they will not pretend that it is a traffic in amenities; they know that it is a spiritual necessity.[5]

The artist prefers to explain himself within such a framework. He resists attempts at declaring him a man totally apart from others. Instead, he sees himself as someone who, by reason of innate talent fused with an early inclination, has nurtured and heightened his best abilities. With no awareness of their source, he also admits to having certain attitudes that are relatively rare in our society, and it is these that equip him to withstand the multiple pressures toward conformity that so furiously bombard all of us these days:

But our talent doesn't make us a special breed. You don't consider a man who can run a complicated machine to be so special because he does it . . . that doesn't make him different from everybody else. It just means that he has had that particular experience. There is a certain aptitude that in every profession is inevitably made more acute by the practice of that profession. But it doesn't make him part of a special breed. Still, any guy who gives up the other type of life to become an artist obviously must have something a little loose in his bolts. I will admit that. To have that drive, taking the whole context of society, he must be in that sense a more unusual man than the layman.

The artist thus reveals the basic conflict with which he must cope: on the one hand, the push toward group membership; on the other hand, the drive which keeps him functioning as an artist, and therefore separate and different. While he resists attempts to characterize him as unique (and this is a consistent stand among those to whom we talked), he is aware that those attitudes, character traits, and modes of adjustment which enable him to persist, and which he shares with so few others, *do* set him apart. Despite variations in emphasis, there is a remarkable uniformity in the orientation of these artists as a group. Despite their denials and protestations, it is apparent, to them and to us, that in certain respects they differ basically from non-artists.

69

In a study comparing artist and non-artist, Bernice Eiduson, although reluctant to see artists as unique, notes that: "Artists, furthermore, were shown to accept reality but perceive it in a way which is different from that of the non-artist. They are extremely responsive to sense data . . . they are able to tolerate ambiguity in perception . . . establish a multiplicity of identifications . . . ego-involvement is great . . ." [6] She does state that: "No developmental or motivational factors which serve as exclusive or crucial determinants for the making of an artist or for the encouragement of his selection of art work could be singled out," [7] but only after indicating that artist and non-artist differ significantly in the following aspects of thinking and perception, personality, and motivation, among others:

> [*the artist*]
> . . . *shows unusual emphasis on the elaboration of fantasy*
> . . . *seeks to depart radically in his expressions and thinking from the usual, obvious, or hackneyed*
> . . . *interests point to the theoretical and abstract rather than the practical and realistic*
> . . . *can loosen or relax controls in thinking without personality disorganization*
> . . . *can convey experiences or feelings so that another's emotional response is aroused*
> . . . *is sensitive to moods and feelings of others*
> . . . *values work primarily as permitting expression of inner personality*
> . . . *strong ego-involvement and conflict expressed in work* [8]

These would seemingly obviate her argument that there is fundamentally nothing distinctive about the artist.

THE PERSONAL QUALITIES NECESSARY FOR THE TRUE ARTIST

In her studies of successful artists, Anne Roe has concluded that "They are extremely hard-working, and although they have considerable superficial freedom with regard to hours and place of work, the self-discipline required to effect the rather routinized life that is characteristic of most of them is probably much greater than is generally appreciated." [9] Phyllis Greenacre, after a study of some of the literature on creativity, sees the artist as possessed of:

1. *a greater sensitivity to sensory stimulation*
2. *an unusual capacity for awareness of relations between various stimuli*
3. *a predisposition to an empathy of wider range and vibration than usual*
4. *an intactness of sufficient sensorimotor equipment to allow the building up of projective motor discharges for expressive functions*

and further, "sensibility of subtle similarities and differences, an earlier and greater reactivity to form and rhythm." [10] When Heinz Hartmann asserts that: "The knowledge of an artist's conflicts and unconscious fantasies often does not sufficiently explain why their working out takes the form of art," [11] he is only emphasizing how limited we are in our knowledge of the sources of creativity and talent.

When artists talk about their own important characteristics, they do little to explain the making of a good artist. They shed little light on the sources of creativity, but they illuminate and amplify some facets of the process of creating:

> *Well, I'd say you have to have a little talent and a lot of character. I've seen cases of people with lots of talent who failed, and I could only attribute it to their lack of character or perseverance or whatever it was that they lacked, outside of talent. Intelligence and courage, I think, would be the basis of the personal traits that would make up character. As an example of what I mean, first of all he has to be intelligent enough to see that his aims are not the aims which are commonly accepted in society. Then he has to have the courage to go against the general stream and the aims which he sees on all sides. He has to be able to set up his own goal and then work out some way of achieving it.*

> *Well, I think in different cases it varies. I hate to say, no, I guess I still say that the really essential things include the*

commonest and the most mundane old-fashioned virtues. You can be as fey and whimsical and imaginative and creative as anybody in all history, but if you haven't got the ability to persist in spite of everything and just keep knocking your head against a wall, you're lost.

Well, character, of course. I mean, what else could it be? I don't think there were any such things as breaks or anything of that sort. We were all faced with comparable situations.

It's possible to say that the artist is involved in ethical problems because he always has to make the ethical choice in his work. He can never, if he is an artist, make less than the most moral choice. He can never compromise. He can never do what he thinks would be good for him to do in terms of recognition or money.

. . . a great deal of enthusiasm and interest that never stops. It requires dedication.

It's a special kind of caring. When you're working it suddenly matters to you that this was a hairbreadth of an inch too much off to the right, or the color isn't right. It would be hard for someone standing over your shoulder to see the difference, but I think it's something in your nature that makes you think about these things.

The average age of these artists is over fifty, and most entered the art world at a time when there could have been no realistic hope of worldly reward, pecuniary or otherwise. They experienced counter-pressures and resistances, at home and at large, sufficient to deter people less strongly motivated. At least for those who entered the art world before the last decade, it can only be these characteristics which made it possible for them to choose painting as a life work. Under present social conditions such a choice may be more ambiguous.

When their statements are broken down thematically, they suggest a number of characteristics consistent with high professional stature. The artist is unable to indicate how they have originated, but he leaves no doubt concerning their importance to him. He emphasizes most: Intelligence, Suffering, Sensitivity, Freedom linked to Independence, Solitude to Privacy, Discipline to Dedication (as well as to Courage), a "Big" Ego, and Innocence. Some of the characteristics overlap, but they receive enough individual attention to warrant separate consideration.

At the same time, an overall analysis of these statements shows that character (variously defined) is viewed as basic. Talent by itself is de-emphasized, since all take it for granted. The artist rejects out of hand the proposition that with sufficient training and practice "an artist can be made," but he is aware of talent that has failed when wedded to an excess of human frailty. This indeed is why he refuses to give it primacy. He accepts R. H. Collingwood's opinion that:

> *The artist must have a certain specialized form of skill, which is called technique. He acquires his skill just as a craftsman does, partly thru personal experience and partly thru sharing in the experience of others who thus become his teachers. The technical skill which he acquires does not by itself make him an artist; for a technician is made, but an artist is born . . ."*

and "All this, properly understood, is very true, and as a criticism of the sentimental notion that works of art can be produced by anyone, however little trouble he has taken to learn his job, provided his heart is in the right place, very salutary." [12]

SENSE OF RESPONSIBILITY AND CAPACITY FOR WORK

Character has many facets, but artists emphasize two. First, they stress the importance of *personal* responsibility (artists, particularly those who are younger, avoid assuming more social responsibility than they have to). They regard personal responsibility as a factor which enables them to develop their own perspective and then empowers them to work toward nothing less than perfection. This is by definition a never-ending quest upon which the true artist must embark. One of the greatest dangers facing him is the complacency and sense of completion which may attend any success. As soon as he permits himself more than momentary satisfaction with his attainments, he is in danger of succumbing to material or other undesirable temptations. Being human, he may desire recognition at some level, but it remains a threatening specter to his integrity as an artist. In view of this danger, he reacts to "arrival" with doubt, suspicion, and anxiety. Besides shunning the very obvious temptations generated by success, he must exercise a peculiar temporal caution. As the artists see it, even the greatest of them is chronically in danger of being overwhelmed by time—past, present, or future; and to paint in response to any force outside the self is to risk surrendering all that is important and meaningful.

Second and always paramount is the artist's capacity for work. Everyone agrees, once again, that if the painter or sculptor does not apply himself unremittingly, he will never be a true artist—even with talent. Growth requires discipline and dedication of a high order. Except for a creative elite in the arts and sciences, most of us find work an unmitigated burden or a monotonous bore performed out of economic necessity and external pressures. The artist's dedication, spurred on and sustained from within, is therefore a rarity, scarcely to be found elsewhere in our society. External force plays a minor role in the artist's life. To be sure, he does not "create" on schedule. His work pattern is a highly personal matter; some artists work regularly and others work in spurts. It is taken to be self-evident, however, that the artist cannot be effective without devoting much time, energy, and effort to his task. All studies of successful artists show that they are persistent and hard-working.

Beyond character, these artists center on specifics about which their comments show an impressive unanimity.

INTELLIGENCE

> *Well, I think I would say intelligence is more important than that sense of emotion, because I think that the emotion that a painting has is communicated through intelligence, as a discipline.*

> *Art couldn't exist without intelligence. It's the one absolutely necessary element.*

> *I do think that John Dewey was right when he said that*

artists' activity is an intellectual enterprise of a very high order. It's not the kind of rational intellect that other disciplines demand. All the artists I know who are good are first of all quite intelligent. Their perception is always keen and off-beat, which requires a certain kind of intelligence.

I have never met a good artist who wasn't intelligent, and I don't think you can divorce the intellect from art. Intelligence has to do with seeing relationships. I think the great intelligence is a unification of all the forms back of it, the mind, intuition, the subconscious, and the superconscious—all of these things working at once.

I think it's being open to possibilities in some ordered way that you can use. I'm not talking about the intelligence that comes with learning facts.

It's a certain kind of cunning; it's a certain kind of quick decision; it's a certain kind of response to colors . . . wit and other definitions of quick comprehension of many points of view.

Intelligence, then, is a necessary ingredient in achieving success. Great care is taken to limit the definition so as to exclude people who acquire only facts and figures, "the kind who do well on IQ tests." (These artists share with many knowledgeable people the fallacious idea that information, in and of itself, is sufficient to guarantee a high score on any intelligence test. Knowledge is certainly useful, but other dimensions are usually included in testing intellectuality.) It is quite likely that artists are not only bright in special ways, but also in the broader sense, as measured by well-constructed ability tests which have a heavy loading of the g (general) factor. Implicit and sometimes explicit in the artists' statements is a fear that intelligence will be confused with routine academic achievement, something they wish to distinguish from creativity. Although in the minority, at least one artist's formulations were unguarded in that respect:

Yes. Essential [intelligence]. Well, I think in order to simplify or to use a code you have to be able to throw out an awful lot that you really know and learned. It's the kind of intelligence that would make you test brilliantly, I would guess, in the kinds of tests that were thrown at me in those different schools—just that kind.

Artists are properly concerned about a popular tendency to use the terms *intelligence* and *creativity* more or less synonymously; however often they may be related to each other, these phenomena are not identical. Phyllis Greenacre has noted that "creativity is a special capacity which may or may not be associated with great ability . . . does not seem to have a great deal to do with superior intelligence in terms of quotients, even though excellent intelligence may contribute to the productions of the creative person." [13] The mental measurement literature helps to resolve this problem by sub-suming intelligence under creativity and seeing it as an element that, along with many others, contributes to it.[14] For artists, per-ception is the crucial aspect of intelligence. With it they can visualize linear and other relationships, form and color harmonies, relevant and irrelevant detail; without it, they are unable to make quick and proper decisions. To verbalize about these matters is relatively un-important for them. They feel that they use intelligence to sift what comes through from the unconscious: "I don't feel I'm giving up my intellectuality in painting. My unconscious is controlling it to the benefit of what I want to do."

On this point then, a final summary comment from one of our group: "I've never seen a good stupid artist."

SUFFERING

The artist suffers more acutely. He doesn't suffer more. Every-body suffers, but he suffers in a way that is more acute, more knowing than the man who may suffer deeply and not necessarily know the extent of his suffering.

No. Suffering is absolutely unnecessary. If it's there and it's unavoidable, then you just take it. But I certainly do not believe in the necessity of it. It's actually such an egocentric conception that the artist has to suffer to do art. He suffers enough mentally and morally and all other ways to be able to work. But the purely physical side or the material side, I don't see why that should be necessary.

Well, I think most people suffer. Some know it more than others.

I've been an artist enough years to have had both conditions: near starvation, no money, uncertainty . . . food every day, secure rent, practical luxuries. And what poverty takes out of you in energy and morale is indescribably terrible. I can do more in two well-nourished hours than I can do in a week in poverty. And it isn't only my experience; I've seen it in other people. Lots of people get corrupted by affluence and lots of people get corrupted by poverty. Just considering people are people, whatever they are capable of doing, poverty and that kind of suffering that comes from deprivation won't improve what they can do.

If there is suffering peculiar to the artist, it's nobody's business but the artist's because it's peculiar to him. He has no right to impose that on the rest of the world.

No, I don't think there's any virtue in suffering for an artist or anybody.

The artist is careful to discriminate between physical or material privation and psychic suffering. Nobody laments the numerical decline of hungry and impoverished artists who must struggle merely to remain alive and feebly pursue their work. Such deprivation is simply defined as an impairment. Artists repeatedly point out that they have enough emotional trauma in their work life, and indigence can only be an added and gratuitous burden. Yet among the strongest resentments which the artist evinces are those related to the popular conception, which still has some prevalence, that his suffering is an integral part of his being an artist. From his point of view, material insufficiency merely obliges him to spend valuable time away from creative work in money-making pursuits. He expresses such sentiments in neither a bitter nor a masochistic way; this is a matter of circumstance, to be handled in as reasonable a manner as possible.

The artist typically can have only contempt for painters and professional people who complain about long hard years of preparation and deprivation:

> *When I talk to a doctor and he tells me how many years he has deprived himself so he could go to school and be a doctor . . . but why did he do it? So he could tell me sad tales? I think he must be a terrible doctor and he's out to get every buck he can because he's suffered for so long. And I'm suspicious of people who impose their special condition on the rest of the world, including any artist who runs around crying about the plight of the artist.*

But this is a relatively minor problem in today's affluent society: "It used to be that we had to decide whether to spend our money on art stuff or food or cigarettes; now it's a matter of whether somebody needs three hundred dollars or not."

Material privation has no doubt kept some artists from succeeding, and has even kept some potentially great artists from discovering their gifts, but it is also true that many of them entered the field when it was necessary to "take a vow of poverty." They persisted, despite practical difficulties.

Non-material or spiritual suffering is a universal condition. So the artist refuses to see himself as a unique sufferer, although he does make some claims concerning his heightened awareness of psychic pain, which is ostensibly more pronounced than that of the ordinary man. However, the artist is able to confront his suffering and transcend it through his meaningful work, an outlet which few others have at their disposal. To this extent his techniques of adjustment stand in contrast to those most others must use to maintain some sense of stability. Most of us rely much more heavily on complicated and frequently crippling defense mechanisms. Art provides the artist with a valid outlet, even though it produces new tensions.

The artist's special preoccupation turns on his struggle to bring something of note into being without yielding to cross-pressures that constrain him to do what he "knows" he must not do. The artist, as a man among men, is also beset by common concerns, but he tries to keep them from impinging upon his creative function—and he very largely succeeds.

Suffering is intimately connected with sensitivity, and in the artist's view, without the deep experience of all feelings no real art can ever be produced.

SENSITIVITY

I think the artist experiences deeper emotions, inevitably, because he deals with them more than other people do; he knows them better. He is more accustomed to them, and so they have a wider range after his years of experience. It's a faculty which is developed through use, and that would be one of the reasons we don't like the bourgeois. They don't enjoy themselves anymore or feel anything.

I don't think you can make a generalization that all artists are naturally endowed with more sensitivity than other people. What I do think is that the kind of work they do, the things they cultivate in themselves are things like that. An artist shapes himself. He isn't even all there. And then he uses the tools. He has to work, and that work means he's working on himself.

I've know good artists who are pretty cold fish, and by that I mean what is commonly meant. But I don't deny them their feeling or even a special intensity of feeling which they choose not to reveal in conventional expressions and dealings. And they are good artists because they have those feelings. However, they may cover them up or drive them underground or disguise them or whatever.

Yes, I think the artist is sensitive to form and color and line and design and emotion and the expressions thereof. But I think oversensitivity is due to fear of dangers, and it is to be avoided.

Again the artist is inclined to ascribe his distinguishing characteristics more to cultivation than to endowment. He believes that certain activities have led to a heightening of his sensitivities, precisely those that are stunted and blunted in most other people. This view contrasts somewhat with that of Phyllis Greenacre, who sees the artist's sensitivity as biologically given; it is manifested in his experience of himself and of other living and inanimate objects: "The increased empathy associated with creative talent would seemingly depend on the sensory responsiveness to the individual's own body state as well as to the external object, and appears as a peculiar degree of empathic animation of inanimate objects as well as a heightened responsiveness and anthropomorphizing of living objects." [15]

There are sensitivities and sensitivities. It is necessary to separate those involved in interpersonal relationships (sensitivity to the feelings and attitudes of others) from a general intensification of responsiveness to internal and external stimuli. The artist can be "crass and insensitive" in the first situation, but he cannot be insensitive in the second, more general meaning of the word. And yet there are limits to the amounts of sensitivity an artist can have and still function effectively. Oversensitivity, related to fears and apprehensions, leaves him in a weakened state of total and therefore nonselective receptivity. This causes him to be indiscriminately responsive and consequently prevents him from making the choices which are so necessary to his painting (in psychoanalytic terms, a weakened ego defense pattern).

The artist is probably correct when he claims that he "trains and develops" himself and in that sense achieves his own fulfillment. Because the artist deals with emotion as raw material for work, he must be conscious of his own feelings to an unusual degree; through the daily experience of actively using and mastering affect, he may well develop a greater emotional capacity than the average person, who will have more trouble allowing certain attitudes or feelings to grow and develop. This selectivity is either necessitated or facilitated by his greater acuity in perceiving the universe. It is in this sense that he shapes himself and, within limits, touches and influences others. Some find it more comfortable to refer to all of this as intensified vision rather than sensitivity, a preference which may stem from various connotations which cluster around that term, especially those that imply effeminacy.

FREEDOM AND INDEPENDENCE

> *I think freedom is a matter of personality, how you feel,
> yourself. Some of them seem to be free; others, I don't
> think they're so free. Like I send my kid to school and I
> don't feel like going over and attending all those meetings
> and lectures. There are all kinds of people writing you letters
> saying they want you to attend this meeting and that meet-
> ing, and you say the hell with it. Maybe that's some kind
> of freedom. But later on you realize it's not. You say some
> terrible things to people by accident and then later on you
> think you really shouldn't have done that. Maybe it's not so
> good. Some of them are able to feel free and others feel
> trapped.*

> *You say, well, I am free; I can go to bed at four o'clock
> in the morning and I can get up at three o'clock in the after-
> noon. Where is there any freedom in that? Just less regular
> hours. But these are his regular hours and they are pretty
> regular. It's his life. They're just as regular as a man who
> gets up at 6:30 or 7:00 to go to work and gets to bed at
> 9:30 or 10:00. They're both regular.*

> *Generally the artist is freer in that he cares less about many
> of the false forms that most people go for.*

> *I think that in a certain sense artists are very lucky, be-
> cause the work they do is the work they choose to do and they
> feel it expresses themselves. They aren't doing a job which
> pays them money and has no interest otherwise.*

> *Yes, I think art gives the individual freedom. It's the one
> thing a person can do all by himself. He isn't a cog in a
> machine. He doesn't punch this button. The activity of art
> is completely done by an individual—the whole thing.*

It is a gross illusion to think of the artist as a completely free,
uninhibited, and independent being: "I think that freedom is a most
essential quality. At his easel, the artist is free. He's not free any
other way, but he has to be free at his easel. Is he free as a member

of the human race? Of course not." This comment points up the two freedoms which an artist must enjoy. The first is an inner freedom which will permit his painting to evolve in its own highly personalized direction. The second is official or unofficial permission from the authorities for him to pursue his painting and sculpting. If either of these freedoms is absent, the artist cannot flourish (although in the second instance there is always a great likelihood of underground action).

The artist recognizes this situation clearly. He sees his freedom at work, where he himself is the only restricting force, as one of the few remaining bastions of true independence, and to that extent he is grateful to a society which has ignored him. But even this "beneficial neglect" is in jeopardy because of the influence now being exerted by business in the art world, as well as by the general political and cultural scene and the human frailties to which the artist is heir no less than anyone else. He will lose his freedom only insofar as he "wants" to, but the potential sources of corruption are many, and some of them are insidious.

Hence the freedom artists cherish is far from absolute. Like most people, the painter or sculptor accepts responsibilities as a citizen. At the same time, he is bound to his work as an independent craftsman, and he disciplines and regulates himself at it in a way that few others do. His indifference to, or outright contempt for, certain social conventions affords him a relatively greater freedom in one area than most others have, but he does not delude himself that this makes him truly independent of the society in which he lives. Only at the canvas can he be really free, and without this specific freedom he cannot be an artist.

SOLITUDE AND PRIVACY

That reminds me of a friend of mine who in school was asked whether he'd rather lead or be led, and he said he'd rather be left alone. I think that's pretty good for the artist— to be left alone.

You only need quiet and isolation for your working hours. I don't mind being interrupted occasionally. I don't like it all the time.

Well, of course he always needs solitude, but the nature of the solitude has to do with your work, what you work in. I think one always manages to establish that. During the period that you work you go into the isolation of your studio for long periods of time. It takes as long as your work is moving, a month, two months, or maybe three months. This doesn't mean that during those months you don't come out in the evenings and things like that.

I think a high percentage of creative people exist in a kind of isolation. It may be in the middle of society, or it may be in the Maine woods. But they do exist in a kind of isolation. I think that's true of anyone trying to accomplish work.

You are always working alone. There's no institution. You can go to art school but that doesn't lead anywhere. It isn't like medical school where the channels are fairly fixed. You know a lot of artists, but even so, you're operating absolutely on your own. I can't rid myself of a certain nostalgia for a situation in which the tradition could exist where one builds on the other, and I think it's a weakness.

To be by yourself. Yes. A lot of painters want to paint, but one of the things you notice about them is that they can never stand to be alone. And that's very important, actually, being able to spend four or five hours in the studio without somebody bugging you or the phone ringing or something. A lot of people can't stand it. I think it's very important.

In disentangling these facets of solitude and privacy, the aspect most commonly noted is literally that of being able to bear the solitude of painting. The act must be performed by an individual on his own, whether in the presence of others or isolated from them. This means that the "group" does not exist in painting, and that the dependent person can only have difficulties in functioning. Put otherwise, the true painter must be self-sufficient. He needs tremendous initiative. After the early period of practice and training, an artist must work independently to find himself. Most painters and sculptors prefer physical isolation while at work. They resent intrusions and distractions of any kind. Some carry this need to the

83

extreme of almost a monastic existence. For them, art involves the disciplined renunciation of pleasurable social contacts, at least during periods of productivity.

The artist alludes to another kind of isolation which he experiences, and which André Malraux has made explicit: ". . . in the nineteenth century a special kind of solitude, at once contemptuous and creative, soon came to seem the natural lot of the sincere artist. This was a new development . . . now the painters ceased catering for the general public or any given class; they appealed to a strictly limited group who recognized the same values as they did." [16] This self-imposed exile was necessary to their development; thus they renounced a large public for their own more meaningful small circle. This willingness to accept a way of life which provided limited recognition could not have been easy, for it is a general human trait to desire attention. To persevere in a situation where there is little public understanding of one's goals and intentions not only requires great dedication but also an enormous capacity for survival under circumstances of prolonged isolation.

If this psychological strength is not just biological, possibly the capacity to withstand isolation has to do with certain types of childhood experience. The self-sufficient pattern manifests itself very early in the lives of many artists. A surprising number of artists tell us they were "on their own" at an unusually tender age, having left the family at or before adolescence. Others report going off by themselves for many hours as young children, studying nature, daydreaming, and playing alone. While our findings do not go as far as Bernice Eiduson's, her material bears on ours: "The artists were lonely and isolated as children, dissociated from family ties . . ." [17]

Working from a different viewpoint, but dealing essentially with the same matters, Phyllis Greenacre has postulated:

> . . . it is possible that in the libidinal phases of development of the infantile years the presence of such collective alternative relationships ["love" involvement with the seen or unseen audience, as opposed to individual object relationships] permits diminution of the effect of critical situations involving the individual object relationships. . . . In the gifted ones, however, the individual object may be only

> *apparently relinquished, to appear rather in a glorified col-lective form which becomes the object of the love for a time.*[18]

Dr. Greenacre thus contends that in his early years the artist may be unable to obtain the intense individual object relationship that he craves (primarily with the father, or so it seems from our data), and that he then, through his work, strives to reach the collective audience as a substitute for the individual object relationship. At an unconscious level, one motive force behind his work is the continued quest for a primary object which, according to Dr. Greenacre, he has never really relinquished. This intrapsychic situation may lessen the artist's need for close individual ties, while helping him to accept the restriction of social contacts imposed by his work.

DISCIPLINE AND DEDICATION

> *I'm the kind of person with sharply defined work habits and routine. I need only so many hours, but I need them at certain times. These are my best working hours and I always like to be working during these hours.*

> *I get up in the morning and have my breakfast, sit around, get a little nervous, and go out and do some work. My days have a certain order. I don't know . . . in the work, I mean. The studio is pretty sloppy, but I know where everything is. In putting down a color, I don't know what discipline means.*

> *That's a question of habit, because I cannot go everyday as a rule to the studio. There are days I don't do any work and there are days when I would stay late in the studio, and come home late, and go early. There are periods when you can't do a damn thing—discipline or no discipline. It doesn't substitute for creative work. There's a technical discipline in addition to a moral discipline.*

> *But with the doubts or frequent downs or depressions, con-fusion is something that forces one to stay with it and push through it. You question yourself. You have faith and sud-denly you're looking back on how you got through it.*

I don't think seriously of doing anything else. I do remember the day the eviction notice came. I started on an enormous canvas which I knew I could never finish, but I did; in four different locations, I did finish it.

I think that we, without undue stress, can use the term dedication. *And we use the term* discipline *because I think without it you're just a floundering dilettante. And I think dilettantism is probably more the reason why we have more people in America painting today than ever before. Unquestionably. Whether it's for therapeutic reasons, told by their psychiatrists, or what have you, or whatever it is, but today there are more dilettantes painting than ever before.*

A guy asked me the other day, "Do you have to paint?" I hate statements like that. That brings up this whole romantic hassle of a guy standing there, with a cloak around him and the storm roaring behind his head; dark and light shadows are on his head; these lights light that corona around his head; he has to paint. Well, I think that's one of the public relations images that don't mean anything. Sure, you have to paint. It's the thing that you do the best. You feel that of all things you've tried to do, this is the thing you do the best. That's the way you can express your interest in life most fully. You love painting because it's good to you.

Discipline and persistence are often grouped together, but they refer to two different attitudinal dimensions: the first tends to be used in a rather narrow sense, denoting the painter's daily regularity at work; the second suggests his devotion to art as a calling. Most spontaneous comments refer to the first level. Relative to the second, our painters all speak of periodic but intense discouragement, times when they think about giving it all up. This transitory melancholia has no true reality for them: "I've only thought about giving up. The only thing I can tell you about whenever I've thought about not being able to paint, the only thing I would consider is going to England and becoming the village drunk . . . like that's the other kind of a paradise that I could think of. But I've never had anything I would care to do more." This exemplifies the prevailing attitude among all these artists. In spite of a certain depression that comes and goes, there can be no serious doubt about continuing. To consider anything else seems absurd.

Regardless of their own idiosyncratic habits, all artists place a high value on regularity and persistence. To the more erratic, steadiness at work is theoretically desirable, and they express envy of those who are able to attain it. They make a sharp distinction between disciplined work habits, however, and anything like compulsiveness. The first means giving systematic expression to creative urges, whereas compulsivity suggests sterile ritualism. One artist comments sarcastically: "I envy a guy like X who, for example, can get up in the morning and have a room for etching, a room for lithographs, a room for painting. He takes a walk and he makes a stroke as he moves around. But this is manufacturing." Looking at it a little differently, in the first instance the artistic product is decisive, whereas in the second, artistic activity becomes the focal point. Artists recognize that inspiration cannot be expected to appear on a "regular" basis. For this reason, painting every day can have very little creative purpose. When they talk about discipline and regularity, it is relevant chiefly for periods of true creativity. "Applying paint to canvas for its own sweet sake" is not considered sensible for a true artist.

Internal as well as external factors may conspire to limit an artist. Inner blocks to performance hinder artists no less than other people. Their attempts to exercise "will power" to dissolve the blocks seem to them to be fruitless. External interference is also difficult to master. It is possible to reduce social participation, but outside work cannot be so easily eliminated. There is more to the problem than budgeting one's time. What to do about a constantly shifting set? How to maintain an adequate level of inspiration? There are quandaries in these questions that make many artists prefer obligatory bread-and-butter work which is completely outside the art field.

COURAGE

Yes, you need courage, and I don't mean in relation to the public either; I mean in relation to not permitting yourself to be comfortable with what you do, but always pushing it further. Now that takes a kind of guts. You know, not to settle for the norm, but always trying to find that next place you've never been to yet. I think that sort of courage is important.

Someimes I'm not sure what courage is. Courage is sometimes based simply on desperation; courage is sometimes based on ignorance. Those who fail are simply lacking in pride or conceit.

Well, I suppose you could say it's a quality that enables you to see things in a special way, that is, you wouldn't be influenced by conventions. But I don't know if you need it in the moral sense.

Moral courage. Moral courage not to conform, to be able to say and to act, both; there are many conditions prevalent now, you see, which I think are very hard to take. You may easily be subjected to them, submerged by them, cut up, or whatever may happen to you, instead of being able to survive these things.

You need loads of it. You need a tremendous abundance of it, because there is every reason why you shouldn't be doing it, painting, that is, money-wise. If you are not interested in merely showing pictures, because you feel you haven't arrived with something. There is conscience related to this thing. It requires more integration as a creative man, while the dilettante has no such idea. I still make this contrast.

I never thought I believed in courage. I always felt it was easier to do the things I believed in and I wanted to do, than do other things. It hurts me to do the other.

"Courage" is obviously evocative to artists, but defining it proves troublesome, and they wonder about different kinds of courage. There is also some, but less, uncertainty concerning the appropriateness of the term. In the more common usage—bravery in the face of danger—it is widely questioned: "Courage? I find people on the battlefield courageous or people running into burning houses. I don't find anything particularly courageous in art." There is possible bravery in an extended demonstration of staying power as an artist, but even this is dubious: "Maybe after a man has lived for sixty years. If you think, well, the fact that if the old boy kept doing it, that was something tremendous. But day to day, I don't know if it's really so marvelous." Another minority view makes much of the difference between courage and necessity: to do what you believe you must do is in no way admirable.

But the dominant opinion is that courage exists by itself and that its presence or absence is a moral question. The willingness to expose oneself to total rejection, to stake everything on success or failure, is of comparatively minor importance. The courage to remain uncoerced, to stand apart, to reject easy and seductive conformity—all this is more germane. Courage also strikes the artist as an essential characteristic whenever he must summon it to avoid work designed just to show or simply out of concern for his present and future stature. He needs it when he breaks with tradition, as he ultimately must (which is different from undertaking innovation for the sake of innovation). There is evidence of courage when he fights against the impulse to be comfortable with his attainments, no matter how widely they are accepted, so he may continue "exploring" exclusively out of inner awareness. His courage means facing himself and acting on the basis of insight, by contrast with the "well-defended" person who lacks awareness, or the opportunist who gives up being true to himself for monetary rewards.

"EGO"

You see, part of the artist's equipment is to have a very tough ego, so that I have never met an artist, except those who quit, without it. But the artists who stuck with it never felt what they were doing was mediocre. They may have felt it was misunderstood and that they had not yet been appreciated.

I think you have to feel that in some way you're absolutely marvelous. This has nothing to do with your judgment of yourself, but with some sort of secret side of you which is convinced. That's what I mean by fanaticism. What I'm talking about is something mad, something so powerfully felt that if there were a steel wall in front of you, you'd go through it.

I think that no artists can survive unless they really think they're the best, the best of their times. You really think that in this department, in this little thing that you're doing, you're the best. Many artists are willing to stake their reputations against Picasso, against Matisse; it requires considerable ego. Other artists are willing to say, "I'm better than any other American artist," or, "I'm best among New York artists."

Americans are too timid and not confident enough. I refer to a certain kind of realism in America that doesn't exist in Europe. The Italian artist very rarely doubts his quality. If at the end of his life he didn't succeed in doing as well as he had hoped, it was because of circumstances—not having met the right people, right situations, not how big is his talent.

I've known quite a few artists who don't think they're very good, and they know it, and have no pretensions about it. But dammit, come hell or high water, they're going to paint a good painting if it takes them eighty years. Going on isn't a matter of being good.

All kinds of people have a facility for performance; they can do something as long as they feel like it. As long as they don't worry about it, it's all right. Maybe they could even convince other people. Sooner or later there comes doubt, doubt creeps in and they succumb to it; they disappear. I mean you've got to have confidence to afford to have this doubt.

These artists habitually use "ego" in the colloquial sense to mean confidence and conviction (rather than ego in the technical psychoanalytic sense). As they use it, the "big ego" is essential; if an artist is to continue, he must believe he is great, or at least potentially capable of being great, irrespective of his present performance. (The so-called modest artist who knows that he's not very good, but is determined to paint for "eighty years" until he produces that good painting, must have just as great an "ego" as the painter who merely believes that he *is* great.) This is a necessarily irrational aspect of the artist's makeup, since it bespeaks a disinclination to deal directly with reality: "I remember one of them saying to me way back when I was just getting a dim awareness of this thing, of the art tradition—I have that scene sharp in my memory of that artist who quit, saying to me—'We may as well face it. We're not geniuses.' And I answered him, 'Well, you can speak for yourself.' It takes conviction." The same artist then describes how this faculty operates: "I'm saying—I've been aware of it so I can say it—that knack of stupidity, maybe, or of ignorance, when I'm working on a thing, that's really *it*." They show considerable awareness of the subjective and possibly unrealistic quality of this "ego"; yet it is also one of the mainsprings of their work and they must be guided by it. There is thus a certain split in their perception of themselves as artists, which does not seem to disturb them. Irrational egoism, self-doubt, critical and keen, harsh or charitable assessments of what they do function simultaneously.

Perhaps this kind of "strong ego" operates only as a reaction-formation against underlying self-doubt. We should ponder one foreign-born artist's suggestion that this tendency is peculiarly American. It may well be that as American artists broke with the past and struck off into virgin territory, "slaying the European father" and establishing themselves as "art leaders" of the world, such uncertainty was an inevitable by-product. On a more primitive level, when a child breaks with his parents there must be a period of uncertainty while he is in the process of consolidating his independence. The same may be true of American artists, especially those who were among the first to initiate the new movement. Possibly the American artist lacks those deep and important roots and traditions which would give him a sense of intactness comparable to that which the European artist has, or had at one time. In addition, the American artist failed to receive psychological support from his society (at any rate, in the formative years of this group; we suspect that the present generation of young artists find their situation more complicated and ambiguous), which perhaps forced him in even more ways to depend only on himself, to remain his own best judge. Doubt, despite the above, is considered by these artists to be as vital to their work as the "ego," for it is doubt which impels them to search and probe. This combination of traits has pertinence for both the younger and the older, more established painter.

Here we touch a significant difference between the artist and the typical "non-artist." The artist is able to entertain contradictory and conflicting attitudes and ideas in relation to himself, so he simultaneously doubts his capacities and the value of his productions and sees himself as the "greatest." He can balance these attitudes within a general state of awareness and use them productively in his work. The non-artist tends to have ups and downs, periods of belief and doubt which, when they coexist, more often produce conflicts and tensions that cannot lead to constructive release. The artist seems generally better able to tolerate ambiguity in relation to himself and to the world. He can contain these contradictions within his consciousness; he is even able to articulate them. The artist, by his "unreasonable" aspirations and his repudiation of extraneous standards, asks for uncertainty and is able to tolerate it, although not without suffering.

INNOCENCE

> *Well, it means every time you look at something, you're not looking at it through a preconceived notion of experience. You're looking at it and nothing is standing between you and your vision—no book knowledge, not a theory, no philosophy. It's the vision and you, and you come face to face with it.*

> *Innocence comes best usually when the painter is a very old man. He is very wise and knows all the corruptions of the world; then he can afford to be innocent in the true sense and achieves it. I think Beethoven was innocent in the last quartets. I think Monet was innocent when he painted the "Water Lilies" picture; he was eighty-five.*

Innocence, I think, is more useful than discipline, but then you get to the point where you are a professional innocent, you know, which is something that has to be dealt with. But I find innocence is at least guiltless. I mean that whatever comes out, if you can enjoy it, all right. If you don't, then it's not. Innocence in a way does away with a point of view. It just means that if a guy comes along and tells you that it is marvelous to be innocent, he isn't any longer.

Artists agree that innocence is a prerequisite for their work. They describe it as a mode of experiencing which is immediate and spontaneous, where there is no interposition of irrelevant intellectual material. It is an envisioning of things, or a perceiving of things, without any preconceived set, which entails treating each situation that arises in all its novelty and particularity. The artist carefully points out that innocence is not to be confused with naiveté. He totally rejects the "innocent as a newborn babe" cliché, because to him it spells "ignorance" and nothing else. Paradoxical as it may seem, he takes innocence to be the same as infinite wisdom; neither verbalized nor symbolized, it is correctly identified by either name. Such innocence can only appear with maturity and "ripeness." Implicit in it is "all-knowing" rather than "non-knowing." It indicates that the artist has experienced "everything" and because of this he is able to eliminate those biases which graft artificial ideas and "foreign matter" onto his work. Innocence cannot be consciously cultivated; to be aware of it is to invite its extinction.

THE COMPOSITE SELF-PORTRAIT

The self-portrait of an authentic artist, then, is that of a person who has an uncompromising commitment to his work; who is disciplined and capable of unusual persistence in the absence of any external rewards or guideposts; who approaches his painting without preconceived ideas beyond being true to his artistic impulses; who feels with unshakeable assurance that what he does is not only worthwhile but unique and essential above any other pursuit or consideration; who is able to endure solitude and finds privacy, along with freedom and independence, a necessity; and finally a person who has the courage to live and act on these premises, without regard for extraneous consequences.*

The fine artist's distinguishing qualities are found directly within or just below his attitude toward artistic pursuits, but they refer principally to his behavior as a painter or sculptor; in his personal and social life he may function in a different manner. It should be understood that even in his professional attitudes, each individual artist, still being human, is no paragon of everlasting virtue. It is clear that his expressed attitudes involve a readiness for many renunciations and sacrifices. But he does not make a virtue of deprivation, regarding and experiencing his work as more important to him. This does not imply freedom from conflict. He is constantly struggling to resist corruption in order to maintain his artistic integrity. What may distinguish the man who remains a "true" artist from the one who goes under and gives up this struggle is the artist's psychological apparatus, which provides him with greater and more meaningful internal gratifications than he could obtain in the external world.

Besides the variables already specified (with "talent" always assumed), the artist also sees himself as possessing certain additional endowments. He is a person of strong sensitivity whose experiences are deep and intense. He is "intelligent" chiefly in his ability to perceive new relationships (and, we might add, in the conventional verbal sense as well). Even though most artists insist on the non-intellectualized and non-verbal nature of their work, the striking thing about their performance in our interviews was not only their verbal facility but their precise and original imagery and expression.

It is interesting to note how closely related the artists' descriptions are to those given by Miguel Prados in a Rorschach study more than twenty years ago:

> *A large percentage of our artists share personality traits which give to their average record a characteristic aspect.*

* This emphasizes the inherent bars to creating true art in a totalitarian structure, where consequences may be of such a nature as to preclude further pursuit of central goals, e.g., an artist faced with the possible choice of physical harm and liquidation or an artistic compromise is clearly in a different situation from one who must be ready to forgo comfort or fame for the sake of his artistic integrity.

> *These common features are a superior mentality which emphasizes the abstract form of thinking, the logical and constructive activities, with an obvious disregard for the routine problems of every day and a certain fear of mediocrity. These intellectual potentialities are efficiently used, since they are accompanied by a strong drive for achievement and a richness of the inner interests and stimuli for spontaneous creative thought. There is also a strong sensitiveness and emotional responsiveness to the outer world with a lack of adaptivity to it. This feature, however, is counterbalanced by the rich, rather mature and adjusted inner life and the refined intellectual control which helps and facilitates the creative sublimation characterizing artistic work.[19]*

Thus, despite the different method of approach used by Prados, and the more or less justified criticisms made of projective tests, the distinguishing features of the artist found in his study are quite similar to the artist's perception of himself as reported to us. The finding that artists are both unusually responsive to the external world and show "lack of adaptation" to it is of special interest. Quite possibly the "lack of adaptation" in Rorschach terms reflects many aspects of character stressed by our artists. It is also important to note that Prados' group contained a sampling of many categories, i.e., academicians, realistic painters, abstract artists, surrealists, and some members of the Royal Academy. Only commercial artists were excluded. While our group is more restricted, from these comparisons it might be reasonable to assume that had our sampling been broader the results would not have differed markedly, at least with respect to the variables considered in this chapter. Perhaps Anne Roe makes too harsh a judgment when she states that the Rorschach and the TAT are of little value in helping us understand artists as a group, but can only shed light on a specific artist and his paintings. Projective tests do not explain artistic talent and creativity, but they are able to underline certain personality patterns which, while not necessarily unique to artists, are projected by them as prerequisites for artistic creativity.

The characteristics noted by Prados and by our group do not

encompass every quality of a "quintessential artist." They *are* presumed to be the significant ones, which the artist himself offers clearly and with definiteness. Questions relating to talent and the creative impulse are less productive. We find a general acceptance of the view that talent is biologically given and that it can wither if appropriate experiences do not take place. The artist also sees talent as radically different from creativity. He regards talent as a static entity that comes alive only under certain circumstances of stimulation. It is portrayed as that portion of the person's native endowment which facilitates the expression (in creative form) of inner preoccupations and private visions. Training cannot create talent; proper training may hasten development. A mixture of talent and training is insufficient to produce true creativity, which flows from a hidden and mysterious "inner" source.

TALENT, CREATIVITY AND "GENIUS"

Maurice Grosser's evaluation of the artist treats talent in a way that is relevant. He uses a principle advanced by George Stoddard to differentiate the intellectual genius from the merely very intelligent person. Stoddard imputes certain characteristics to the ordinarily gifted person but assumes that an enhancement of these characteristics only increases the individual's natural endowment; it does not produce a genius. The genius has a special amalgam of talents and characteristics.[20] Similarly, Grosser argues that another factor beyond talent and training produces the great artist. This crucial element is not easily defined, but it is related to motivational factors, whose source or sources Grosser is unable to pinpoint:

> *The distinguishing feature of the amateur is his lack of original ideas. . . . Talented and skillful as his may be, it will nevertheless be adapted from some painter or some school of painting he admires. . . . Real painting is the expression of visual ideas . . . a thing of the mind. Anyone can have talent. Talent is only the grease that makes the wheels go round. But if the painter has somewhere to go, he can creak along perfectly well without it.*[21]

The creative impulse presumably consists, to begin with, of energy that starts and keeps an artist on his particular life path. Characterizing or defining its sources poses a problem:

You know, this is impossible. This is the essence of a man's life. I don't think it's because of a sense of devotion to humanity; it was a fulfillment of my own personal need. I never felt in any way I was uplifting the human condition. When people wanted to know why I thought it was possible to continue working while some of my friends were fighting Hitler, I could only say that this is my contribution. This is the only way I can fight Fascism. It may be less harrowing and less dangerous than to go into the battlefield, but it has its own dangers—of the mental and psychical kind.

I think there's a great inner pressure in a real artist that he can't control. I mean, I've known in my own work that there's been very little outside pressure that I can think of, except maybe the general style of painting. Over a period of years my work will take some sort of a radical shift that I hadn't anticipated, and it has something to do with some inner force.

You're really sitting on a powder barrel; you've got very little control over it, I feel. The only control you have is to try and keep all foreign matter out. I'm like a receiver and transmitter of things that are in the air. I want to control and direct it, but you know you've got no control over your talent. The people that you admire are all people who you feel were terrifically strong in listening to their own inner promptings on what their work should be.

Possessed might be a word for it. They've tried to analyze it—a special kind of neuroticism or pathology. It's hard enough to describe, much less analyze. It's something like an animal instinct. Why do hornets build those paper nests? Just because it's in their organism to do so, their genes, or whatever. The good artists all have some sort of secret little spring wound up that makes them go and go and go.

97

It's something they can't get out of. It's a fate. They're almost not the authors of their own lives but subject to it.

Well, I think it's pretty simple. You need to have to do it. You have to have to do it. If you can't live without doing it, you're a natural. If it's anything less than that, you're better off teaching high school. If you can do it or leave it alone, then you're out of the picture. You have to have to do it, that's all.

When confronted by the "Why?" of his aesthetic bent, the artist can only depict his feelings; he cannot explain them. He reports these feelings as insistent pushes or drives which clamor for expression. Finding the purest and most suitable way to express "inner promptings" becomes the essence of his life. He sees himself as having little choice, and in that sense he finds himself a prisoner of his fate. His own role is limited to being the agent, as it were, who mediates and finds the channels for expressing that which the inner force commands. Childhood experiences relating to this condition, reported in our interviews, are well summarized in a statement by Malraux. His response to the question of what makes a genius (in painting) was: "A man who is destined to become a great painter begins by discovering he is more responsive to a special world, the world of art, than to the world he shares with other men. He feels a compelling impulse to paint . . ." [22] This certainly matches the reports of our artists, but it provides no further clarification.

Perhaps Anne Roe is correct in her guess that creative talent and ability come from deeper levels of the personality than can be measured by such instruments as the Rorschach. Probably they are outside the sphere which has thus far been conceptualized by students of personality. Dr. Roe drew this conclusion after her study of highly ranked painters showed, among other things, that: "As far as Rorschach offers any indication of perceptual facility and creative imagination, it can only be said that about half of these are startlingly lacking in both . . . ," [23] and the others, who showed positive evidences, were not considered to be greater artists. Bruno Klopfer, one of our foremost Rorschach authorities, examined these records and concurred in the statement that "few of them could . . .

by any criteria commonly used, be called the records of 'creative' personalities . . ." [24]

The secret of creativity, its origins and nature, remains impervious to such inquiry, or indeed to any inquiry. We have merely skirted the mystery without attempting to penetrate it. "Creativity" may be as impenetrable as "creation." If so, we are ill-advised to despair. After all, it was Sigmund Freud who laid down his tools rather than apply them to the creative act.

4

Origins: Familial and Cultural

No people known to us, however hard their lives
may be, spend all their time, all their energies in the
acquisition of food and shelter, nor do those who
live under more favorable conditions and who are
free to devote to other pursuits the time not needed
for securing their sustenance occupy themselves with
purely industrial work or idle the days in indolence.
Even the poorest tribes have produced work that
gives to them aesthetic pleasure, and those whom a
bountiful nature or a greater wealth of inventions
has granted freedom from care, devote much of their
energy to the creation of works of beauty.

—FRANZ BOAS, 1927

Down THROUGH the ages, and in every civilization, art has been accepted as a touchstone of human achievement. Every society, regardless of its primitiveness or sophistication, has produced a body of works meriting its legitimate place in any historical or archeological consideration of art. The children of all peoples have been observed drawing or expressing themselves spontaneously in the plastic or graphic media available to them. They have used various art forms to communicate feelings, attitudes, and understandings for which their verbal or merely discursive capacities were insufficient.

As we all know, children often display artistic facility and originality. Yet any attempt to predict from such productions which child will have a future as an artist would be folly. Even if early appraisals of talent reliably indicated aesthetic potential, there are still too many other variables to contend with. Will the individual develop enough drive to make art his vocation? Does he have the personal qualities to carry through with such a drive? Examples of competently evaluated ability eventually coming to naught are all too frequent in this as in every other creative field. How or why talent flowers in some cases but not in others remains a mystery.

Conversely, when looking at the life histories of successful artists, causality deduced in retrospect is as difficult to establish. We still lack adequate information about the relevant factors, or mixture of factors, which would foreshadow such an outcome. At present there is no known and validated amalgam of inner qualities and external conditions which will predictably lead to fruition in the artist.

The critical questions can easily be posed: How does the child who is a potential artist differ from the child who is simply "expressing" himself? Assuming artistic endowment, what conditions (psychological and environmental) must exist if his talent is to be properly nourished? And finally, what factors will influence his decision to dedicate himself to an artistic calling? In answer to these questions we find only an embarrassment of speculations and partially supported judgments. The absence of definitive answers is a rough gauge of the complexity of the problem: successful artists come from enormously varied backgrounds, and attempts to establish unifying developmental factors or to isolate significant conditions appear doomed to failure. When examining artists' recollections of their formative experiences, we note a great variety of responses with extreme differences in emphasis. What is considered critical by one is irrelevant for another. This heterogeneity stands in sharp contrast to the consistency with which artists delineate their essential characteristics.

Some offer early discovery of talent and encouragement as prime movers; others view contact with art and art objects at home and in museums as decisive. Some consider artistic development as possible only within a middle class setting; others adhere to biological explanations. Education in the classical tradition is considered necessary for some, but others presumably succeed with a minimum of formal education. Commonly held perceptions and narrowly restrictive interpretations of painting as simple sublimation of unacceptable impulses are uniformly rejected, but with few proffered alternatives. Yet each of these positions is stated convincingly enough to warrant more detailed consideration. Before we examine them, however, it should be noted that our interviews do contain certain common elements relating to developmental matters, which we will also take into account. Our artists may not ascribe any particular importance to them, and for that matter, they may not have any particular awareness of them. Yet these elements appear often enough in the biographical data to have at least speculative interest.

THE EARLY APPEARANCE OF TALENT

Much has been made of the importance of discovering and encouraging talent as early in life as possible. Bernice Eiduson's statement is fairly representative. In her study of artists, she contends that:

> *What stands out more significantly than any single factor for the development of artists, however, is the early recognition of artistic talents which subsequently led to many gratifying experiences and relationships. Natural endowment,*

then, seemed to be given encouragement by many experiences
which tended to place a premium on artistic capabilities and
helped crystallize these over-valued activities in later voca-
tional choice and performance . . .[1]

Our findings definitely confirm only one part of this picture. With
striking frequency these artists, while still children, already exhibited
their artistic gifts. They began to draw, and well, at a very early
age. Subject after subject could remember achieving recognition for
the quality of his pre-school drawing and painting. This quality
was apparently spontaneous; their precocity often evidenced itself
through an unusual amount of detail and an emphasis on form as
well as expression. Their productions were in this sense advanced and
atypical for children of a comparable age:

> *. . . from the very beginning. From the time I was about*
> *three. I have drawings . . . very detailed drawings, which I*
> *made from this time when I was about three years old. And*
> *with fingernails and eyebrows, you know . . . that kind of*
> *detail.*

> *I remember my very early recollections . . . even before I went*
> *to school. I don't know how young or old I was then but*
> *I was scratching a picture of a steamboat on our best china*
> *cabinet . . . [Four or five?] No, earlier than that. But even*
> *about that time I remember I had some vague idea about*
> *being in art. And later, when I got to be a little older, still*
> *very much a kid, I used to be the one who drew the pictures*
> *on the street or on the fences.*

> *They said that I used to be drawing at the age of three . . .*
> *very very frequently . . . and they had until recently a big*
> *collection of stuff . . . it was very detailed . . . remarkably*
> *detailed with respect to observations of externals. At from*
> *four or so, I was away from the family for a while. I used*
> *to send very copious volumes of drawings . . . of things that*
> *I had observed . . . so that the kind of cactus or the kind*
> *of cowboy was very important . . . they had just the right*
> *kind of spines on it and flowers.*

PARENTAL RECOGNITION AND ACCEPTANCE

The quality of parental recognition, as well as its timing, must be underscored. All parents reacted during this early period with at least tacit approval. Later on—and often enough—they opposed the artistic line, but there seems to have been no attempt to pressure the young child into more formal intellectual pursuits. Embryonic propensities were never questioned. In his formative period, the child never had reason to doubt the appropriateness or acceptability of his creative interests.

But after this period of unambivalent acceptance, the adult world became much less consistent in its response. As a group, these artists were then exposed to the whole spectrum of possible adult attitudes, ranging from continued acceptance and approval to indifference, and finally, in most cases, complete opposition. Only occasionally did artists report that their parents gave them much encouragement during latency and adolescence. As their childish interests merged into more mature involvement in an art career, opposition was more and more often the norm. Life patterns which could be fitted into the "accepted" category became rare. By then, parents offered their children virtually no unqualified support for a career in art. We suspect that it would be different for young people entering the field today. The social role of the artist and parental attitudes toward art as a life-work appear to have shifted that much. In our group there are only isolated instances of early and continuing recognition, support, and encouragement: "I was always talented. I was encouraged early, encouraged by my family. I had formal art lessons when I was nine years old. I was one of those compulsive drawing children. I was always drawing—and they saved my things during the war, things I did when I was four and five years old."

It seems doubtful that the talent could have survived if active resistance had been encountered at pre-school levels. The problems for a child facing active opposition, as compared with one facing even indifference, are self-evident.

There are two facets to encouragement and they are intertwined. Encouragement from the outer world seems to be critical during one's earliest years; without it, inner motivation may never develop.

The child comes into the world with no sense of himself or his productions. He learns to interpret himself and his world on the basis of reactions from important adults around him. So to assume automatic gratification from the art activity itself is unreasonable. It may provide some emotional release, but the world has to recognize it as "valuable" before it can take on any broader significance. When artistic maturity is achieved, the need for an external response may be lessened or extinguished. But during the early period of personality formation it would seem to be a necessity. The artistic act comes spontaneously, but its perpetuation may well depend on how it is initially received. If the response is positive, the art activity *per se* can produce sufficient gratification to motivate its continuance. Even if there is a period during which inspiration seems to die, as so often happens in latency and pre-adolescence, at least the basis for a later positive response has been laid. Without this firm basis it is unlikely that anyone would burst forth spontaneously as a. talented artist-to-be. Thus, in those cases where our artists did not begin to find themselves until adulthood (an apparent cultural bleakness at home notwithstanding), some positive source of encouragement or acceptance during their earliest years can almost always be uncovered. In certain cases approving parents, although themselves without apparent interest in art, gave support to the child. These parents were able to view their children as separate entities upon whom it was not desirable to impose their own predilections:

> *Well, they never really heard of painting until I started to do it. They were very good about things like that. I went to Europe when I was very young. They thought that was a good idea. They were very cooperative. I think they would have been so for anything I wanted to do.*

> *They were very proud of the fact that I was an artist. They happened to be very sympathetic, and they wanted me to feel happy in whatever I was doing, and if that made me happy, then it was fine with them.*

> *My mother didn't have too strong a feeling; she just wanted me to be comfortable, I guess, but she has absolute convictions that whatever I do is gold, so that didn't mean much.*

> *My father, I think, for many years just waited and hoped I*
> *would get over the nonsense, but there certainly was no*
> *active opposition.*

This kind of support was apparently granted without regard to the
sex of the child. It is reported as frequently by female as by male
artists.

There were also those parents, personally uninterested in art,
whose support was based on intellectual grounds. They felt in-
tuitively or philosophically that talent should be nurtured for its
own sake:

> *My parents didn't encourage me really. But I don't have*
> *that middle class bit of the hostile parents that were horrified*
> *and resisted to the last ditch. As a matter of fact, I had*
> *private art lessons when I was eight or nine. I went to an*
> *art class when I was seven. My parents weren't particularly*
> *interested in art, but they do have a philosophy of always*
> *encouraging a talent in art.*

PARENTAL OPPOSITION

But acceptance of art as an adult occupation was unusual. Typically,
the child was indulged or even encouraged until he showed evidence
that his interest was more than transitory, that it went deeper and
meant more than just a constructive hobby. As an avocation, a whim,
or even a certain kind of harmless rebellion, his painting and
drawing could be supported. When he showed a persistent inclination to treat it as a serious pursuit, then resistance hardened. This
usually happened during adolescence, when vocational decisions
were made, although occasionally the indulgent pattern persisted
into early adulthood. Some parents granted their children considerable time and latitude for experimentation.

> *They were rather pleased with it, and I don't think they cared*
> *one way or the other. [Ever?] Oh, eventually—when it got*
> *to be more than a childhood thing. Then they clamped down*
> *like the dickens. As soon as it became apparent that I was*
> *going to take this a little more seriously than simply a high*

school major . . . then they became increasingly concerned for my future.

I don't think they knew exactly what it meant or whether I was very serious about it. But when I was in Europe and I ran out of funds, they did send me an allowance so that I would be able to stay there. But then the family wouldn't send me any more money, so I had to come back. They were concerned about my staying there so long and they felt I should come back and try to adapt myself, to be practical. They thought I should learn some kind of trade or profession.

There was no opposition in early times. When I was older and in the Depression days I was supposed to apply myself to the very practical problem of earning a living and contributing to the family's economy. And I had ideas of going to art school and won a scholarship once on my own, and that bit of initiative started up a storm. That wasn't the type of thing to do. I don't think my family had any idea of what it meant except that it certainly didn't mean to make a living.

The principal focus of parental opposition was money—and its alleged unavailability to artists. This attitude may have had its roots in the Depression, but it was equally prevalent in financially secure and financially uncertain families. Parents said little about the dubious sexual role often attributed to the artist, although they probably harbored unexpressed reservations. Our hunch is that openly expressed sexual doubts and anxieties were more frequent in previous generations. Within this century, earning a respectable livelihood and achieving success in the "American" tradition is the overriding consideration.

Perhaps parental concern bespeaks more of a cultural attitude than a specific anxiety. One artist, whose family ostensibly allowed him full freedom in his work decisions, analyzed the underlying attitudes in such cultural terms:

My family wasn't aware . . . didn't care whether I was an artist . . . If I wanted to be an artist, well, okay, go ahead. My father, I know, secretly felt I was a damn fool because he knew artists didn't make any money. It was obvious that

> *I was not going to follow in his footsteps . . . and this brings me back to your whole subject of America. In America your family would be proud of you if you're successful . . . and that's the only basis. The fact of being an artist would make many families proud of you, if you're successful. The key word is "success," not "artist."*

Another artist, of similar antecedents, sensed his permissive family's preoccupation with money and success:

> *They thought it was a big joke. They were very silent about my being an artist. They thought it was foolish, like I ought to be making money. They really didn't care. "If you want to do this, okay." They were delighted I was doing something honest. When you're eighteen you are a man, you see, and you have to go out. I mean you are like your own boss at eighteen.*

At the other extreme, one budding artist encountered parents who opposed him actively and unremittingly once they grasped the seriousness of his intent, and who never relented even in the face of apparent success:

> *Well, this is a remarkable thing. Today, I don't think they are any happier about the fact that I'm an artist, although when they see my name occurring over and over again—and occasionally somebody says something nice—this naturally assuages the hurt a little bit. But the most important thing now is that I'm a college professor. If I had not been a professor, I think there would have been hell to pay.*

But disapproval and resistance did not prevent this talent and others like it from coming to fruition.

Evidently, talents which meet with acceptance and gratification in their initial stages are able to survive the strong opposition they may soon confront. Thus at first these artists received that modicum of respect one needs to establish a separate and independent identity. Each of them enjoyed sufficient support and had sufficient opportunity for differentiating himself. For that reason, these young people, when they felt it necessary, were able to remove themselves from old family ties and controls. This turns out to be the pattern, not only within families where manhood and separation arrive early, but also within close-knit families where children are bound to their parents far beyond childhood.

On the surface, it appears that early positive reactions from parents may have enabling effects; "normal" negative reactions later on may simply constitute additional obstacles which must be overcome. Perhaps opposition is even a useful, if not a necessary, test of seriousness of purpose and degree of commitment. Not altogether facetiously, some artists claim to have welcomed antipathetic reactions, because they were then forced to concentrate and consolidate their energies in order to survive. They were compelled to resolve any doubts and ambivalences in favor of an artist's life—or surrender and conform to more conventional work patterns:

> *Well, my folks hated it so much that I figured it must be a good thing. No, in all seriousness though, that played a part, I'm sure. It was a kind of stimulant. The opposition was helpful in crystallizing my determination.*

> *There was a negative attitude toward it all. But maybe that was an asset. It made you think pretty deeply about what you really wanted to do. Then I left early. I left the family early.*

In some extreme instances, it also supplied them with "acceptable" justifications for severing home ties with unsympathetic and uncomprehending bourgeois families, with whom by then they felt strange and uncomfortable:

> *They kept saying, "It's nice for a hobby," and it was absolutely ridiculous. I never even bothered with them after that. It didn't make any difference. Actually, I was very cruel, but I felt if they're not going to help me, then the whole thing is over . . . because I can't listen to what they say anymore. And so I had nothing to do with them.*

But few of these separations were violent or dramatic; the spectacular rupture was the exception. The decision to pursue the artist's life may have been viewed as wrongheaded and imprudent but not as a "major" disgrace. There was no reaction of horror; direct interference and condemnation rarely took place.

On the artist's side, his choice did not represent an act of defiance or rebellion directed against his parents; it was not even a repudiation of them. Rather it was a disaffiliation; the emerging artist was driving toward a different life pattern because it had more meaning for him. It was less a disavowal of his previous condition, or that of his family, and more an affirmation that there was another way of life which held more promise of true satisfaction for him. To achieve this, only disengagement was necessary; a break was seldom required.

The relative calm of these separations testifies to the remarkably high degree of differentiation and individuation these artists must have achieved at an early age. With comparative ease, many of them could contemplate their physical and emotional autonomy at adolescence, or even sooner. They were able to set out on the path of "adventure" without evident qualms or trepidation. We have inferential evidence that their parents were themselves fairly well differentiated, and that they were remarkably free of ambivalence in their attitudes toward their children. They were neither overprotective nor overcontrolling. They never reduced their children to the point of impotence where, in order for them to have achieved separateness, the children would need to resort to infantile bursts of rage, passion, and rebellion. It is important to realize that parental opposition to an artist's life was based mostly on the question of material practicality; it never reflected an underlying desire to limit the child as an individual. Only under those circumstances could the departures have been effected, for the most part, without permanent and painful schisms.

Herein lies a possible difference between the true artist and a certain type of "beatnik" with middle class origins. The latter is so bound to his home that his psychic economy is totally dominated by one objective: to break and separate. Other goals pale in the face of this overwhelming conflict. Generally, the beatnik has had parents who are overwhelming and controlling, who have failed to permit adequate self-differentiation. He feels engulfed, a state that is abhorrent to him, and he attempts to escape. But he then reveals his weakness and dependency in the agonies which separation usually precipitates; what remains is a never-ending need to proclaim his "freedom and independence." The truly autonomous man does not need to reassure himself constantly, publicly, and dramatically. But the child who is reared under circumstances of envelopment and control never attains real independence. The classical beatnik feels that he is always in danger of being drawn back into a frightening family situation. To avoid being swallowed, he runs—like the Gingerbread Man. Unfortunately for him, his freedom is a will-o'-the-wisp. He gyrates desperately to escape entrapment and thereby assures it. It cannot be otherwise as long as he responds only to external conditions. Though the reaction to him is negative and rejecting, his behavior nevertheless continues to be ruled by the primary prototypes. To be opposite to his parents, or the values they represent, becomes as compelling or driving a force for him as "conformity" is for the more conventional product of the middle class.

In striking contrast, one of our artists comments: "Just because I'm an artist doesn't mean that I have to wear a pink shirt. I can wear a tie and jacket, too." *He* has his independence; he does not have to prove it to anyone. The artist is not escaping; he is going to something. The consequent difference in life patterns between the beatnik and the artist is clear: it is the difference between "breaking only in order to reject" and "disengagement for meaningful action." This may explain, without disparagement, the limited creative output of the beatnik.

EARLY EXPOSURE TO "CULTURE"

The significance of exposure to art objects at an early age remains ambiguous. Many of the artists in our group came from culturally barren milieus; others had rather rich and varied experiences; some fall between these extremes:

> *Art books? No, there were no books in the house.*

> Q. *Did you go to museums?*
> A. *Oh no. We never did that.*
> Q. *How about art books?*
> A. *We didn't have any books.*

> *If I had to think back to my childhood I would say we always had records around with music and quite good literature in the family library. I can remember no exciting examples in the area of art, no art objects that I can think of. . . .*

There were no books and there were no pictures of any account. I didn't even know what an oil painting was until I was about fifteen or sixteen. I'd never seen one. I guess the only culture was basically talk, more or less stories and fantasies. Mother would always tell us old stories about Italy and tell us about fairy tales and what not of that kind.

My mother used to have reproductions of Vermeer and Rembrandt all around the house. So I became interested. And then she used to give me very opulent art books, but she wanted me to be an appreciator, not a creator.

If there were a range, say, if a hundred represented the artist and his exposure to art . . . and then there's zero which means some sort of institutionalized individual who has no connection with anything . . . I would say my parents ranged at about twenty-two. They had no interest, no interest in art.

For some, cultural impoverishment extended beyond childhood. Several artists seem to have had no awareness of art as a cultural phenomenon until adolescence and, in several instances, young adulthood.

In high school I did a few drawings . . . I had never been to a gallery nor to an art museum until my last year in college. I had not heard classical music until after I had entered college.

It just all of a sudden hit me to take up painting after my military service. I didn't even think about it when I was young. I just sort of got interested in it at this period. When I was young, I thought maybe I'd write or something, but I never pursued it. I dreamed of it for one year in high school.

I might have been an artist sooner if my parents had been involved in education and things like that. As it was, I became an artist relatively late. I was in my twenties before I became an artist. It's a supposition and I can't say. I don't think that it necessarily would have made a great deal of difference. It might have; it's possible.

These comments surely indicate that cultural advantages while young are not necessary ingredients for the eventual emergence of a talent. The artists just quoted were all culturally disadvantaged as children, and yet they ultimately became well-accepted painters. As we shall see, however, no artist in our group remained indefinitely isolated from cultural experiences. There is some evidence to indicate that contact with "real" art sooner or later gave important impetus to their own work. Whether a delayed encounter with art in any way handicaps or limits the artist cannot be adduced from our information. Nevertheless, it is clear that many of our high-ranking painters and sculptors had little or no contact with art until adulthood. What's more, some of our respondents are even concerned about *premature* exposure to art. They stress "readiness" and not chronological age for the profitable use of aesthetic experience. Without readiness, an indifferent or negative reaction is always possible:

> *I didn't go to museums very much and I'm glad I didn't. I think most kids who are dragged through European or American museums never really learn to see a painting. I mean, I learned to tell a good one from a bad one, or how to feel that one moves me, when I was in my twenties. I didn't even learn that in college. I didn't really start until well after that. In college I knew the facts, but I didn't get the feeling. When I did go to the Met as a child I was bored stiff. They dragged me.*

"Readiness" develops at such disparate age levels that it is difficult to establish what one needs to attain this condition. Also, it often appears out of nowhere with great suddenness and specificity—like a revelation:

> *It almost did really happen overnight. A required course in my sophomore year at college was clay modeling. From the moment I touched it I knew sculpture was what I wanted to do. I suddenly had a tremendous natural talent that I had never been aware of.*

> *During my last year in college I happened to be in a building on campus that I hadn't been in before. I was walking*

down the corridor looking at people in some of the doors,
and in one room they were painting. And I stopped and drew
a long breath and then I thought, "Why, I'd like to do
that." But I didn't go to my room and think it over or wait
for the next day. I walked right in and asked the instructor
if I could audit without credit for the rest of the term. And
she said yes. I knew immediately that that was it and that
I had always been an artist. I didn't have to speak to an
artist to tell me to become one. I had never known anything
about art, but the moment I became involved with art, I
felt that I had always done art.

Generally my brother and I went together. I remember when
I was nine and he was eleven, friends of my brother took
us to the museum for the first time. From that time on, we
knew where we were going to go every Saturday.

There were always very nice people there at work that were
interested in painting, and I used to go around with these
people. They used to take me to museums and all that. I
never had any feeling at all before that. I really didn't have
a chance to see, to be exposed to paintings and sculptures
and things like that. It was a big thing, all of a sudden, and
I got terribly interested in it after the war.

ENVIRONMENT AND EDUCATION

"Exposure" for the child is clearly less important than for the developing artist. Here there is no ambiguity. We have full agreement
that without such culture-contact growth is totally impeded. No artist
can develop in isolation from art. Malraux has written that the artist
sees things differently from the ordinary man just because his sensibility has been conditioned by extended association with paintings
and sculpture. Every great artist, he says, traces his vocational interest
to emotions aroused in reacting to some specific work of art: "What
makes the artist is that in his youth he was more deeply moved by his
visual experience of works of art than by that of the things they
represent . . . and perhaps of Nature as a whole." [2]
While our data would not support so sweeping a statement on the

centrality of youthful exposure to art, they would affirm and reaffirm the significance of major art works, as well as art history, for mature or maturing artists. There is a pervasive awareness that artists exist only within the historical setting of art:

> *Well, this is another old art saw again . . . that art breeds art, that art is learned from art, that art is not learned from nature, but art is learned from art. I'm implying that this is one of those chicken and the egg stories. You know, what comes first? I had no museums or art books. I had no exposure to the arts. So I say that it's kind of miraculous that I became an artist. I really don't know how it happened. But then when I went to Paris it unfolded the entire art world to me. I went to the Louvre every Sunday . . .*

> *I remember the first time when I went to the Museum of Modern Art, in 1939, when they had that big Picasso exhibition, and I was quite dumbfounded by the whole thing. I remember it very vividly, but it didn't actually make me want to be an artist or anything like that. That just sort of came gradually over a long time. My first contact with painting was very, I suppose, typical of anyone who wasn't exposed to it. I was amused by modern painting.*

> *I would have been an artist anyway, but I think that being able to go to Europe at that formative stage was very beneficial, and it gave me a background which I think has been very valuable. I must admit that most of the time I was there I wasn't painting. I was in museums. I spent my time in museums, and in a certain light this may have seemed frivolous. But when I look back on it I feel like that was the best thing I could have done. It was like going to college, that is, like a physicist going to MIT, and I think it had that value.*

While there is this recognition of an eventful need to confront true art, there is wide disagreement concerning the value of formal education and art training. Regarding educational background, there are those who failed to complete high school and there are those who have secured advanced degrees:

I never went beyond high school. I did go to European universities but I never matriculated. I went to three universities and audited for a period of about three years. I never took a credit.

I went to the High School of Music and Art and from there to college. I got my B.A. there and then moved on, taking my M.A. and part of my Ph.D.

I had no schooling because I was brought up at home and I had tutors who taught me to play chess, but nothing else. I literally had no formal education. Everything I know I had to get by pieces.

I went to grammar school and went up to junior high school and the first year into high school. I played basketball and football, and I was very good in most subjects, especially mathematics, geography, and history. After the ninth grade I had a row with my father, and he said it would do me good to go to work. So I went to work. I got a construction job. I was employed when I was about sixteen, and I never finished high school.

I just went to the ordinary public schools through high school and mostly at the direction of my parents. I was oriented generally in a technical direction to be an engineer. I found that stuff interesting enough in a way, but it wasn't what I really wanted to do.

Most of our respondents found their formal education burdensome. It diverted their time, attention, and energy from art, which had primary importance for them. This is not a "sour grapes" reaction; they were all good or excellent students. When they submitted it was because of family pressures and other practical considerations:

You have to remember that being a teen-ager means you are in a very disadvantageous position, because the people who direct you and who tell you what their expectations are, are very much older than you and have all the authority, and so you go along. I think rebellion very seldom succeeds, and in many cases it's completely hopeless. So when your whole

> *family and the school counselor and everybody says "Do this," it's very hard not to.*

The practical considerations are also related to financial survival. The artist, when he must supplement his income, finds himself turning in a pedagogical direction. Formal education may become his ticket of admission to Academia, although it is still not required in all teaching situations.

Not that every memory of school is negative. Some artists see their academic training very positively for its broadening effect, and more specifically because it provides a cultural cache or reserve which they may consciously or unconsciously draw upon in their work:

> *Twenty years ago I would have said it was a great mistake to stay in school, but more and more of the contemporary American artists that I respect and who I think are good seem to be emerging from that background. When you go to college many areas of knowledge are revealed to you. Your eyes can be opened up. I think it's important in that respect, but I don't think that college is the place to learn to become an artist.*

> *I guess I was lucky. They had a wonderful high school. It was on a very high level and it was like, you know, a good private school in New York, where you get a good education—Latin and Greek. In English you studied the Greek drama and its plays. You studied the classics and things like that. How else can you be an artist?*

The potential impact of this cultural reservoir is clearly outlined by one of our group:

> *I think that there is a lot to background in the making of an artist. You've got to relive a whole cultural history. For instance, I know damn well the way I'm going to develop that [sculpture]. It's going to have some reference to early Greek figurines. When I began it, I knew it, and I've seen those things for thirty years, see? And when I develop that thing, I'm drawing upon my knowledge of Gothic art.*

Beyond supplying this cultural background, formal education is not felt to have much instrumental value. There is no relationship between schooling and artistic accomplishment. Artists are not made in the university:

> *I found out in college that what you learn in classes there doesn't have anything to do with becoming an artist. So I quit. I quit before I got my credits. Afterwards everybody was very upset. Art is a field that ·you get better in as you work at it. I don't think it matters what school you go to. I was never so miserable in my life. The atmosphere was very unartistic.*

Formal education and artistic success do not seem to be correlative, but newly emerging artists tend to have an advanced education. This may simply reflect the increased affluence of our society which makes it less and less necessary for the adolescent and the young adult to be self-supporting. Changes in parental attitudes toward art and a willingness to support the student in his pursuits are also operative factors.

The change may also involve recent trends in a few university art departments where majors are given increased opportunities for actual painting. Previously this had been possible only in professional art schools. But such occasional policy shifts are not typical. Most art departments remain traditional and academic in outlook and are criticized as such by almost all of our artists:

> *I enrolled for a Master's degree, but I loathed it. I stayed only four or five months. It was very dry and academic and torture. I wanted to paint.*

> *I started in college and was an art major, but I never got near a paint brush. They had no workshops whatsoever, so I quit after six months.*

> *I had an art class . . . The teacher was doing her papers for another class. She had cut out all the pretty pictures, the colored ones, from magazines over the years. She had a big envelope of them and we used to go through them and pick out something to copy. I picked out all the Titians*

clipped out of Life *magazine—the good ones—without
knowing anything about art. You can't call this influence
from school education.*

The relevance of technical art training, whether provided by professional art schools or working artists (as distinguished from the
university art department), is less clear-cut. Almost our entire group
had some formal art training, but individual patterns are very
dissimilar. In her study of artists, Anne Roe found that each of
her subjects had attended art school for a year or more, either in
the United States or overseas, and after that their development pro-
ceeded without assistance or further instruction.[3] Our results are
much the same, with a minimal confluence of individual patterns:

*Art schooling? I've been self-taught. I've not gone to any
art school. My background with an art school was extremely
limited, of very short duration. It was so inept that I cleared
out.*

*I started drawing and painting in high school, and I didn't
go to college. I just went right to art school.*
   Q. *Was art school important for you?*
   A. *No. Not at all.*

*I went to a commercial art school for two years and that
showed me that I could not be a commercial artist. Then I
went to an academic art school. This was beautiful because
you gained the technical understanding, not the spiritual
understanding. And then the Art Students' League for a
year. Then to Hofmann, and that was it.*

*. . . and then I went to an art school, but chiefly to discuss
God and tea and art, but never to work. That was the only
training I had.*

*I took my undergraduate degree in art history. Subsequently
I studied sculpture at the Art Students' League. Later when
I had a Fulbright scholarship, I also studied sculpture in
Paris. That would pretty much outline my formal studies.*

Degrees of need and enthusiasm for formal art training thus

range from fairly strong support to faint derogation, such as, "Well, it gave me a chance to paint." These contrasting opinions are a continuation of the mixed picture of specific background factors. Most artists recognize formal art training as a valuable source of information and an aid in developing basic technical skills not easily acquired elsewhere. These benefits accrue from both group and individual study. Beyond that, and more emphatically, there is the teacher's inspirational importance. The following tributes to Hans Hofmann are typical:

> *The only schooling in art that I got that was really valuable was with Hans Hofmann, and that was quite intangible in a way. But it somehow made me feel that I was an artist after I had been to that school.*

> *He didn't do things directly. He gave myself and many other people encouragement to go on, but I wouldn't say directly. The majority of his students were kids, at least in relation to* ART *in capital letters. They would come to the school and they would feel inadequate. They were afraid to mix paint on the palette, because how did they dare? And at weekly criticism meetings he would begin to talk in a general way about something, and every once in a while drop a phrase, "We artists must remember," and in this way he sucked in his students and involved them in artistic problems and made them feel it was their problem, and they really do deserve to cope with this problem. He had a lot of little ways of giving people a sense of self-respect.*

SOCIO-ECONOMIC BACKGROUNDS

If we apply the six-class system set forth by Lloyd Warner and his associates [4] to our group, these artists are distributed within its four central categories, that is: from lower-upper class through upper-lower class. They are most heavily concentrated in the lower-middle class. That they are not represented at the two extremes (upper-upper class and lower-lower class) is hardly surprising. A careful quota sample would not materially have altered this picture. The extremes of poverty and wealth rarely produce artists. While an occasional aristocrat or a stray proletarian achieves critical recognition in the arts, most painters and sculptors originate in the middle class. Some artists did point to individual exceptions, but this is the general tenor of their observations:

> *I don't know any very poor boys who have become artists. Almost every one of them has been fairly well off. Of course I don't mean rich. I'd say middle class.*

> *I repudiate the general value of the middle class life, but artists come out of the middle class. They don't come out of Park Avenue and they don't come out of the slums. Actually, if you have to scrounge around for a living, it's pretty tough to be a painter. You have to be able to live by your work. To that extent, an artist is a middle class character.*

> *You never find great upper class artists and you never find proletarians. I think it's the lower-middle class, a lower-middle class that reaches out. I don't think it is the middle class of what is called the "subsidized middle class" which is at heart the bourgeoisie, because the artist is anti-bourgeois at heart.*

But although middle class origins and the rejection of typical middle class values exist as vague unifying factors, other regularities of social and family background are hard to find. Differences in family attitude toward art as a life work have already been noted (although each artist experienced a high degree of family acceptance), as has much variation in early cultural opportunities. The educational status of artists' parents is also highly variable: some artists' parents were lacking in any formal education; there were others with advanced degrees. Although we came upon only one case of severe economic privation (despite the Depression), financial circumstances were exceedingly variable.

Furthermore, though they now live in New York City or its environs, these artists came from widely scattered locations, both inside and outside the United States. It is true that with time they all gravitated to this urban center, but many were reared in a rural setting. Apropos of Harold Rosenberg's remark that "Immigrants and sons of immigrants predominate in the list of the originators of America's first identifiable style in art. . . ," [5] the greatest number of our group would be similarly classified. But daughters of immigrants should also be included, for they make up an unprecedentedly large segment of today's well-accepted artists. Most of these artists came from intact families, although a few had lost one or both of their parents at relatively early ages. There is a larger concentration of Jews and Catholics than might be anticipated from their numbers in the general population. (None of these come from families which could be called rigidly orthodox; they professed varying degrees of religious feeling or conviction.)

Family size varied greatly; one artist had as many as twelve brothers and sisters, whereas others were only children. Where there were brothers and sisters, their involvement with art covered a range from those who themselves became artists to those who had no interest in art or learning. Arid cultural climates were found as frequently where parents were educated professionals as where they were uneducated semi-skilled workers, and vice versa. Family political and social involvements were just as unpredictable. Museum attendance was not related to family income or place of residence, and art objects were present or absent in the home at all class levels.

This information suggests threads of similarity, but how far these threads are related to stimulating an art career is a question that remains unresolved. Many factors we can isolate are used unsatisfactorily by the artists to explain the paucity of artistic representation by certain minority groups. We fear that they will no more effectively explain the absence of these groups than the presence of others.

Our findings continue to bear a remarkable resemblance to those reported by Anne Roe in 1946. Her study of highly ranked artists showed that their backgrounds encompassed a broad continuum of social and economic levels and that they had a varied assortment of early family experiences. As children, they seem to have been subjected to a greater number of stresses than most (especially because of race or religion), but since many non-artists have suffered equal trauma and some artists have not, it is doubtful that this would prove to be an important motivating factor in their selection of art as a vocation. Some of them decided to be artists very early in life, but for others inspiration did not come until adolescence or early youth. Parental attitudes toward art differed greatly. Where there was opposition it usually stemmed from "the economic uncertainties" of this career, but there are occasionally clear evidences of another consideration: that painters are popularly considered "queer," and this may have activated more family opposition than is apparent on the surface." * And, as in our group, their cultural experiences ranged over a wide spectrum.[6]

It is significant that some twenty years later, a second group of artists selected on essentially the same basis as the first (that is, acceptance by art authorities as being of high rank) reveals such a general similarity of background. It would be an exaggeration to say that nothing has changed for the artist in the last twenty years, but the similarities in these two groups lead one to suspect that whatever nurtures an artistic bent has remained more or less constant. All this may be changing before our eyes—the artist's social situation is in a state of violent flux. Our own group sometimes cast doubt on the motivations of those entering the art world today. Whether this is their chauvinism or an objective fact has to be studied, but the reality of ongoing extra-aesthetic pressures can neither be gainsaid nor discounted.

EARLY FREEDOM AND THE MODEL STIMULUS

Despite the seemingly thin threads of consistency among all these variables at a descriptive level, our interview material regarding motivation is perhaps more rewarding than might appear at first glance. When asked directly to specify those factors which contribute to the awakening of talent, artists showed little uniformity. But an

---

* In discussing the focus of opposition which our group experienced, economics is always given major emphasis. We did not encounter the perception of the artist as a sexually perverse individual. The question as to whether the stereotype of the artist in the culture at large between Dr. Roe's generation of artists and ours has shifted, and whether concerns about sexuality have had to go underground, cannot be answered from our data. Conceivably, the emerging artist will meet only encouragement as the new social line includes embracing culture and decrying concern with material gain. This position is reinforced by the fact that there is less realistic need now to be concerned about the financial position of the artist.

examination of their life histories turns up at least two clues. The first clue consists of cumulative evidence that regardless of how they felt later about their children as burgeoning artists, parents displayed extraordinarily little ambivalence toward them as children. The second clue derives from a consistent element in the early life of each artist who speaks of a significant figure, usually a male, acting as a catalyst to the expression of his artistic talent. If the interplay of these two factors could be found to foster special kinds of adaptation, and especially a tendency to use "sublimation," some beginnings might be made toward answering the questions of why and how an inborn talent is expressed successfully by some and not by others who appear to have equal potentialities. We make no claims that we can explain an art career on the basis of these elements, but they seem to have more than coincidental relevance. Since they are regularly conjoined in the lives of our artists, it is reasonable to assume that, given talent, they may constitute necessary, if not sufficient, conditions for the development of artistic expression.

The artists have either directly stated or repeatedly implied that their parents showed little ambivalence toward them as children. Response after response has indicated that they felt fully accepted by their parents, that they were treated as unique, separate, and highly valued individuals during their early years. Since children learn to evaluate themselves primarily through identifications with their parents, consistently accepting parents are likely to induce a strong sense of security and, ultimately, of self. Willingness to allow their children unusual freedom at an early age without significant emotional upheaval accounts for their high degree of individuation. Obviously, these parents, much more than most, accepted their children's separate identities. What this means can only be appreciated in the light of recent psychoanalytic investigations which stress both the significance of such differentiation and the unsuspected difficulties that so frequently block its achievement.

While many parents love their children and many are eventually able to cut the silver cord, a mixture of high valuation and healthy separation is less common than the layman might suppose. That this type of relationship prevails among these artists is even more impressive, because it is most atypical for the social classes from which they come. Love which was not "smother love," followed by a free grant of individuality, may have helped to endow these future artists with a sense of independence on the one hand and self-confidence on the other. These qualities would, in turn, have permitted them to make the choice of an unusual occupation, even against general opposition, at a critical juncture in their lives. For many this point came at adolescence; for a few it came earlier, and for others it came later. In no instance was an artist hopelessly tied to the family's "apron strings."

Of course, artistic expression is too complex a matter to be explained simply on the basis of inborn talent plus a sense of separateness and freedom: "It was the thing I did best and so I did it," is an honest but naive oversimplification. Limiting it this way obscures the fundamental components of drive, purpose, and dedication. It yields no point of entry into the problem of why emotions at all levels are more readily available to the artist than to most others. It gives us no help in understanding why the maturing individual bucks widespread opposition and in time comes to "see" himself as an artist. Despite their systematic appearance in the lives of artists, relatively unambivalent and differentiated parental attitudes toward gifted young children are only one of the possibly necessary conditions for their full development.

The second stable element that can be pieced out of artists' pre-adolescent years is the presence of an important stimulative figure who, in varying ways, gave impetus to the expression of their talent. If this stimulus has a more direct bearing on the successful use of talent, artists are no doubt able to take advantage of it because of strength gained from early acceptance. As young people (through pre-adolescence), each of our respondents had a model with whom he could identify—a significant figure whom he greatly admired, or someone whose approval was crucial to him. Most of the models with whom aspiring artists allied themselves showed some interest in art or in other creative activities.

No matter how culturally barren their lives seem to have been, there was one figure, almost always a male, who played a significant stimulative role for them during those early years. We do not mean just the ordinary personal model so essential to psychosexual development, but rather an individual who, in one way or another, made it clear that an art response would please him. For example, after describing the total lack of cultural stimulation in his youth and the absence of artistic opportunities in his home town, one artist related the following anecdote, based on an incident which occurred while he was working as a twelve-year-old helper in a bar:

> *My art interest just came up spontaneously. I think because of having to be in the bar at twelve, doing nothing, taking glasses and washing them and things like that, having to be confined, I started to draw then. I was doing some water colors and of course I couldn't get them as smooth as the originals I was copying. This disturbed me and I announced this in the bar . . . and there was a man there who said, "You can't do that with water colors; you must have oil." When I asked what that was he said he'd show me. So one day he came back and he brought this little box of oils with little tubes. In addition to that he brought some oyster shells and banana oil. And then he proceeded to tell me that I should take these colors and squeeze them into the shells and take the banana oil . . .*

One can only guess how large this man loomed in our artist's life, but one might speculate that his impact was more than casual. One might also assume from this account that the artist's early years were not quite the void that he now recalls; his having water colors to work with would by itself raise some doubts about the cultural vapidity he describes.

A stimulating role was more often assumed by the original accepting person (usually one or both parents), but where, as in the above example, the parents' own response to the child's gift was limited, a substitute figure appeared some time before adolescence. It needs further substantiation, but in our group this was a recurrent finding. As time passed, other persons reinforced the initial influence, but a primary figure always appeared before adolescence in the artist's history. This process is apparently at work even when the expressive response lags far behind the human stimulus. It seems likely that such a stimulus is necessary, and that contact must occur early (before maturity) for the later influences to take effect. Whether or not they currently make much of the early figure, artists in recounting their lives, in many random remarks and comments, testify to his importance. Broadly speaking, our study confirms the opinion of those psychoanalysts who have studied the creative individual in clinical detail, that identification is crucial to fostering the use of talent,[7] a theory to be discussed more fully below. In this connection, it is of more than passing interest that the central figure, with few exceptions, turned out to be a male—father, uncle, brother, peer— a male who showed interest in the creative process or its product:

> *Father had a great interest in foreign languages and he taught himself several languages. He's a very lively and adroit man. My mother is just a housewife, a simple woman, good-natured. My father was always pro-education and very sympathetic to culture, and I remember my father once taking a few of my little drawings and putting them in his wallet because he liked them, and he kept them there for a number of years.*

> *My uncle was sort of a black sheep in the family. He had spent all his money, and then suddenly he disappeared. One day I discovered him walking up and down along our street selling window glass, so I ran down. He was the only one, apart from my grandmother, who had some, shall we call it understanding, or warm feeling for me. So I used to slink out of the house and go to him. And he lived in a basement with his boxes of glass all around him. He used to paint on glass; little flowers, still-lifes, things like that. That was actually my first fascination with paint.*

> *I think that the earliest memory I have of anything that had to do with drawing had to do with a certain admiration I had for a boy in class. He did drawings of horses, marvelous ones. I mean realistic, with a very fat pencil point. It had a certain physical effect on me. I'm not inventing this. I remember it. I've thought of it a few times. I mean, trying to think back, what was my first memory . . .*

You see, my father did all kinds of wonderful things, handicrafts. He used to carve airplanes, weather vanes. He used to do these things with wood. If you're a molder, you make things. He used to cast things, his own things, at the foundry.

I don't know whether it is from my own predilection or from the fact that my brothers did it. My middle brother, the one just older than me, and I were always together and always making things, constructions which involved drawing and putting them together. He was really an artist. We went to the museum and we drew together on Saturdays. We made books, animals.

If the significant figure had no perceptible interest in any of the arts or crafts, the child was still able to sense it. At least an underlying interest had to be established. It was somehow necessary to see him as potentially, if not actively, involved in the creative world:

My father is in the wholesale business. This isn't what he really wanted to do. It was not his real love, so to speak. I think my father was a frustrated artist.

My dad is well-educated and his education is a pretty good one, too, but he's also aware of the implications of too much education regarding one's financial future. And this, coupled with his irrational hatred for art . . . He wanted to be a musician, amongst other things in his youth, and he was frustrated. But he has a profound sensitivity for things artistic. But he shuts them off so much that anyone in his family who shows these tendencies is going to have some trouble.

Psychoanalysts have always stressed biological make-up in explaining talent, although they have occasionally speculated about its psychodynamic roots. While leaving the sources of artistic capability essentially untouched, they have centered their interest on the meaning of creativity and of the art work itself. In detailing the path followed by the artist while creating, Freud characterized him as a man who originally

> . . . *turns from reality because he cannot come to terms with the demand for renunciation of instinctual gratifications as it is first made, and who then in fantasy-life allows full play to his erotic and ambitious wishes . . . with his special gifts he molds his phantasies into a new kind of reality, and men concede them a justification as valuable reflections of actual life. Thus by a certain path he actually becomes the hero, king, creator, favorite he desired to be, without pursuing the circuitous path of creating real alterations in the outer world . . .*[8]

In this oft-quoted statement, Freud makes no assumptions concerning the origins of talent or, for that matter, the factors which must coalesce to elicit its expression. He merely outlines the steps involved in making the specific kind of reality adaptation which is characteristic of artists, that is, one which permits an unusual latitude of instinctual expression and gratification within the realm of work. But while delineating this "sublimation," which Freud saw as basic to all artistic creation, he also called attention to motivating forces of a different order within the confines of the artist's object relations. For example, in his study of Leonardo da Vinci, Freud wrote that: "The replacement of the mother by the vulture [an error in translation which in no way modifies the underlying premise] indicates that the child missed the father and felt himself alone with the mother." [9] Freud went on to demonstrate how Leonardo must have suffered several years of disappointment and loneliness with his mother before he was finally taken into his father's house. Freud felt that this was a deprivation to which Leonardo was never reconciled, and he saw it as a crucial factor in this genius's life adjustment. But he never attempted to generalize from this one case about the role of the father in the personal development of *the* genius or *the* gifted creator.

Freud's line of inquiry remained virtually untouched for more than forty years. Then, with the growing psychoanalytic interest in "object relations" for all phases of ego development, there came the work of such analysts as Ernst Kris, Phyllis Greenacre, and Kurt Eissler. To them the artist is a person who, in his work, symbolically attains a longed-for position of acceptance relative to certain crucial figures in his life. Among other things, his art makes it possible for him to seek the symbolic approval of an idealized object. But he does not strive directly for his original object-choice. The primary object, although never fully renounced, is transformed first into an idealized image, then reprojected onto the collective audience to which the artist addresses his work. Through this collective audience, or "public," the original love object, which was not adequately available in the past, is eventually regained. Such, in broad outline, is the position taken especially by Dr. Greenacre.

In discussing the emergence of talent, Ernst Kris has been quoted as saying:

> *I have never seen any concrete material on a gift where identification did not play a part. In the literature, there are many cases reported. I have never seen one. My personal experience has been that in every instance it has led to a model. It could be a three times distant model, and I am not saying that the model would be sufficient to explain it, but there was always a model.*[10]

And Dr. Greenacre, while continuing to emphasize the biological basis of talent, has stated:

> *Identification plays a very important role in the selection and zeal for a field of development of talent. . . . The problem of identification stimulating inheritance is probably as great in the development of talent as it is in the appearance of certain neuroses in successive generations. . . .*[11]

And then she elaborates. It is "unlikely that artistic performance or creative product is ever undertaken purely for the gratification of the self, but rather that there is always some fantasy of a collective audience or recipient. . . . The artistic product has rather universally the character of a love gift, to be brought as near perfection as possible and to be presented with pride and misgiving." [12]

These newer formulations, while representing a breakthrough in psychoanalytic thinking, are still compatible with more conventional views of maternal primacy. Gardner Murphy sums up these widely held beliefs:

> *In Walter de la Mare's collection of early memories of those who later became creative men, there is much evidence of the importance of an intimate and stimulating mother-child relationship. It seems legitimate to conjecture that the warm response of the mother may in the experience of many children give quicker life, or her prohibitions may mark off areas through which exploration becomes less and less feasible and ultimately less and less interesting.*[13]

Murphy also discusses studies of Herman Witkin on the mother's role in blocking development of finer perceptual differentiation: "It is almost as if clinging to the restricting mother has entailed an unconscious attitude that there are some distinctions not to be made, some explorations not to be permitted, some realities not to be broken down and seen in all their sharpness." [14]

From discussions with colleagues, one artist claimed that they feel this maternal influence continues beyond the early years and becomes more and more of a dominant influence with the passage of time. Only fugitive references of this kind can be found in our interviews:

> *But my mother is the one who took me to museums and to the opera and to plays, and so on. As a matter of fact, most artists have discussed this question with a good many people, and their mothers, the mother was always very important. I'd say influential, even if she didn't eventually take them, the way my mother did.*

> *My mother was always giving me ballet lessons or something like that. And I used to be shown prints of the old masters. I was taken to the museums, and she always said I would go to New York and copy the pictures of great masters in the Metropolitan Museum.*

But most artists picture the male as the operative influence after those earliest years of unambivalent acceptance. We do not infer from this that the roles of the two parents must be mutually exclusive; rather they may be complementary. The love of an "all-accepting" mother in one's tender years, with or without father's support, is perhaps a precondition for the vital "male identifications" which have yet to take place. That the mother is generally given short shrift as a direct contributor to the professional art career may reflect that common amnesia which develops around all our earliest experiences. If so, it would help us understand why there is more awareness of the male influence, which comes along at a later period in life and is thus more available to consciousness. In speaking of their mothers, artists do not bristle with hostility. They just give mother her due as "mother," ungrudgingly, but with little specific credit. They reserve this for father or the father-substitute. Undoubtedly both are necessary for a full flowering of expressive ability. Good "mothering" probably lays the groundwork for that force through which the individual is catapulted into his own professional niche through identification with an idealized male. It goes without saying that he is in prior possession of talent.

Why does the energizing parent so often turn out to be the male? Psychoanalytic theory would suggest that father is most often experienced as the parent who controls or regulates his child's flow of instinctual impulses. These impulses are closely tied to the child's oedipal constellation, but their active expression toward the mother is prohibited. The usual resolution of an oedipal conflict (for a male) consists in accepting frustration and limitation, pending ultimate identification with the father. The truly creative person seems to resist this typical path. Rather than temporarily renounce gratification out of fear of the father, only to identify with him later on, the artist resorts to symbolic expression at a fantasy level. By actively and aggressively expending his energy along creative lines, bolstered by inner resources and armed with fantasy, he unconsciously continues his search for the idealized father who would give freely and without condition, who would unstintingly support and encourage the expression of his instinctual impulses.

All this assumes that the original parent-child relationship was not "worked through" properly, something which Phyllis Greenacre feels is always the case with creative artists. The intensity of their feelings, accompanied by equally strong demands for reciprocation, is too great to permit it. But rather than withdraw or surrender in the face of this dilemma, the gifted person doggedly but unconsciously perseveres in his struggle to achieve an ideal relationship with his father, eventually using the projected collectivity to attain that most cherished goal. This seems to mean that personal feelings must be diluted and that the group achieves ascendancy. Indeed, this would be so but for a simultaneous "push" toward alignment with the idealized father who will allow instinctual gratification by licensing it with his authority.

Details of the lives of gifted men in various creative fields tend to corroborate these findings. The families into which such men are born center most often around a warm and good-hearted mother who is initially close to her child, and a father (or father-substitute) who, while he may run a wide gamut in talent, temperament, achievement, and interests, is either devoted to the boy or unusually involved in having him achieve. As he passes through childhood, the son comes to feel more and more strongly that he must please the father. Not always, but frequently, the boy proves himself by locating an area of self-expression related to the interests of his father figure.

Examples of this family pattern are abundant. Edward Hitschmann, writing about Johannes Brahms, points out that "his father was a diligent muscian who quickly recognized the uncommon musical talent of his Johannes. He took him to qualified teachers. We must imagine the boy, filled with musical ambition, inspired by his identification with the father but aspiring beyond him." [15] As for Brahms's mother, Hitschmann says, ". . . the treasures of her soul, her goodness and piety, influenced him long afterwards." [16] Dr. Greenacre, writing about Lewis Carroll, notes that his mother was reputed to be "one of the sweetest and gentlest women that ever lived." [17] However, the greater importance of Carroll's relationship with his father is easily established. The extent to which this father, with his own interests in mathematics and his own puckish sense of humor, was involved with his son can be gleaned from some of their correspondence. The boy Lewis had asked his father to get some things for him on a trip to the city, and the father responded (in a letter quoted by Dr. Greenacre from Derek Hudson's book on Lewis Carroll) :

> *I will not forget your commission. As soon as I get to Leeds I shall scream out in the middle of the street. Iron mongers— iron mongers—Six hundred men will rush out of their shops in a moment—fly, fly in all directions—ring the bells, call the constables—set the town on fire, I will have a file and a screwdriver, and a ring, and if they are not brought directly, in forty seconds I will leave nothing but a small cat alive.*[18]

After reviewing the meager documents that shed light on the kind of mothering Leonardo da Vinci received as a very young child, Kurt Eissler feels that no conclusions can be drawn. He points out, however, that there were important male figures in Leonardo's early life: "The relationship to the grandfather is hypothetical, but Leonardo's closeness to his Uncle Francesco, eight years younger than Leonardo's father, is documented." And while conceding that this uncle was not very ambitious or energetic (he did not seem to mind a subordinate role in life), Eissler comments, "I presume he was a welcome playmate of the boy Leonardo . . ." [19] It may also be taken as evidence of their unusual intimacy that Francesco made Leonardo his heir, in preference to the latter's legitimate siblings. That the male model be successful in his own right is unnecessary; perhaps a passive and otherwise inadequate type can more easily commit himself to the child and applaud the child's accomplishments without rancor.

Marcel Proust's close ties to an adoring and enveloping mother have been well publicized, and his is considered a classic case in that respect. Proust's relationship to his father has generally been ignored. One can deduce that it must have been very important. Until he was thirty, Proust was making educational and vocational decisions to please his father. Even though it flew in the face of his own desires and interests, Proust did these things to satisfy a father universally described as kindly but aloof. Passivity alone does not explain why a frail and ailing Proust entered the Sorbonne to study law, a subject to which he was totally indifferent; it does not explain why at twenty-five he took and passed a civil service examination, at his father's insistence, and then gave at least lip service to his position for the next five years.[20] In *Jean Santeuil,* a book by Proust which is clearly autobiographical, the hero may be seen voting not as he wishes but as he assumes his absent father would have voted.[21]

Recognizing the presence of many psychodynamic involvements, we can observe a general pattern of motivation to please the father. Nor does it matter whether the father is warmly and closely devoted to his son. Martin Luther's father, rigid, driving, and parsimonious as he was, made sure that funds were available for his son's education. Erik Erikson, in his brilliant study of Luther, points out that: "Only a boy with a precocious, sensitive, and intense conscience would care about pleasing his father as much as Martin did." [22]

THE ABSTRACTED MODEL AND THE OFFER OF WORK

Two more steps are necessary for artistic expression to fulfill its psychodynamic function. David Beres has formulated the third step as follows: "The artist substitutes an idealized image or an abstraction, particularly the latter, for the parent." [23] By dedicating himself to perfecting his work, the artist attempts to endow it with qualities which will symbolically secure parental approbation; the artistic creation may then be seen either as an idealized self-representation or as a representation of the idealized image of the parent. Through the medium of his "collective" audience, he ultimately strives to reach a state of harmony with his idealized parent. He thus hopes to gain the full measure of acceptance for those "sublimated" instinctual expressions which he was denied in their unsublimated form. To accomplish this he must achieve the same degree of perfection in his product as that with which he has endowed the idealized parental image. Thus the never-ending struggle for perfection.

The final step is self-evident: ultimately the work must be shown. Otherwise the whole operation is short-circuited. But to exhibit or not to exhibit then becomes an anxiety-laden conflict. If we follow Phyllis Greenacre's thought that the product is intended as a sign of affection for, as well as appeasement of, the father's symbolic internalized image, then this conflict is not mysterious. If the creative product can be seen as a gift, particularly a love gift, then Dr.

Greenacre's characterization of the artist's attitudes toward his art ("to be brought as near perfection as possible and to be presented with pride and misgiving" [24]) is apt.

Throughout our interviews, we have seen the artist preoccupied with perfection but vacillating between extreme confidence and complete uncertainty. In this light, the artist must react to criticism of his paintings as acceptance or rejection of himself in the context of an all-important relationship with the father; he cannot detachedly view criticism simply as an evaluation of his artistic achievement. To expose himself to the danger of personal rejection via his work is a step, then, that can be taken only with hesitation. The artist's conflict about audience reaction is made all the more acute because his artistic commitment demands that he do nothing which aims directly at gaining external approval; he must be guided solely by his artistic impulse. Thus when artists say that criticism, even from those they respect (to the extent that they are aware of it), seldom influences them, they catch themselves on one horn of their all but insoluble dilemma. This necessary independence from audience reaction by no means implies that they are insensitive to it. Their struggles must continue until, in fortunate instances, they gain a full sense of self-possession. At that point some artists seem to achieve a kind of inner harmony and spiritual serenity which renders them truly invulnerable to external reactions. One might speculate that such harmony is achieved when the idealized image to which the artist aspires becomes sufficiently integrated within his inner psychic organization as to be above reprojection onto the collective audience.

Thus, four stages may be hypothesized in the public emergence of inborn talent: first, the child and his work must be unambivalently accepted during his earliest years; second, there must occur "identification" with a model, usually a male, which provides specific stimulation of the talent; in the third stage, which may overlap the second, the internalized model takes on an abstract and idealized form, which the artist attempts to express through his work; and the fourth stage, again overlapping in time those which precede it, consists of the artist's offer of his perfected—but never perfect—work to the "world," which has the unconscious meaning of attempting to attain a specific position vis-à-vis the symbolized parental image.

This unresolved relationship to the father, as analyzed by Dr. Greenacre, may provide a partial basis for fathoming another side of artistic creativity. Because artists' oedipal relationships are not resolved in an expected manner, usual childhood repressions may not occur. Dr. Greenacre postulates that this might result in

> . . . a diminished firmness of the barrier between primary-process and secondary-process thinking and imagery, a condition which seems characteristic of gifted individuals. . . . Primary-process thought remains vitally present in the creative person, and is carried throughout life. . . . This continued access to states of early childhood may be the basis of the innocence of the artist, and his ability frequently to utilize the direct vision of the child.[25]

In this connection, it would be interesting to study the earliest memories of artists and the extent to which their infantile amnesias follow "normal" patterns. In our interviews we have only incidental remarks relating to this question. They do suggest that the early memories of at least some artists are more complete and that they go back further than most. But much more study would be required before meaningful generalizations could be made from this hypothesis. The artist, partly because he does not have the usual defense barriers (and consequently does have fairly free access to the primary processes), is a person who expresses universal truths in symbolic language. He is probably not aware of their full meaning. Such psychoanalytic propositions might help us explain why truly great works of art have many levels of meaning and are able to stand the test of time, regardless of the era in which they are produced and the forms which they take.

Dr. Greenacre's formulations may also give us some insight into the peer group as a determining force in the artist's development. His transitory dependence on his peers may relate to the steps involved in gradually evolving an internalized collective audience. Until his art achieves the level of complete self-possession, the alliance which he establishes with his peers helps to sustain him. The artist speaks of this group as a necessity during the years that he is seeking to find himself. As he gets older and finds "his" way, he generally has less and less need for others. But until he achieves the self-reliance necessary to exist in "isolation," and establishes necessary distances between himself and his social world, his life and his life's work are enmeshed in his search for external representations of the idealized parent. The peer group then exists as a special supportive public which provides the external sanctions that the real object failed to give.

But if a creative talent is to fulfill its potential, this phase must be transcended and a level of self-sufficiency must eventually be reached. When it is, the standards of perfection to which all artists aspire are dictated by a fully internalized ideal, independent of external judgment or support. Part of the suffering that true artists undergo may well be related to this struggle to attain full inner integration. The resolution of an artist's efforts eventually requires that he surrender his dependency, his "other-directedness." In the course of this struggle he must renounce reliance on the external cues and rewards which guide the lives of most people in our culture. The artist is free to enjoy worldly pleasures, but his inner psychic organization demands that he stand ready to relinquish them if their pursuit should conflict with his artistic conscience.

Our most significant finding, then, is the consistency with which initial acceptance by the mother and later active and specific stimulation by a male appear as elements in the elicitation of creative activity. Goethe, in whom this pattern is epitomized, may serve as one final dramatic example. Kurt Eissler, in his monumental work on this creative genius, convincingly substantiates the extent to which the almost unqualified and continuing parental acceptance and stimulation that Goethe received from his earlier years influenced his capacity to make optimum use of his talent. Goethe received almost unlimited maternal love and support from birth; surprisingly, as soon as his younger sister was old enough, he received the same from her. But it is in his unique relationship with his father, one in which the elder Goethe devoted himself in an apparently selfless and wholly unambivalent manner to his son, that we have the clue which helps to explain how that son's talent could be realized in such a magnificent way. As Eissler assesses it:

> . . . *this boldness, this urge to penetrate into all fields of human knowledge and activity, and the corresponding expectation of proficiency were certainly based—aside from the inherited store of endowment—on the fact that the parental world was not kept as a mystery, but the child was invited into partnership, the strong, authoritarian father focusing his existence on the welfare of his son.*[26]

5

Alienation
and Integration

Who is responsible for ugliness? What is "ugly"?
The question, if raised by "salesmen" of "beauty,"
is ugly.

The ugliest spectacle is that of artists selling
themselves.
Art as a commodity is an ugly idea.
Art as an entertainment is an ugly activity.
Painting as a "profession of pleasing and selling" is
an ugly business.
Art-dealing, art-collecting, art-manipulating, art-job-
bing, are ugly.
Art as a "means of livelihood," as a means of
"living it up," is ugly.
The expression, "An artist has to eat," is ugly.
(An artist does not have to eat any more than anyone
else.)
Economic relations in art are primitive and ugly.
Artists once led less ugly lives than other men.
Today artists lead the same kind of life as other
men. The artist as businessman is uglier than the
businessman as artist.
. . . Knowing on which side one's bread is buttered
in art is ugly.

—AD REINHARDT, 1962

ART IS a formal, yet somehow free and spontaneous expression of the aesthetic impulse. That impulse seems to lie deeply within all of us as a distinctive characteristic of the species, animating every culture man has ever created. No circumstance in human history or pre-history, however brutal and oppressive, has proved powerful enough to extinguish all artistic representation. There have been relatively sterile periods—which may later look like stages of incubation—followed by extraordinary bursts of creativity, unforeseen flowerings that abate as mysteriously as they begin. No one really understands why these fluctuations occur; they have no fixed periodicity; the social scientist cannot even specify what conditions are likely to yield which outcome. We know only that, great or mediocre, "original" or "derivative," art persists everywhere.

THE ARTIST AND THE ARTISAN

Like the family and religion, with which it has always been closely identified, art is universal.

Artists have mostly occupied an auxiliary position within the larger whole—adding cultural continuity to ineluctable change. They have therefore tended to be an integral part of the overall institutional enterprise in which tribes, bands, city-states, civilizations, and nations were engaged. Their social situation in the pre-industrial past cannot have been seriously anomalous. Indeed, the role they played must have been defined as indispensable, for art was a mainstay of the general effort to give life meaning, to guarantee immortality, to propitiate and glorify the gods. The production of plastic and graphic, aural, poetic, and terpsichorean symbols served a number of generally intelligible ends. Above all, it helped to supply the members of a specific society with the cohesion needed for survival. The artisan who made art objects was like any other artisan. He was not yet an "artist" nor yet a marginal man. A silversmith or a woodcarver did not suffer by comparison with an armorer: the work they did was equally "useful."

Obviously all this has changed, if only because modern, industrial mass society has swept the world—and it precludes most forms of artisanship. Some men still work with their hands (though they too will forsake manual labor as cybernation advances), but nowhere in the economically developed countries do many men produce things, from first to last, with their own hands and their own tools. The artist is a statistically insignificant exception. He is no longer one among many artisans, each trained to make a special contribution within the same social and economic context. He is, instead, the last of a dead or dying breed, virtually the sole survivor, and thus, strictly from an occupational standpoint—an anachronism.

ALIENATION FROM SOCIETY

That the artist does not fit, that he is dependent upon an anonymous public composed largely of ignorant bourgeois buyers, is a theme at least as old as Romanticism. We may lay it down as law that wherever roles are vaguely or ambiguously defined, those who are expected to play them will experience acute discomfort, e.g., mothers-in-law, middle class women, old people, and adolescents at large. He who does not know if he belongs can be expected to suffer substantial disorientation.

As his ancient and medieval status collapsed, the Western painter found himself bereft of social support. At the mercy of an impersonal market over which he could exercise little control, the artist sought to reestablish himself at certain interstices of his culture.

The picture should not be overdrawn, for it differs over time and from place to place. Nevertheless, for about two hundred years the Western artist has been a displaced person, alternately or simultaneously proud of his independence—an ideological heritage of the Renaissance—and abashed by his isolation—a direct consequence of revolutionary change in the social order. As we observe another shift, this time back to some kind of integration but on a new footing, plangent echoes of the familiar lament come back to us. Hence, an old-timer, contrasting the distant past with the uncertain present, asserts that:

Now there is no responsible patronage. The artist is adrift

*and footloose in a society that has no rational way in which
to use him. There is nothing in this society that makes it
possible to use the artist as everybody in any other profession
is used.*

Or this outburst from another painter, several decades his junior:

*It's better for the artist to be a hole-in-the-corner type,
because that corresponds to his real position in this society.
Even if it suddenly takes a great interest in art as a symbol
of attainment, actually it's a very inartistic world we're living
in. Certainly nothing important is primarily motivated by
aesthetic considerations. . . . People are constantly talking
about the Seagram's building. That seems to be the last
refuge of the philistines. They say, "Oh, look at the Seagram's building! There's a little plaza in front of it." The
builders were practical men; they would have filled that
space up. As it is, a great architect built this sheath into
the sky, and he decided a thing like that needs scale, has to
have a plaza in front of it. But what kind of plaza is it?
There's room for about three café tables and a waiter. That's
the type of place it is. The Venetians, when they built a
church out of the mud, sank six million stakes of wood in
order to build a plaza which was commensurate with the
size of the building. But in New York, in America today,
every organized, highly collective activity is primarily swayed
by practical considerations . . . Somehow, art's not part of
the scene.*

The artist feels that he is an invisible man, so far from the mainstream of activity that others put up with him simply because they do
not realize he is there:

*Whatever we do, we do because it's allowed to be done.
But nobody cares or knows it. In other words, that we live
in lofts and fixed them up, that we have these galleries on
Tenth Street, that they've been built up and torn down—
because nobody gave a damn. We were allowed to have them
because nobody noticed it. If we had asked permission,
somebody would have said, "No!"*

147

On the positive side:

> *That's one privilege the artist has in this country. If nobody loves you, nobody pays attention to you either. And in a sense, you have some freedom because of this neglect.*

Asked whether as a youth he had any conception of what it meant to be an artist, a prominent sculptor replied:

> *Well, I did and I didn't. I knew it wasn't going to be easy. I knew I would sort of be outside of society, and that financially I would have to find other ways of making do. . . . If you set out to become a professional man or a technician or even if you just work with no training on some job, you exist within the social structure. But who employs the artist? That's why I say he's been on the outside.*

THE DISENGAGEMENT OF THE ARTIST

Romanticism is a sustained gesture of rebellion against the bourgeoisie, an active revulsion from its commercialism, a head-on collision between antipathetic values. Neither marksman nor target can mistake the meaning of *"Epater la bourgeoisie"* when that exclamation is hurled by a defiant nineteenth-century poet at his respectable enemy. Our vanguard artists are less trigger-happy, and they find their target more elusive. One of them, with as much experience abroad as at home, sums it up as follows: "In America you don't have many bourgeois with any dimension to hate. The French did. We have an amorphous middle class . . ." To say this is to say that we have an amorphous society. (Our respondents use the word "society" as a synonym for "middle class.") In short, artists by and large view themselves as occupying a void within the general penumbra. The shadowy and insubstantial world, by which they refuse to be enclosed even as it repels them, produces a proletariat (more like Arnold J. Toynbee's than Karl Marx's)— signifying persons of the society but not in it. No more than the American industrial proletariat does this creative minority seek to overthrow the system; but the artistic, much more than the industrial, proletariat does wish to disengage itself from that system. Thrust out, and still inappropriately complaining about exclusion, it does not actually want in—and begins to worry about absorption. Meanwhile, coexistence is the keynote:

> *I don't spit in a bourgeois' face just because he is a bourgeois. I don't share anything with him—except the kind of apartment I live in, my car, my clothes. But, you see, these are very minor matters. If it's more convenient for me to wear a white shirt and collar because everyone else does, I wear the white shirt. . . . We live side by side. Yes, I'd call it coexistence. Live and let live. As I say, we are certainly not compatible, but coexistence is painless.*

> *A clash? There's a difference in what we cherish, but I don't see a clash. . . . That is, professional people are really involved in making money and manufacturing or on Wall Street or big business. I'm just not involved in all that.*

> *I vote. I have to go to my butcher, to my grocer, and I have to relate myself to them, behave as anyone else does to them, and take care of all the other things that anyone else takes care of. I think it would be too much of a distraction to do otherwise. It would mean fighting the world all your life, which is ridiculous.*

> *Of course the good painter is a non-conformist, but it's manifested in his work more than in his person. Now, I'm not saying there haven't been times when the painter was a non-conformist in his person, too. Only in most cases he burned himself out. We had that after the First World War: a whole group of painters who lived it up and who died very young.*

> *I've managed to work out a* modus vivendi, *a certain detachment. . . . Consider the example of where we live now. Up until recently, we have always lived in some hideaway, an old barn or house out in the sticks. I like privacy, and since I began teaching we've lived outside New York. I like that kind of contrast between the quiet country and the terrific hubbub here. Well, now we live on Long Island. I bought*

*an old house. I couldn't live in a new one, both for prac-
tical reasons—they're too small—and aesthetic reasons—I
can't stand them. So this house is in an older neighborhood,
but around it is quite a large development of newer ones,
these boxes, split-levels, and so forth. Now my wife is
rather friendly. She likes to know the neighbors. It's very
interesting for me to observe what's happening because we
never had neighbors before. Here's where I come in—
because I haven't. My wife tells me about these nice people,
but essentially they're stereotypes. She doesn't have more
than a few words to say to them herself, although they
would like to be closer because she has some of the eccen-
tricities that go along with the wife of an artist, and they
are intrigued with me and want to know more about it.
But we really can't either of us spend much time with them
without getting bored. On the other hand, she sought out
the oddballs who, incidentally, live in the older houses,
and their children have become more friendly with my children than with the split-level children.*

Such is the typical accommodation of artists whose attitude toward
non-artists turns mainly on being cool, subdued, and not quite accessible, rather than angry, combative, or flamboyant. This is a
state of nearness and farness, of inwardness skirting withdrawal but
stopping short of it, of superficial yet real contact, and civility at all
times used to preserve a certain distance. Their world is a subculture tied by delicate filaments to the larger culture. Upset the
precarious balance between the two, and another pattern is sure to
emerge. Either the filaments break and the artist is removed, or they
tighten and he is assimilated. Many living artists are conditioned
to the danger of removal or of flight, against which they have
learned to steel themselves. Now, to their widespread dismay, they
face the problem of assimilation. "How to remain separate without
being cut off" is, one may say, a traditional question for practicing
artists. Lately for more and more of them it has been unexpectedly
abbreviated. The question becomes simply: "How to remain separate." Put otherwise, "How not to be swallowed up by well-wishers
who embrace and reward what they scorned only yesterday." If

before the artist struggled to preserve his sanity while being pushed out, today, while being sucked in on all sides, he must fight for his autonomy.

THE AFFIRMATION OF WORK

Artists are "peculiar" not only because they continue to be craftsmen in an age of bureaucratic industrialism, but also because of their commitment to an ethic that estranges them from most modern men. Self-actualization in work is the first tenet of that ethic. Artists regard their work as an end in itself. Thus they are unable to regard it as a means to anything like the attainment of salvation in another world (the true Gospel of Work which best expresses Calvin's pristine doctrine), nor as a means to the attainment of worldly success (the Calvinist doctrine secularized to stimulate and sustain early capitalism).

Nowadays the majority of people work not because they like to, or for the sake of their immortal souls, but in order to acquire money and "the good things that money will buy." Artists do not ordinarily find money or material comforts unwelcome; not one in our sample idealized poverty, and several attacked those who see it as a virtue. Starving in a garret or lacking the wherewithal to buy necessary materials does not appeal to them. At the same time, they decline to join in the hot pursuit of money. And the pecuniary evaluation of worth is absolutely abhorrent to them, although they know that it prevails in most areas of contemporary life.

> *Well, I would like to earn a little bit more money. I don't know what I would do with too much more. . . . Put it this way: I don't need money that badly. I just wouldn't go to the same lengths for it that other people do. If it comes my way, fine. If it doesn't, I'll manage.*

For the artist, and for those among whom he makes a resonance, his work has other functions which cannot bear even remotely on money or prestige. Given this disparity between what he cherishes and what "the world" cherishes—given, further, his need for other artists, with the mutuality of attraction and repulsion implied thereby, the rapprochement he achieves can only be an uneasy one.

Voluntary internal exile (in New York), as opposed to involuntary isolation, is one way of dealing with the problem:

> *I think the idea of a lot of painters coming to New York is an exile. They are exiling themselves from the love of their families, from the love of their friends who perhaps do not understand them. There's nothing worse than being in a situation of that kind, having your mother and father looking at you and pitying you. You must get out of that. It's bad enough that you have to go through it yourself, let alone seeing anyone else suffering with you. I think that's what really drives most of the artists into a center like this. Likewise Paris in its heyday.*

Or again, from a painter who thinks that an artist "must have the strength of an elephant and the innocence of a saint to live in this society."

> *You have a feeling up in Maine that the world is your oyster, and you're going to suck the last little bit of juice out of it. Then you come across, say, a garage mechanic, like there's one guy up there with a terrifically attractive personality. I'd love to be great friends with him, and we are—as long as I'm like in his field, on his side of the fence, if I take an interest in his work and his folks, and if I talk about clamming and fishing. But the thing that I really care the most about in life, art, my work, that's something where he's uncomfortable because he's got no way of getting in, and I'm uncomfortable because I've got no way of really letting him in. That happens everywhere outside of New York. Which is one reason the artists are here. It's a miracle, but here there are enough people who do not consider artists as a bunch of hoot owls. So we're congregated in New York where we can feel more or less like members of a community.*

The occupational enclave, with its periphery of aficionados, provides understanding as well as stimulus—by example and intellectual exchange—for people bent upon similar tasks. They find a high measure of consensus about matters of taste and preference that need not pertain only to their sphere of supreme interest. Everywhere else they are outside the swim. Conventional clothes and manners cannot fully conceal unconventional ideas:

> *I was down in Ohio, staying with an astrophysicist friend of mine, and there was this pretty girl living next door. But she was one of those real American girls. I kept trying to get her interested in me, you know. I was very interested in her, but she refused to take me seriously. She said she was very concerned over me because I was always putting down everything that she thought was great. So finally she said, "You are not happy. You don't like anything." You know, because I didn't like Jack Paar on television. All the things she admired so much I told her were far short of the goal. But she was fully satisfied with these tidbits that society throws up to her, whereas I felt that they were nothing but garbage. I guess I am very unhappy when you come right down to it on that level.*

THE REJECTION OF "APPLIED ART"

On that level the common man, or the all-American girl, cannot expect to meet the artist. It is not surprising that he should diverge even more profoundly in his judgment of commercial art, which is so much a part of "that level." Yet, knowing full well that Madison Avenue misappropriates and vulgarizes the latest aesthetic innovations, the artist does not characteristically denounce vulgarization or wax indignant about advertising. His attitude toward this phenomenon is wholly consistent with the division he makes between "them" and "us" in all matters. "They" are perfectly free to do commercial art; "we" needn't; indeed, "we" mustn't. Let "us" not bemoan or condemn "their" activity, which may be better or worse than ours: it is different from and forever incompatible with what "we" do. The above seems a fair summary of the nearly unanimous opinion evoked by our discussion.

Superficially, the graduate of an art school appears to be well equipped for a job in advertising. He may even have had courses in advertising, and he will almost certainly have had them in lettering and graphics. His technical training would seem to be suitable for commercial art. Nevertheless, those of our artists who, at one point or another, have had a fling at it, claim dismal results, for they lacked proficiency in a métier not their own:

> *Actually, I didn't have a gift for commercial art. I mean, I really express myself when I'm painting, and I'm very self-conscious, and I find it impossible to perform under restrictions. When somebody said, "Do this," in the office, I found that I was sort of untalented. I have to want to do something in order to apply myself to it. . . . I tried things like textbook design, too, but I couldn't even begin to do it well. Somebody who isn't a painter probably would be much better.*

Furthermore, the feeling is that if you do have a gift for commercial art, you had better do nothing else. The fine artist who needs employment should seek it anywhere but on Madison Avenue. He will either be inept as an ad man, or it will become apparent that he should not have called himself a fine artist in the first place. The same element in his work that makes him acceptable to art directors in advertising agencies makes him unacceptable to serious artists. He stylizes that element fruitlessly and loses the artistic point of view, a certain perspective which obliges him to stand for something whose importance he personally and strongly feels.

To the question, "Can one be both a fine artist and a commercial artist?" a fairly typical answer is, "No. Absolutely not. That's like asking can you be a slave and a free man." Some say that it may be theoretically possible to reconcile the two, but:

> *You'd have to be a certain kind of nut to get away with it. The only example that comes to mind is Mondrian. He did medical drawings for doctors and publications: intestines, cartilages, livers, that kind of thing. But I think it's a very special case.*

And no one was able to suggest another case. Of its opposite there were numerous examples:

> *I've known many of my friends who took that path, and*

it's always been an unhappy one. They said, "Well now I'll work ten years and then paint." They never do, and if they did their painting wouldn't be very good. You can't mix these things. At least that's been my experience, which has been considerable. I know about a dozen people who have told me that.

An artist who also teaches tells of a former student:

I heard that he got married, had a child, and then he had a house and he had a car and he had one of the top advertising jobs in the city. He came down one day with a long face, moaning, and finally I said, "What's the matter?" He said, "I can't paint." So I said, "Oh, all this and heaven, too." I said, "Look, forget about painting."

Despite the rapidity with which a new art style or a new aesthetic image is picked up by advertisers completely receptive to modern art, skills required for one are evidently not transferable to the other. Practitioners of the parasitic discipline unfit themselves for creativity. By flitting back and forth, dividing themselves, keeping "a hand in," and risking a split sensibility, they contaminate their vision. Clever in many ways, they are creative in none. The upshot is dilettantism:

An artist should be stuck with what he's doing. Because, I mean, how many people do you know who have all kinds of abilities? They can write, they can play music, they're interested in the theater, they paint. And somehow they can never bring themselves together in one specific thing. I think that's a tragedy.

And these reflections prompt others that bring us to the heart of the matter:

I think the whole business of going to a studio, sitting there, and creating a world is essential. When you step into your studio, your sanctuary, it's almost a religious world. I think the artist must create that world. Whatever distractions he allows himself, when he walks into his studio and closes the door he is in one piece. Now, I think the whole idea of ad-

155

vertising, of commercial work, the whole idea of assignments that have to be met, deadlines and things like that, is what's most important. You know, the fact that he gets a job and he's got to do it no matter what. It must be finished by such and such a day or such and such a month. And then after he does it, maybe it does something to him. *Maybe he's got a week or two now to sit down and paint, but what if the painting takes more than a week or two? I've known commercial artists, some of them on top, who try to soften their difficulties. They say they do this advertising now to make a lot of money and then they'll retire and sit down and paint. That's also disastrous because, there again, what it's done to them. . . . You see, I don't really know how to account for it. Maybe what's missing is time . . . to chance upon things or discover them . . .*

Even free-lance artists who escape the office routine by taking on an account here and there must cope with pressures, likened by one who tried it to those of a typing job. And that partial immersion in commercial art produces foreign matter which "creeps into their work." The job may be technical and exacting, and so characterized without disparagement, but it is also "completely lacking in style," and "dead." You use a paintbrush in both, but they are otherwise incommensurable. The distance between them is not readily apparent to laymen, nor always to young artists who, however, if they *are* artists, will soon learn better. One tried it out to please his folks, "to prove I could make a living and all that," but mostly, he says, "to meet Miss Rheingold." He did meet her that year, and many other models besides. "And they all proved to be so disappointing to me that that was the end of my commercial art."

A woman painter was asked to draw a pelican for Pelican Books. She went up to the Bronx Zoo and made hundreds of drawings of pelicans, then came home and showed them to her husband (also an artist) who declared that they were fascinating:

But then I couldn't mat them properly and so on. I kept bringing a great many to choose from. They kept saying, "No." So I gave the whole batch to my brother and said, "Render me one, and I'll split it with you." He just made

> *one very neat drawing from mine, matted it beautifully, and brought it in the proper presentation. In commercial art the matter of presentation is extremely important. Which is one reason I would have no way of doing it.*

For her, even commissioned portraits smack too much of commercialism. Usually a successful portrait painter, she recalls two portraits that failed. In both cases she was commissioned and paid:

> *I just never found my way through with them. I don't know whether I was inhibited by the money or whether it was because they said, "Do me," and I would not otherwise have picked them.*

Commercial art entails the making of "little things," the routine use of a drafting board to produce "the symbol of a bottle next to the symbol of an orange." The residual effects of this "small painting" are hard to efface:

> *If you learn to draw in a certain way for commercial purposes —in a style acceptable to whoever hires you—it is difficult to forget when you're doing your own work. And you have to do more than leave it in the background. You have to kill it altogether.*

The technical objection prevails. It is not a question about which artists wish to be considered snobbish. If most of them prefer housepainting, furniture-moving, or schoolteaching to advertising, it is not because these are more beautiful occupations. To them commercial art represents a deadly interference; once acquired, its techniques rub off and destroy the real thing. Whereas all outside work is a drain on one's energy, commercial art drains, taps, and poisons creative energy, and is therefore viewed as a total nemesis.

The technical objection is uniform, strong, and no doubt valid. Still, we suspect that artists would recoil even if it could be demonstrated that they run no stylistic risk by doing commercial work. Painters see people who undertake "little things" in advertising as "professional designers"—an image irreconcilable with their self-image.

Q. *Can you combine them?*
A. *No. I don't think so.*
Q. *Why not?*
A. *One type is a designer who serves a social need, who has, you might say, a social use. The other type is involved in his own problems, his own education. Doing both is impossible.*

Exploration and education of the self presuppose its preservation. That "self" is under heavy attack—less from enemies, who may help to provide the artist with useful foils and obstacles which strengthen him in his resolve to remain independent, than from friends of art who may love it to death. Aunt Polly was probably not insincere in her feeling for Huck Finn, nor he in his reaction to her, "but I reckon I got to light out for the Territory ahead of the rest, because Aunt Polly she's going to adopt and civilize me, and I can't stand it. I been there before."

Advertising deflects very few real artists from their calling; other forces propel them into the clutches of Aunt Polly. Commercial art is tangential and avoidable. Dealers, directors, buyers, publics, and critics, their number greater than ever and growing every day in an unparalleled cultural explosion, are central and unavoidable. They are the Aunt Pollys who warmly embrace artists and then lead them to higher status in a business civilization.

THE NEW SUCCESS AND ITS DANGERS

In New York, where not long ago there were only two or three galleries, there are now over four hundred. The artist who now has an international audience recently had none to speak of even at home. An earlier generation understood that "no one could live off his art." At this moment there are more graphic artists who do live off their art—without working wives, their lifeline in a less affluent age—than there are poets, dramatists, novelists, and composers put together. This is partly the case because a graphic artist produces things with real present or future cash value. The buyer can own them as he cannot own a poem or a symphony. They are his to hang on a wall, display in a garden—or hide in a vault.

Artists, scientists, and intellectuals, inured to the derision they had every reason to expect (until, let us say, Sputnik I went into orbit), all at once found themselves the recipients of an unwonted respect. It quite suddenly dawned upon decision-makers in every sector of public and private philanthropy that these people—previously regarded as useless and subversive—could be very useful and supportive. Useful people, deserving of respect, must be rewarded. They must be supplied with larger sums of money, a *sine qua non* for prestige in the pecuniary culture. And they must be made into celebrities, culture heroes who will prove that America is not as barbarous as foreign critics make it out to be.

Thus we witness the intrusion of politics and commerce on an unheard-of scale, and with the most benevolent intentions, to promote intellectuality, or spirituality, or both. Clear historical lines of antagonism have been blurred. Artists who were not greatly gifted long ago made their peace with the Establishment; they manufactured *kitsch* for mass consumption; the greatly gifted comprised a lonely *avant-garde*. From antipode to antipode, it was a long continuum. With the popular triumph of nonrepresentational, geometric, or completely abstract art, this continuum dissolved. Now the vanguard painter and sculptor find it as hard as the radical intellectual (such as Paul Goodman, C. Wright Mills, or Norman Mailer) to outrage a public that seems to have become shock-proof. Contempt, anger, and laughter have been widely replaced by respectful, if still uninformed, interest mounting to real or synthetic, but in any case clamorous, advocacy.

Ad Reinhart is a painter of distinction whose most recent work consists exclusively of plain black canvases in various shapes, with brush strokes scraped off; they sell to museum directors and private collectors with an ease that confounds their creator. The sharp turn of recent events, presaged by WPA, disturbs Reinhart so much that he has taken to merciless flailing of his fellow artists. Writing in *Art News* (May 1957), he sums up the last few decades:

> *The business boom of the twenties orphaned the alienated artist, but the great depression of the thirties witnessed the tender engagement of art to government. Ten years after that, the ardent marriage of art and business and war was celebrated with Pepsi-Cola in ceremonial contests called*

"Artists for Victory" at America's greatest museum of art. By the fifties armies of art's offspring were off to school and Sunday School, crusading for education and religious decoration. . . .

From "Artists for Ashcan and Dust-Bowl" to "Artists for America First and Social Security" to "Artists for Victory" to "Artists for Action in Business, Religion, and Education," the portrait of the artist in America in the twentieth century shapes up into a figure resembling Al Capp's "Available Jones," who is always available to anyone, any time, for anything at all, at any price. . . .

The "ice has been broken," the ivory tower flooded by unschooled professionals, the walls of the academy washed out by schooled primitives, and the sanctum-sanctorum blasphemed by Fauve-Folk, Bauhaus-Bacchuses, and housebroken Samurai.

Among many others, Jean-Paul Sartre has reminded us that: "Beribboned turncoats have proven time and again that painting dies whenever it is made to serve alien purposes." [1] That is to say, painting dies when it is made to serve such purposes as those excoriated by Reinhart. Sartre's range is wider than Reinhart's, and that of another worried critic, the art historian Quentin Bell, is still wider. He encompasses the whole Western tradition from medieval to contemporary art. Bell ingeniously applies to the Western artist categories developed by David Riesman for completely different ends in his famous analysis of American character structure. In Bell's opinion the artist has evolved from the anonymity of medieval tradition-direction, through Renaissance individualism and inner-direction, to the marketplace and other-direction. We doubt that other-direction is an accomplished fact. Our data much more strongly suggest confusion and ambivalence. But we do not doubt that Bell is pointing toward the principal danger:

Both abstract painting and action painting have a congruous relationship with what may be called "functional architecture," the former as an extension, almost a parody, of the structures of the machine age, the latter as a decorative foil to the regular unbroken surface of the modern building, giving relief to the eye, but at the same time, harmonizing by reason of its similarly impersonal character. . . . Thus it would appear that the artists of today may be returning to a position in which they can be fully integrated in society. They are swimming with the current; they give the public what it wants and are rewarded accordingly. To an ever increasing extent they are ready to submerge their personalities in the common artistic personality of the age. Their art is no longer a protest; it has become part of a general assent.

In all this the artists may seem to be returning to the position of the medieval painter or the craftsman of primitive society. But their conformity is of a new kind; they remain, in a sense, revolutionary because they explicitly reject tradition and have little or nothing to do with the past. Their revolutions are quasi-unanimous movements, however, and they change direction in the manner of a school of fish, a flight of starlings, or the designers of women's clothes. Their nonconformity is essentially conformist and provides less and less scope for the lonely eccentric or the pre-eminent leader.

If this tendency continues we may perhaps see a progressive disappearance of the man of genius and an ever growing conformity in manners, morals, and ideas until the artist is indistinguishable from the rest of the community.[2]

Bell has perhaps put the matter in terms that are too stark and simple. We find more complexities than he does, and therefore less reason for derogatory generalizations. Nonetheless, every charge that he makes must be examined with care. Bell has hold of something which sounds real danger signals; and he is the authoritative spokesman for a position frequently taken by less sophisticated observers.

Can the artist become "indistinguishable from the rest of the community" and still project his basic removal from its values? Can he be totally absorbed while protesting about business affairs?

I'm not made to do these things. How could I do them? I don't even have the interest or the ability or the idea of starting in the beginning and taking an interest.

Both centripetal and centrifugal forces are at work here. The painter who says it is necessary for him "to buck up against some things in society *in order to be private*," who believes in "some kind of ancient polarity" out of which "a dialectic of creative friction" may be expected to arise—such an artist is struggling representatively, if not very coherently, to proclaim that he is still his own man. So is the painter who asserts that, although he "just isn't cut out for making money," he neither envies nor resents those who are. The attitude could easily puzzle "those who are," since they so often make him and his kind into objects of resentment and envy. He habitually refuses to reciprocate. The dominant feeling remains differentness, separateness:

> *My values and the values of most artists I know are abso-*
> *lutely different from those of lawyers, doctors, and business-*
> *men. . . . We need less of certain kinds of façade. Now I'm*
> *not saying that artists don't have their own, but it isn't the*
> *kind that gets on a Madison Avenue bus and has to keep*
> *up with the country club in the suburbs and depends on how*
> *neat you look.*

There is an edge to this reaction, but it sharpens only when the artist feels directly threatened. One, speaking for most, muses in this vein: "I think I'm fairly free from generalized hostility. I feel hostility toward people who won't let me be myself." And, we believe, this artist captures the prevailing mood much better than Bell when he tells us:

> *So now, one of the things that I need to fight is a tendency*
> *to want to be on good terms with the powers that be. But*
> *I want to be on good terms on* my *terms, not theirs. I am*
> *sufficiently an artist anyway not to be that realistic in wanting*
> *to figure out what I could do to ingratiate myself. As a*
> *result, I get along with very few of them. As soon as a person*
> *is in power, in some position where he might do me some*
> *good, I start feeling very shaky and strange.*

Such symptoms stem from the peculiar nature of any confrontation in our time between artists and the "powers that be." What it can be like was dazzlingly illuminated for us in an anecdote whose historicity our informant earnestly avowed, but which, if apocryphal, suggests the truth all the same. It concerns a New York painter recently catapulted into fame and fortune who until a few years ago was known only to the cognoscenti. At this writing, his canvases command a price of approximately $25,000 each. Somewhat tipsy one day in the Museum of Modern Art, the painter, feeling emboldened, approached a rich and powerful patron to whom he put a question that had been gnawing him, namely, "Why do you buy my work?" "To keep guys like you quiet," came the instantaneous answer. There is no recorded riposte to that thrust. The buyer did not dissimulate; he did not profess to like, much less understand, the work; he did not claim that it was a good investment, or that, being fashionable, it would add to the luster of his collection. He chose instead to be brutally frank, stunning the artist with words that implied nothing less than the intention to tame him completely.

Contact for the purpose of deliberate and conscious emasculation cannot be very common. But there are subtler risks by which the world comes to be too much with an artist, first by destroying his solitude:

> *With neglect, you had a sense of freedom. Now it hasn't begun to hurt me yet, personally, but I have a lot of friends whose careers are far more remunerative than mine and who are better known than I am. We've all grown up together. So in the last fifteen years since we were kids just starting out, I've noticed what's happened to them, and I can see it happening to me to the degree that more and more people from the journals and so on call me up. With the growing interest in art in the United States, sponsored on the one hand by the big mags, on the other hand by the colleges, and sort of ordained by our king and queen, lack of privacy will be a big problem. . . . I don't know whether in our generation as things are changing so rapidly with greater and greater attention given to us, whether we can stand it. I've seen too many of my friends going down the drain artistically. They're miserable creatures.*

The stern judgment of a man like Bell is everywhere matched by artists who feel the same impingement he describes and express even more anxiety about what it means. They see the "atmosphere poisoned" and "life among artists polluted" by commercialism, invasion, publicity, and vociferous but synthetic enthusiasm. They condemn as "phony neo-Dadaism" that highly perishable art which is designed to be impermanent, as well as the appearance of gimmicks, "blown-up funny sheets," "happenings" which are alleged to have a profound philosophical basis but are in fact much more a matter of "window display—commercial art." They deplore, with some savagery, the arrival of too many young people "who become artists the way their predecessors used to become lawyers or doctors," converting a vocation into a profession, a mission into a career, just because it is "considered a possible way to make money." Here we find no more complacency among artists in relation to society than we do in relation to their work—which is a constant source of criticism and doubt. Nor are they unaware of the connection that may obtain between social pressure and the quality of that work. Concerning artists and society:

> *A lot of them seem to get swept up into it. I mean this phenomenon recently of artists becoming very successful commercially, and you find many of them who act more like businessmen than they do like artists. I'm sure it has an influence on their work, causing some of them to produce things that are successful, and then keep turning them out. . . . But I don't think it has to be that way.*

There it is: a plea of guilty, at least for others who have forsaken their birthright. The devoted artist fears that his own integrity is imperiled, but he exempts himself from the general indictment. He has not, and the others need not have, capitulated. One can cope with a difficult situation if its lineaments are known, as they are known even to those who "wretchedly" yield where they should resist. To know is presumably not enough, but it can carry the man with independent resources very far.

Some fine artists, lacking internal fortitude, have probably always given up the ghost. One cannot tell how much greater the greatest of them might have been, given even more strength than they did summon to withstand patrons and publics. A recent case, discussed with some asperity by Jerry Tallmer,[3] is that of the modern painter

André Derain, who early in the century appeared to be on his way to becoming a master. Derain, with his companions Picasso and Matisse, brilliantly contributed to the creation of Fauvism. But after the First World War, Tallmer writes, "Derain turned glib. He turned cheap. He turned—one cannot avoid the ruined word—reactionary. . . . In short, he took the easy way out: easy cynicism. The canvases through the remainder of his life poured down a downhill slope of easy illustration, sub-Impressionism, crowd pleasingness, charm." And Alfred H. Barr, Jr., curator of the Museum of Modern Art, comments in his notes for a retrospective show that "when he died in 1954 Derain's work of his last thirty years was regarded with condescension, sometimes with contempt; and often it still is." The ultimate verdict, if there ever is one, may be different. Now, however, Derain's final phase is held in very bad odor. It exemplifies, no matter how complicated Derain's undiscoverable motives really were, exactly that which artists sense they must not do.

ARTISTIC AUTONOMY AND PERCEPTION

Artists believe that they should be true to their own standards which, if they are at variance with a value system that exalts getting and spending, prompts them to ask not for extirpation of that system but for toleration of its opposite. They are proponents of cultural pluralism who ask only to be unmolested. As such they are also nearly the last proponents of laissez faire. They want little or nothing beyond their own freedom: "After all, society has no obligation to help the owner of a shoestore get out of bankruptcy. If a poor devil miscalculates by opening his shoestore where everybody goes barefoot, that's his tough luck." But they do contend that, without encroachment from above or outside, they have much to give. Indeed, they regard artistic autonomy as a necessary condition for the production of their gifts to society:

> *It is most important for the modern artist that he work alone. He is most creative when he is alone, and very likely before he is recognized. That's what makes an early Chirico better than a late Chirico. Statistically, historically, creation takes place in isolation. I don't mean like the six hours you go to*

165

your studio. It's not just physical isolation, but isolation in the sense that you're attacking something which nobody else is involved in. Or maybe another friend is, or a few other people. But where you are is new territory. And the excitement, the push, the simple push of energy that is necessary to get into a new territory, is what makes that art better.

Q. *To what end?*

A. *Well, I certainly feel that what I'm doing is not just for myself. It's not just a personal expression. It's what people say about an expansion of consciousness . . .*

Q. *Not only your own?*

A. *When I expand my consciousness, I expand the consciousness of everybody who looks at the painting. That kind of thing is obviously happening in the twentieth century. I don't know if the art has been good or bad or whether it has gone ahead or backwards, but it certainly has expanded consciousness. Just look at the enormous variety of stuff that's being done.*

There is much conviction in all this that the painter and the sculptor, as they deal with the physical aspects of reality—not merely the surrounding landscape and its beauty, but "cracks in the walls and on the sidewalks, old newspapers, dirt and disorder"—help all of us come to terms with the world. Indeed, coming to terms with visual reality or becoming aware of a certain poetry in the external world is usually emphasized by artists as their first, if not their foremost, contribution. They recognize in themselves an occupationally heightened sensitivity, not to all things but surely to color, mass, line, and the other ingredients of their trade—which cannot but stimulate those exposed to it. Thus the artist, permitted to work without let or hindrance, has within him the capacity to make men more alive than they could be without his special services. By seeing our common environment with greater profundity than we can, he re-creates it, while transforming himself and the rest of us—if we care to commune with him. Unmediated by art, the banality of everyday life, its disorderliness and evanescence, would be too depressing to bear. Numbness or paralysis of the senses—and of the spirit—would inevitably set in. That condition already exists among many, the neutral or indifferent, toward whom artists say they bear no grudge. By contrast, there are "the real philistines":

> *I think that if I have any social purpose it's to reach people who* could *respond. I think the real philistines are the professional aesthetes who have an idea about what the perfect world of beauty is and go out to make it . . . like a group that's represented by Duchamp, who declares that there's no such thing as art, and that therefore the thing to do with the world is give it an artistic environment: rubber foam chairs, tile bathtubs, refrigerators that are absolutely straight—so they live in a world of beauty.*

It is not the substitution of arty objects for art that painters and sculptors have in mind when they speak of transforming the physical environment. They mean a new sensory experience which begins but does not end with the vision itself:

> *Those developments, like the growing realism of Greek sculpture or Renaissance painting, were part of a separation from existing ways of seeing, and presumably, therefore, of existing ways of relating to society; so the fourteenth-century painter didn't paint in a Byzantine manner but assumed something different and was necessarily out of gear with his society.*

The artist is a visionary; what he sees, he sees with greater clarity than the non-artist; this gives an inherently prophetic quality to his work. First this has to do with visual and tactile phenomena, with otherwise unperceivable sense data that materialize in works of art. Their initial impact is such that we come to look at things in a new way, to notice what has hitherto escaped our attention, and thereby to redefine the perceptual boundaries of life. Viewed in this light, great art is always subversive of our most elementary prepossessions. We begin to understand what the artist means when he says that art, though "useless," always changes the world. The artist creates his world, and with it an image of man—so that ultimately he creates our world as well—and all this regardless of his specific subject matter. He is engaged in a sustained attempt to achieve clarification, endlessly exploring himself and the existential reality around him. The good artist who translates his sensations, perceptions, and apperceptions into meaningful form finds that he is in advance of any but the tiniest audience. Viewers, and even colleagues who have not struck out for the same new territory, will lag behind, and by the time they catch up the creative artist will have outdistanced them once again. Consequently, we have to do with a chasm that can never be fully breached. The psychophysical distance between art and those it may ultimately reach is too considerable even today—perhaps more today—in an age when art is avidly consumed.

With this conception of himself, the artist—occasionally apologizing for the metaphysical cast that it takes—will undertake to resolve an apparent paradox: he does not feel particularly rebellious, his behavior is for the most part socially acceptable, he rarely acts like a maverick, lately people seem to think better of his occupation, surely he is not at war with them—and yet he regards himself as a revolutionary man. Thus:

> *I think that in the context of American society today he is really a revolutionary man—but really! The art public certainly doesn't realize it, and very few artists themselves have any idea, but I suspect that there are implications in the things we do that, if fully accepted by society, would revolutionize it. There is a great revolutionary power in what we do, but I don't think it's seen. I feel this instinctively. I can't put my finger on it.*

Another artist offers an illustrative story. Years ago he was seated in his studio with two friends, one of whom has since become an eminent art critic, the other an eminent painter:

> *We were sitting where we are sitting now, and I had that little brown painting on the wall. We were speculating and bouncing the ball around, and finally H. said, "What the hell does this mean to the world?" He said, "You painters have no feeling for the world and society" . . . and you know how H. gets, like he knows how society works. So I said, "Well, H., if you understand my painting, you'd realize that it could destroy all state capitalism." B. was there, too.*

> *Both of them were stunned. I don't know whether B. or H.*
> *said, "Do you really think you can do it with that little paint-*
> *ing?" I was perfectly serious.*

So much for the here and now from this painter for whom art
is the freest, most powerful force on earth. More important for him
and his peers is that art always makes the *Zeitgeist*, puts its durable
stamp on everything, and by effecting real revolutions—not like those
of the politicians—anticipates the future.

> *Historically, we always talk about periods in terms of Classi-*
> *cal, Romantic, Baroque, and so on. There are a couple of*
> *exceptions like Victorian or Napoleonic. But still, even*
> *though those are non-artistic terms, when you think of the*
> *Victorian Age, who the hell remembers Victoria? I don't*
> *even know what the issues were in Victorian times, except*
> *maybe India and Disraeli. But the artistic things that are*
> *left and the artifacts determine the historic spirit, the time*
> *itself.*

Our age is no different from any other; its special tone, color, and
flavor, its distinctive appearance come from art:

> *I mean, the girls walk around with mascara and they look*
> *like Picasso figures—right out of a picture. Their eyes have*
> *changed. Suddenly they look like harlequins. I'm giving you*
> *a lousy example. Maybe Dubuffet would be better: he's in-*
> *fluenced the beatniks, you know, the way they look.*

Yet from this relatively superficial plane on which life imitates art,
we move to the enormous power which is believed to inhere in a
single private vision of the world.

On the one hand, artists disclaim any militancy whatsoever. They
point historically to a whole spectrum of social types from, for instance, the roughneck Gauguin, who was a fighter and a big drinker,
to the outwardly serene Cézanne, who more than anyone else in his
age made a successful revolution. Compliance or non-compliance
with the normative demands of society is historically and individually
variable and not really relevant. It is the inner fire that counts, and
it is to this that they persistently allude in characterizing their breed.

So, curiously, one need not defy the mores and folkways or overtly threaten existing institutions to be an anarchist, an insurgent, a rebel, indeed, a revolutionary man. From his elegant home in the Upper West Side of New York City, a good (and prosperous) artist urbanely asserts that the artist is by nature an anarchist, chronically in opposition to the status quo. He explains, "The fundamental thing we are expressing is a certain kind of freedom—which implies revolt against any authority from above." Such revolt, he adds, would have to be articulated politically in a fully totalitarian country like Soviet Russia, but while still subversive here, it takes on a different and more muted character in America. Whether politicized or not, the subversion remains. It can scarcely be otherwise because:

> *The artist represents his time, but he also* makes *his time. In other words, the artist who is an innovator—and I think that all great art in modern times has been involved in the* avant-garde—*forces people to* see *in a new way. In that sense the artist can't help changing things and making his time.*

This prepotent feeling is repeatedly verbalized. "Some shout about it, and others are very discreet about it," as one artist remarks, but he wants us to know that his "stuff is pretty subversive," for he guesses that: "To make something new is a way of saying I want to change or add to the concept of life." Or the ultimate objective of art is delineated as unsettling people, "not letting them rest too much." The artist, "a queer duck" even when decked out like the average man, puts his active critical faculty to work, consciously or unconsciously undermining all those certitudes most men take for granted.

REJECTION OF THE MIDDLE CLASS LIFE

His marginal position is likely to help any fine artist endowed with exceptional intelligence to describe the pathos of American life, not only in abstract pictures but in moving prose. A vanguard painter not native to the United States broods over his adopted land with much insight and with a verbal facility graphic artists are not supposed to have:

Most of what happens here belongs to a life of missed opportunities, hopelessness, false and artificial pleasures and ignominies which can only be covered up or hidden by money. Despite the extravagance of personalities and situations that present themselves to us, to point them out is to be automatically despised. . . . I see a drama more profound than that of America itself. The excesses of wealth, and then on the other hand, the absence of memory which gives to Americans a liberty without usefulness, a goodness without destination—which in turn delivers them to all sorts of violence and all sorts of calamities.

This is direct social criticism, free of the Marxist jargon in which some "realistic" artists of the pro-Communist left still indulge. It is delivered in fairly fresh and poetic, if also lugubrious, tones; they are those of an experienced, melancholy, involved but disinterested observer. The artist's voice is seldom shrill, and we are taken by surprise when one does reach the higher decibels with strong and strident emotion. It is triggered by our customary question about middle class values: Is the artist at war with them? On this one occasion, respondent bellows his affirmation: *Yes,* and follows that with a still more emphatic *Yes, sir.* Then he begins to sputter: "I say that with great immediacy. I say that with the most instinctual feeling about it. This is no little game, I am anti-middle class, *per se."* And what does that mean? "It means middle class security. It means middle class judgment. It means middle class reflected glory . . ." The explosion ends, but it reverberates. And no one else erupts. The rest are cooler or cagier.

The attack is most often oblique or impersonal or darkly implicit. Sometimes it is simply displaced onto others, and only somewhat breathlessly and partially accepted as one's own. A painter, describing the generation (to which he belongs) of American artists who grew up in the twenties and thirties, avows that if you scratch any member of that generation you will find an anti-bourgeois, tending toward anarchism. These men were more or less formed, he explains, by the liberal socialist kind of literary thinking which prevailed at that time. But he himself was in France during most of the period:

I never really experienced the whole Left view—when all

America moved to Moscow, as Lionel Abel recently put it. Probably I am therefore an exception. I would suppose that the anarchist substratum is stronger in those of my colleagues who didn't go abroad at that time. They would no doubt express themselves more strongly. . . . So I would limit your question and say, yes, I get along fine with the middle class. But at bottom, if you pin me down in a corner, I'll say that I really think they aren't leading the full life, that they don't begin to know how. Does that answer your question?

Indeed it does—and almost as much for what it omits as for what it includes. The artist does not stalk his adversary with murderous intent, and in point of fact may not even define him as the adversary. A business hustler is usually envisaged as the pathetic victim of his false consciousness—or he is not taken into account at all.

Fortuitous events have yoked the artist to the businessman and threatened one with conversion into the other, Yet they remain worlds apart. Their physical proximity is inverse to the social distance that separates them. And this applies not only to such a painter as the veritable Gulley Jimson who, at the time of our interviews, worked sixteen hours a day, and who, following a fifty-year retro-spective show of his at the Whitney Museum, was being widely and belatedly hailed as a forerunner of the New York School. He placidly asserted that art is guided by an anarchic spirit, that the art of our time, if understood, would contain a revolutionary message, and that for the artist to accept bourgeois society would be to invite destruction. It applies quite as much to the artist who, seeing that he "has a bull by the tail," insists that his primary duty is to twist the tail, and that this is what every artist worth his mettle has had to do since 1780. Is it any less applicable to the artist who, though "he *could* spit on the goals of society," finds rather that they "just don't concern me except in a large, most abstract way?" The range of affect from heated denunciation to unconcern turns out on inspec-tion to be rather narrow, a difference merely in degree and not in kind. It may be comparable to the limited range of difference in temperament between one creative individual and another.

Over and over, there is that "other world" peopled only by artists, their imagination, its "absolute hold and complete dominance." Says a woman artist:

> *Very often, after I have painted and I walk through the apartment, I see that nothing in it has value or meaning or identity. It's all lost. I think this is a special kind of projection: you concentrate for a number of hours on one object, and everything else—even when you look at it—falls by the wayside.*

For the painter, she continues, his work *is* reality, and it draws upon the imagination or unconscious "which will always be infinite." To come out of that reality into the mundane world of things without value or identity where, moreover, she must act as wife to a professional man and mother to their children, can only result in some bewilderment: "Being in both worlds, swinging back and forth between one and another, you never know where you really are." Yet the balance is maintained. We see every evidence of productivity in her work, and genuine if less intense satisfaction outside it. The descent from creative reverie to things and people is rarely disabling, and no artist can live exclusively on one of these two levels.

Among our artists, there is only one, a sculptor, who swings back and forth so far that he may be said to lead a double life. For over thirty years, twice a week this man has practiced dentistry, and not satisfied with that, "I had to be a scientist as well as a practitioner. I've done a great deal of research in dentistry, published twenty to twenty-five papers. That took a lot of conscientious objective thinking—which is a little different from the conscientious subjective thinking you do as an artist." Successful as a professional and applied scientist, a role he plays out of expediency but with some relish, his primary allegiance is still to the plastic arts. The combination of dentistry and art is not unknown: two or three other prominent examples come to mind, but all of them are men in or beyond middle age, who if they were starting out as young artists in the 1960's would probably not opt for the double life:

> *The advantages were those that accrued from having an income which was not as difficult to get in those days for a*

dentist as for an artist. Also the simple respect and adulation which the middle class pays to the scientist in this country was a great help in keeping me on an even keel. As artists we are a deprived group; even now, with all the money that some artists are making, we don't belong to our society. As a dentist I could be lifted out of the feeling of not belonging, into a situation in which I was functioning as a regular member of society. In other words, I think the artist is an outcast—and it's hard to live as an outcast. Artists who manage to teach in professional schools also do better. They receive the homage of their students and the respect which teachers get in our society—to some extent. However, the break between responsibilities to other people and doing art, where your responsibilities are only to yourself, makes quite a break in living. It's difficult, but I've gotten used to it.

Two lives, each compartmentalized, with layers of conflict in both, and despite that this man has preserved his equipoise and effectively synthesized the creative elements of his personality. The adaptation he has made is far from perfect and not without psychic wear and tear.

Another artist, in remarking that it takes courage to resist the opinions of others and that such courage is essential, lowers his guard a bit and admits that there are times when his vital forces are a little low and he needs "confirmation." Other people, by responding favorably, can confirm or not confirm him, and at certain periods —when troubled by illness or any reduction in energy—their not confirming may hurt the artist severely. Only when feeling well, or feeling well with himself, is he invulnerable. Otherwise he is open to self-doubt, for after all, "the artist's work is very largely experimental. He's not performing a single skill. He's not just doing one thing well. He's not making boxes of a certain kind. He's working with a highly fluid affair, often in darkness and doubt . . ."

Yet how rarely, with all the crises and uncertainties and agonies he undergoes, does the artist turn for "confirmation" to the great public whose approval is no more to be coveted than its disapproval. "I had this show at the Collins, and there was no response whatsoever, and it just didn't matter a damn." How so? "Well, artists lead a very sheltered life, because they shelter each other." And, "We really never need anyone else."

More so than America's dispersed poets, composers, and novelists —with whom they like to mingle as kindred spirits—graphic artists tend toward social solidarity. True, the segmented, casual, economic encounter cannot be avoided: it is the fate of every city man who diffuses his associations as they multiply. If these associations make most of us who live in the metropolis oblivious to people we never meet beyond the point of formal contact, so that deep interaction occurs only within a narrow circle, or not at all, the same may certainly be said for artists. Extraordinarily responsive to urban tempos, sounds, shapes, and smells—and stimulated by them—they are less likely than their neighbors to extend the glad hand of artificial affability. Their associational reach is both wider (often cosmopolitan in scope) and narrower (excluding those in the immediate environment). They are déclassé: "I never thought of myself as belonging to any class, lower, upper, or middle"; impatient and impolite in the presence of too much small talk: "It's the triviality—I can't stand the triviality"; comfortable with men of letters: "I associate with artists and with poets, chiefly poets, and writers because they're articulate"; and though no more subject than anyone else to the world's cruelties, more heavily burdened with them because: "The artist *knows* what he's feeling, and he must know to make art. He's trained to it. And his awareness intensifies the problem."

THE ARTIST AS PROPHET

Occupying his no man's land, which is also Everyman's land, further from reality and closer to it than non-artists, at home everywhere and nowhere, the artist goes about his strange business. What is he, after all? An anarchist? To be sure. But he does not throw incendiary bombs. Just aesthetic bombs. And he is not less of an anarchist if he has a home and a car and a family: "He may have a house that cost $80,000 and three cars. He's still an anarchist. The mechanics of life don't matter. Throwing those bombs does. It's his essential justification for being an artist. Otherwise he couldn't

175

paint. He would have nothing to say." The artist is a prophet, a rebel, a subversive. These are labels he is unwilling to relinquish though he knows "they are just clichés, generalities—that happen to hold true." And once again, that condition has nothing to do with the artist's personal appearance, the "front" that he presents, his outer and inessential self: "I mean I could still wear a top hat and spats and go to church on Sunday and be a sculptor."

To *be* a sculptor or a painter, howsoever attired, is to be subversive. Is this true for the reason suggested by W. H. Auden?

> *In our age, the mere making of a work of art is itself a political act. So long as artists exist, making what they please and think they ought to make, even if it is not terribly good, even if it appeals to only a handful of people, they remind the Management of something managers need to be reminded of, namely, that the managed are people with faces.*[4]

Artists would broadly agree with this declaration and vindicate it by pointing to their work. That work, as they interpret it, has two vital sources: identification with the universal human condition and identification with the great social revolutions of our time, the permanent predicament and its modern ramifications. In addition, on the formal side, there is art history with its own organic evolution. These are the components out of which the artist makes his prophecies, and it is as prophecies that he sees most of his output. "The great artist has a premonitory capacity. . . . That's what I would call it. He can associate and anticipate, and kind of jump beyond the present." In the most succinct terms:

> *Obviously we come out of our time, and we very closely relate to our time. But, what we are saying in its implications is no mirror reflection of our time. Quite the contrary. I think it's after a whole realm of new values. I think it's really revolutionary.*

Lesser artists are content just to reflect the spirit of their own time and place. But it is, from this point of view, a superficial reading of the best modern art to see in it, let us say, the disintegration of contemporary values, without seeing their prospective reintegration.

Granted the prophetic quality of his best work and "the premonitory faculty" on which it is based, a gift such that he can not only envision the future but help to bring it about, there is every internal reason for the artist and his art to be rejected. For a long time they were. Now, if they are being accepted, lauded, embraced, and rewarded, the reasons must be largely external to themselves. Our best artists, far from catering to public opinion, defied it completely, went all out into total abstraction, courted contempt—and won Success. They fear the price may be too high—if that price is institutionalization:

> *There was the artist, off by himself. Then you got all the institutions, the museums, the schools, the newspapers, all the organs of communication, and all the foundations, all very, very eager. Oh, there's a lot of money around, and there are dealers, and as soon as anybody has anything, everybody's involved in a search, and as soon as somebody finds the smallest nugget, or what looks like a nugget, he brings it to market. There it's eagerly exploited, not to ruin it— but everyone wants to give it a fair shake; everyone wants to know what's going on; everyone wants to help.* It's like the artist goes out into the wilderness and, suddenly, there's a concrete road under him. *There are an awful lot of roadbuilders.*

It is worthwhile to hear this artist out at greater length:

> *Look at the classic case of the Abstract Expressionists who in 1945 were unknown, or let's say, most of them were unknown. I don't think you could speak of them as a group at that time. But then, on the part of some artists and some critics, some institutions and benefactors and so on, there was a certain coalescence. And then came fame and then purchase and then influence, I mean influence on younger artists. Within ten or a dozen years,* these people who had been prophets became high priests. *The office of High Priest carries with it certain very alarming and disarming characteristics. You know, like Israel became a state, something impure. There are knotty issues. You make all kinds*

of compromises. Everybody is on your neck watching every move you make. Every move you make has significance of a sort it would not have if you weren't in the public eye. In any case, so many people are involved now in exploiting it—not necessarily profiting from it, but canonizing it, buying it, and distributing it—which is pretty stupid because it can't even be exploited fully either by the original artists or by the younger generation. Everybody now has to go on to something new.

Further, and even more significantly:

I believe the artists instinctively recognize what's up, and they say, "Well, we want to go underground. We don't want anybody to be near us." But there are six dozen people to pick them up. Every museum has adept assistant curators who try to come up with something new. They go underground to find the artists who go underground.

Everything about this account has the ring of authenticity. It is highly compressed and in need of qualification, but fundamentally we are on the right track in recognizing that men and women who were "strugglers" did rapidly find themselves "in the saddle" and were actually "pushed into the saddle" by newcomers—all in the course of ten years or so. Not a few of them have vainly attempted to gallop away or burrow underground or return to the uncharted wilderness. The escape hatch proves harder than ever to find. Privacy is shattered and cunning must be used to restore it. Public institutions, once so laggard, now pursue the artists like some secular Hound of Heaven down every labyrinthine way.

6

The Artist and His Publics: The Ambiguity of Success

In America everyone buys art. . . . Bankers always did it but now farmers, taxi-drivers, and plumbers also do it. Rich men, poor men, women, students, the young and the old—they all do it. And their choice is diverse as their own characters. Expensive, cheap, advanced, conservative, obvious, hermetic, all find their admirers . . . let us call them the buyers. . . . They are huge in number and represent vast amounts of money coming from all income levels, from the very rich to the lower income brackets. Their taste, if it can be so called, is indiscriminate, shapeless, and spreads over the whole broad field. Their intensity is momentary and evanescent. Consequently they are easily led and easily influenced by fashion, publicity, and ballyhoo. They do not seem to want knowledge or to miss the lack of it. . . .

—FROM "A Nation of Art-Collectors" IN
The American Imagination, 1960

THE AMERICAN economy has been expanding at a sustained and dramatic rate for twenty years, and while not all segments of the population share the general affluence, quite a few artists do. Prosperity, accompanied by a "culture" boom, has provided painters and sculptors with a measure of material success and public attention never previously contemplated. The poverty that artists experienced until very recently is no longer the norm. Where in the past purchasing necessary art materials might present a serious economic problem, many artists now support themselves solely through the sale of their works. Others maintain themselves comfortably by supplementing their sales with income from teaching. Most artists do, of course, continue to have financial concerns, but they are now of a different order.

There is scant need for us to document the recently acquired interest in culture and art. For a traditionally sports-oriented nation, "culture" is now ascendant: ". . . there are more piano players than licensed fishermen, and as many painters as hunters. There are twice as many people listening to concerts and recitals as at Major League ball games. Boaters, skiers, golfers, and skin divers are fewer than theatergoers." [1] The private sector of our economy has provided $160,000,000 for the Lincoln Center complex in New York City. The Metropolitan Museum of Art, even without the artificial stimulation of Rembrandt's "Aristotle Contemplating the Bust of Homer" (which boosted attendance 30 percent in 1961) and the "Mona Lisa" (responsible for an extra million admissions in 1963), draws over three million visitors each year. [2] A commemorative postage stamp honoring the fine arts was issued in 1964, and commemoratives are generally "reserved for people and events that have the deepest and most lasting significance to the nation as a whole." [3] Howard Taubman is probably accurate when he writes that:

> *The arts are riding the wave of the future. Wherever you turn, centers are rising to serve and glorify them. States and municipalities are spending money on them. Indeed,*

*they have become so respectable that even the Congress has
dared to embrace them.*[4]

As late as 1948, José Ortega y Gasset declared that the primary
characteristic of twentieth-century art was its unpopularity: "Moreover it is antipopular. Any of its works automatically produces a
curious effect on the general public. It divides the public into two
groups: one very small, formed by those who are favorably inclined towards it; another very large—the hostile majority." [5]
That this is no longer the case in America is very clear; today it is
the "accepting" majority; the rejecting minority is vocal but small.
The base of support for modern painting has expanded enormously.
A $25,000,000 drive by the Museum of Modern Art was over-
subscribed in short order. Art auctions now replace church bazaars;
organizations accept paintings for sale on a commission basis as a
routine method of fund raising. Many cities use community chest
"united fund" approaches to support the arts successfully. "The
arts market now runs about $2,500,000,000 a year . . . it will go
up to $7,000,000,000 by 1970." [6]

Painters agree that their share of this booty is sizable:

> *As a matter of fact, I was talking to some artists who have
> income tax problems, and this, the income tax situation,
> has produced quite a droll situation in which it behooves
> artists to be generous. Many artists I know who are very
> well off just give it to all kinds of benefits. They give a
> painting and when it sells for $2,500 or $3,000—that's
> what they give to the cause. Composers are still very broke.
> They all have to do something on the side. A group of
> artists I know thought of getting together and setting up
> a foundation to give money to composers—which I think is
> terrific. They're not so generous to artists.*

> *Some artists make money. More artists make more money
> than they ever made before.*

> *. . . even second- and third-line artists, not the first group,
> are making it now without too much trouble, living on their
> painting. I see it all the time.*

> *Let me tell you that I know poets and artists—musicians above all, who have a lousy life. Painters are better off than a poet. A poet still gets his three bucks for a poem. Composers? Well, that's a misery. I can say without hesitation that there are many more painters who live off their work than there are composers or poets.*
>
> *Painting is in a rather favorable position because the painters are not so badly off as the poets and the musicians. I think that the poets and the musicians are completely demoralized. They have absolutely no opportunity and they cannot make a dime and it's a completely hopeless situation. I think that the fortunate thing about the painter is that he can't make enough money to be corrupted, nor so little that he can be demoralized.*

As Virgil Thomson puts it:

> *. . . all artists, certainly all artists today, aspire to the conditions of the painter, envying him his regular life, his cheerfulness, his fecundity, his vigorous energies, his complete lack of emotional complexity, and (among the higher-flight ones) certainly, yes, very certainly, his income.*[7]

CONFRONTING SUCCESS

Painters react to their success with ambivalence, as they do to everything and everybody associated with it; their gain in status and growing financial security often increases their discomfort and even produces bewilderment. There are no feelings of triumph or vindication; it is much the opposite:

> *Artists have a negative reaction to this success. I don't think it has made them happy. They haven't gotten happy under the circumstances. They haven't expanded and gloated or basked in the glory of their success.*

Many respondents actually decry the shift that is taking place in their lives:

> *The artist needs an artistic integrity—he needs an artistic consciousness and an artistic conscience—he needs an artistic guilt and an aesthetic guilt. The artist who compromises pays for it himself. Guys who monkey around in artistically disreputable ways, like with things that have got to do with business and careerism—they're going to have trouble.*

> *One of the most interesting things you could study is what success has done to the artist in America. This success story is really quite lamentable. In my mind, the commitments made by most of the artists in my generation precluded the fact that there was any success. We became artists like entering the priesthood. There was no money gained or fame even possible. We never conceived of the fact that some day—we wanted to be artists, and certainly, inevitably, as human beings, we wanted to be famous in some way— we wanted to make it—but we never considered any possibility of making it in a monetary or prestige manner.*

Artists obviously perceive the many faces of success, and here, too, in characteristic manner, they confront their own complex and ambivalent reactions. Positive aspects are easiest to delineate:

> *My concept of an artist never included making money or achieving success. But I find it invigorating; I can get all the canvas, all the paints, everything that I need for my work, and I don't have to think what it will cost. I can have a very nice studio in which to work. In other words, the frustrations of not having adequate materials or a proper place to work have been relieved.*

Yet they cannot leave it at that; there is too great a sensitivity to those potentially corrupting elements which turn success into something destructive. It is this awareness which makes success a source of conscious conflict for them, and they articulate the problem in a variety of ways:

> *I think the motivation for the artist, by and large, is that he wants to produce what he thinks is good work, and I think he's dedicated to, and preoccupied with, this sort of*

184

notion of success. But let me say that an artist is human and has all the foibles and tendencies of anybody in any other field. You know, we want to make money and we want to have success.

A senior painter enlarges on this:

But an artist can get corrupted by success. Not just premature success—just success. That is the most dangerous situation for the artist to be in. He dare not change. You know the reason as well as I. That success, that kind of success is very destructive because it captures the artist in a very limited stream. Should he go over the line to where his image-makers—what a horrible term—say, "Well, I don't know what he's doing now. I can't buy it"? That won't trap the real artist. Somehow he can remain the person without tricks. But these men are few and far between, and let's give credit and proper respect to the human being. He's spoilable; it's just that the artist will be spoiled less. It isn't necessary to blaspheme the artist by saying that poverty is good for his soul. Therein lies our ambivalence. Success is hard to resist when prices are blown up beyond any point of rationality.

The perils of recognition and reward are constantly reiterated; they shed some light on the seemingly bizarre behavior of some artists, although few find it necsssary to go as far as Carl-Henning Pederson, who is widely considered to be the best painter in Denmark and who, to avoid the dangers of success:

. . . has about 1,000 canvases stashed away in the storerooms of a Copenhagen brewery, and he turns as frosty as a glass of Carlsberg when anyone suggests that he might sell one. He recently refused a substantial check for 15 paintings because he said it would raise his standard of living, so he simply gave the paintings away. He is indifferent to what the critics say, and dealers who try to see him at his lonely house on the west coast of Jutland seldom get inside his door. . . . For privacy's sake, he has no phone or radio.[8]

But some highly placed American painters approach this level of secretiveness, and all artists easily empathize with Pederson. While rarely resorting to such extreme solutions, they are deeply concerned with the same problems:

> *I assume that in the past when a man reached a position in the medium of painting, it didn't take fifteen minutes to get it. So when he got it, it didn't take fifteen minutes to destroy it. Today, speaking of my paintings, I get many thousands of dollars for them; they're all over the country— in museums and collections, and in lots of collections in Europe. Yet I still wake every day and say, "I've got to make a great painting, I still haven't made it yet," and things like that. This "success" doesn't really convince me. I don't want to seem modest, and I probably exaggerate, but that's how it is. I've been given recognition, or at least people pay a certain amount of money for my work. Then one wonders if that will continue and you become like a petty businessman. Is the business going to keep up? I mean, it's ludicrous. One loses sight of what the heck this is all about. We forget that it's—"I don't like that yellow so much and I think I will put a little more orange in it. You know, I don't like this over here; I will put it over there." We forget that.*

> *I'm sure nothing is an unmixed blessing, and I've seen enough examples of those successes whose lives turn out horrible. But it's nice to be able to try it. You know, if you don't have it, it's easy to understand why you want it.*

> *Publicity can be a big boost for the artist, but he's supposed to be bright enough to know what it means if he's in art. It means practically nothing except that he can pay his rent. And paying his rent means that he can continue to be an artist and devote more time to it. So that's what it amounts to, period. However, if he is interested in being a celebrity and wanting other things, then it can mean other things to him. It can't do it to you. You have to cooperate a little with all this business.*

> *There are many difficulties that arise when you are success-*

ful that you never anticipated when you were not successful, such as, "Am I to continually paint a certain kind of painting because it's successful?" Or if you stop that, are you doing it just to be perverse—because you wanted to assert your independence? So you have to be able, in that situation of success, to be very much aware of what your motivations are and whether you're doing a thing in order to maintain your success or not; are you still being as free as you were before you were successful? And I think we all want to be as free.

I think if you really know yourself, you don't pretend you're not a celebrity. You also don't let it change your own life to that extent. It does change it somewhat, but it doesn't have to run it. I've seen many go from anonymity to fame, and I would say none of them have changed especially. In other words, those who were anonymous and power-happy are now power-happy and not anonymous. But I think if you have a sense of yourself, I mean, if you're thoughtful, you're going to stay thoughtful; if you're charitable, you're going to stay charitable; if you love your mate, you're still going to love your mate. The people who are really changed by success didn't have, or rather lacked, a great deal to begin with, so that if he becomes a star and it throws everything into a new perspective, there was something all wrong anyway.

These statements stress the importance of self-awareness—an unclouded view of one's inner motivations—and the need for constant vigilance in counteracting the deleterious influences of success. There is no particular feeling that artists should avoid or reject deserved accolades in order to achieve safety. Rather, the prevailing attitude is that if they are to be truly successful as artists and as human beings, they must be strong enough to walk the tightrope and resist compromising themselves for the proffered temptations. They do convey the sense that it is a tightrope—that prosperity, despite its practical advantages, necessarily becomes a source of intrapsychic tension.

Inner conflict is old hat to the American artist; it merely has a new basis today. In the past his struggles centered about the "simple" matter of continuing as an artist. Lack of recognition and tardiness of acceptance caused him severe hardships; to persist as an artist required the firmest resolve, an unbending drive. And all the while he had to resist the temptation of following paths which might lead to greater material reward. Continuing as a painter, in that sense, is no longer the question; it now becomes: "What kind of an artist am I going to be? Will I be able to stick with what's important or will I go down the drain with so many others? Can I be strong or will I give in to the almighty dollar?" A new conflict has replaced an old one, and it strikes him as potentially a more serious threat.

A minority of artists even question whether artistic values still survive in the face of this onslaught of popular interest. They see the battle as already lost. New "Art" is viewed as a clear indication that aesthetic purpose has been defeated; that artists have surrendered their integrity for acclaim; that artists work on terms dictated to them; and that they ignore their aesthetic consciences. Concern for achievement is said to be gone; pleasing is now the theme:

> *There's a lot of camping around with pop art, junk art, and happenings—I guess it's very entertaining, but it doesn't entertain me because art shouldn't be entertaining or entertainment. I want to keep it free—not a means of making a living.*

> *There's a danger to success. Maybe you want to change, but you don't dare, and maybe the next thing you would have done would be alive or something. The big change has been this—people have left the traditional method of painting. In order to avoid the problem of time in art, the idea of doing it in some terrific way, they went and started monkeying around with pieces of junk and assemblages. They went in for collages. Very gimmicky now, very gimmicky. Everyone wants to make it now. It's like a contest for attention now in the art world. It's not even competitive. You stay awake nights and you come up with an idea; you produce this thing and it goes off—an accident, a crazy thing. People hang it in their apartments and like it. I don't know. It has nothing whatsoever to do with art.*

> *Painting is one of the big mysteries. It's a thing that every-body has to do by themselves. This so-called success is the very thing that eventually kills off those few that are so successful. That's because they cater to people's needs. They say artists are leaders, but I don't believe it. I think there are certain people who have some kind of need for something and certain artists are only too glad to fill it in for him. That's why everyone runs around saying that this is terrific stuff and then two years later some new guy comes along with a new product and everybody seems to enjoy his work better than that other guy's. Somehow he's conveniently for-gotten about by that time.*

Misgivings are sometimes anecdotally documented:

> *I know of a situation where there were some fresh million-aires, and artists used to waltz them around and sell them a couple of pictures and then pass them on to the next one. It was a real kind of contempt; seemed like the idea was that these guys were suckers. But I guess since all those paintings went up in price about ten times there can't be too much trouble in that situation anymore. The maneuvers are still going on.*

Such artists' observations coincide with certain persistent attacks made by modern critics:

> *A generation of hard work by colleges and other institutions in devising effective "art appreciation" courses and the skill-ful adoption of high pressure publicity techniques by muse-ums has certainly enlarged the knowledgeable audience for painting. But it has also encouraged the production of spuri-ous work by lifting art in this country from the status of something half suspect to the status of something accepted blindly as worthwhile.*[9]

> *But painting, in a time of easy money, follows the taste of those spending that money. And the taste of today's ruling group in the West favors a minimum of imagery.*[10]

While there are differences in emphasis, then, there is general agreement that success, especially when it comes too soon, should be viewed at least with skepticism and caution, often with fear:

> *If the young man has the ability to stick to it and a great deal of courage, he'll still find that the path is not clear; he'll still not know whether to jump this way or that way to find himself. When does he find himself? Young men are told by stupid teachers that they have talent because they have little idiosyncracies. But that isn't the thing. Lots of people can have talent and they fall by the wayside. What you do with the talent is the thing. That's a long time ripening. If it has a short and quick ripening, it can pass out like that, too. Aging has its difficulty, but people also become riper and more innocent—destroying the baggage they have acquired, that they always thought necessary to accomplish things. Success, especially early success, destroys, sir, it destroys.*

A similar point is made elsewhere:

> *A too sudden or too early fame may easily overwhelm the painter and neutralize his talent ("Thank God," says John Sloan, "I never had success before fifty"). And the fame obtained through high pressure publicity is the most sudden and, to the painter, the most dangerous of all. . . . It is likely to leave you dead on the floor one morning with your head snatched round. This, in our time, has happened to many promising painters.*[11]

Since prosperity in art is a phenomenon of the last decade, some of our respondents feel it is the younger groups which have been affected most profoundly.* The older generation sees the younger as "pandering to outside powers, viewing art as a money-making proposition, and subverting their artistic souls":

> *I think that there is a tendency now beginning among young painters—I may be doing them an injustice but I think I*

* Which is why we have chosen to deal with the question of inter-generational conflict in extenso. See Chapter Two.

*perceive that there is such a tendency—to go into art as if
it were a legitimate profession in which you kind of expect
to have success and to make money and to have three children and a house in the country and a nice car like everybody else—like anybody in the middle class who has a middle
class standard of living. It was never my conception of an
artist. It still isn't.*

CONFRONTING THE "PUBLIC"

Thus the material rewards of success eliminate certain practical
hardships but become added burdens in themselves because of the
ambivalence they arouse in the artist. "The Public," which is responsible for this success or lack of it, in turn becomes the object
of similarly mixed feelings. As we have repeatedly noted, real
artists are unanimous in declaring that they paint out of inner
necessity and not in response to external influences; but they are
also agreed that their painting, while not "therapy or a hobby or
a commodity," is at the same time intended for a wider purpose
than simple self-expression. They differ a bit in their definition of
this purpose: whether, for example, it is to reflect the times (which
few believe), to anticipate the future, or to disturb people's complacency, but there is a confluence of opinion that "paintings are
painted to be seen." Therefore, an audience or a "public" is a
necessity:

*If it's not being lived with, what's the point? In short, I
guess artists want very much to be involved in other people.
Painting is a calling, but I think there's a question of comradeship. You have found something, discovered something,
and you want to say, "Hey—look at this" to people. They
will share it with you. It's not simply someone superior who's
conveying words.*

*Naturally I like my paintings to be bought where as many
people as possible can see them. I think I even resent it a
little bit when I have a painting that I like and somebody
buys it and I have to think, "Oh my God—is that painting*

going to be closed up in that place?" I think that the painter likes to feel that a painting, once it leaves his place, will get a chance to be seen.

I think that there is at least one truth about artistic life and that is that you do it in order for it to be seen. I mean, what is it all about if it isn't that? If it got stuck in vaults then I would be very disturbed, and so out of a bad reason, something marvelous might come. I could be bugged by the idea that there are ten paintings now that no one will ever see. I might think to myself, "I've got to work twice as hard now."

It does matter to me; otherwise I would be inhuman. I have my ego, my life, and so does everyone else. But it doesn't matter to me in an extreme way inasmuch as I do these things because I have to do them. I am always surprised if somebody buys my pictures, even today. It's not pleasant what happens to some of them. Because I don't believe that pictures and music and poems—poems have to be read, books have to be read, pictures have to be seen—they're not things for storage. I guess I like to hang in good company and be looked at.

We should say, somewhat parenthetically, that this so-called "public," or audience, while often referred to collectively, is not viewed as an undifferentiated whole. What Virgil Thomson describes for music obtains equally for art:

It is a false image of the truth, nevertheless, to group all the people who like listening to music into a composite character, a hydra-headed monster known as The Public. The Public doesn't exist save as a statistical concept.[12]

But while *The Public* may not exist, *publics* do, and our artists view each with strangely differing feelings:

I think that there is nothing to do but recognize that there are very many publics. There is just no such thing as The Public. *I think there never was, and I think that now, since there has been an enormous increase in population and an enormous increase in education, it is impossible to speak of a public. There is no such thing as there being a closed and absolute audience.*

FRIENDS

It seems to us that painters and sculptors deal with four more or less distinct publics that may be arbitrarily designated as: Friends, Buyers and Collectors, Viewers, and Critics. Multiple group membership accounts for some overlap among these four, but the artist still has a range of specific feelings about each category. Of these, Friends constitute the only segment more or less free of conflict. Artists wistfully but unequivocally agree that this would be their ideal audience—a body which with few exceptions would include mainly other artists. Such a group would be small, compact, responsive, and empathic with the artist's outlook and strivings. It would receive his work critically, but its responses would stem from a common orientation which excludes those personalized and extraneous considerations that color the comments and judgments of so many others. Artists are dismayed when "The Public" at large willingly seizes upon everything and anything as "art"; they are equally disturbed when serious work is rejected out of hand and without a hearing. The ideal audience of fellow-artist–friends would eliminate this situation. It would criticize with sympathy and understanding and provide stimulation for further growth, without encroaching upon the relationship of the artist to his work. However, no artist deludes himself with the possibility that such a group will become his effective audience. There are too many practical considerations involved:

> *I know damn well I have no control over who buys and so I just take it in silence. I'm aware at all times that while I get in touch with my public through my paintings, they've got nothing to do with me and I've got nothing to do with them. In order to make a living from your work, you can't sell your paintings to your friends or people who really seem to go for your work, because they know your work and you; people who are in sympathy with your way of life*

and who thus want to have your paintings. Like it is some-thing that they can stand on—this is their symbol of the world. How many people do you have like that—that are intensely involved in a painting? And yet the artist would like this thing to be viewed as such.

Well of course it matters who gets my paintings. It matters very much. If I lowered my—if I was completely, if I was desirous of selling my paintings regardless and no matter, I could sell them all. But it matters very much to me who buys them. Very much, oh, very much. I think that it's of great significance when the buyer can have some pleasure, because that gives me pleasure. I would put it this way: since you are always putting this in a personal way, I don't think you can see my work without being disturbed by it in one way or another, and yet if you don't see it, it's another matter.

Of course it matters who buys it. I like people I like to buy my paintings.

You are gratified if in rare instances there is someone who really loves the work and wants it for himself. But this, of course, will always be extremely rare. How many real friends does any artist have?

BUYERS AND COLLECTORS

To get their work before a sizable audience, artists feel they are forced into alien procedures; they must also accept the fact that much of their work will be acquired by aesthetically unappreciative buyers. They are elated when things go otherwise, but there is rarely any expectation that they will. Few can hold out for the "perfect buyer." The size of the purchasing audience often makes it difficult for the painter to know who his "customer" is, let alone appraise what motivates him to buy. The pervasive feeling is that the patron of yesteryear and the collector of yesterday have been replaced by a new and difficult-to-define breed of art consumers—a group whose motivations are at best suspect. Painters seem to accommodate themselves to these realities without excessive rancor. Understandably, they deplore the fact that the buying group, which can in practical terms make them or break them as artists, is often guided by extraneous considerations. Yet only occasionally is a voice raised in unrestrained condemnation:

> *Well, personally, I think all those collectors are practically morons anyway. They have very low taste. People tell most of them what to do. Once in a while you get a collector who is foolish enough to buy something out of his own motivations, but they usually give that up after a while. They always fall back on "expert" guidance and advice from other people. It helps them to ride on in comfort and not worry whether or not the guy is an artist. Maybe they like the decorative qualities of the painting. I don't know.*

This man is expressing his personal frustrations, but they do not stem from material failure; like so many of his colleagues, he also has been a beneficiary of today's art boom.

Other respondents are more temperate in their reactions, although they leave little doubt as to their mixed feelings. Artists are not inclined to dramatize this dilemma, which turns on having the fate of their work, whose purpose is partly communicative in nature, determined by factors unrelated to its intended meaning or any other genuinely aesthetic consideration.

John Canaday, often an outspoken foe of modern art, describes the situation facing today's painter:

> *People now hang paintings on their walls with the idea that somehow something called culture will be exuded for absorption much in the way that they install an efficient humidifier in order to impregnate the air with beneficial moisture for breathing.*
>
> *This concept of art by which the purchase of a picture becomes instant education is not entirely new. Pictures on the walls and books on the shelves, whether or not the pictures were seen or the books ever opened, supplied "a cultured*

atmosphere" for our grandmothers' houses. The trouble today is that mass communication, mass color reproductions, mass museum programs, and mass cultural attacks in general when they propagandize for art will be most successful when the product being sold is flashiest. It is much easier to make a bad painting sound good than it is to explain why a good painting is good. When this misfortune is compounded by the misconception, peculiar to our century, that only the novel and "original" painting is worthwhile, we finally reach the idea of the standard novelty—the mass product that people think of as something not mass-produced but special, the pseudo-esoteric item for general prestige consumption.[13]

With all of this, the contemporary artist successfully resists withdrawal into self-pity. He responds to, and focuses on, those few channels of genuine communication which remain open. Despite his contempt for most buyers and his frustration with prevailing conditions, he makes generally reasonable—and reasoned—observations. Each painter accommodates himself in his own non-ulcer-producing way. He accepts the situation, knowing that to attempt to combat it head-on would be futile as well as debilitating. In making his modicum of peace with things as they are, the artist resolves much of his conflict; he relegates selling and exhibiting to a secondary position among his functions as an artist, and then passes them on to others. These maneuvers help him maintain objectivity in viewing himself:

It's mixed. I like selling a picture and it does make a difference. It would matter if somebody put them in a vault to wait for them to get more valuable. But really, the sale shouldn't matter. It's the painting of it and the idea you have at the time which is more valuable than the painting. After all, the painting is never exactly what it was meant to be anyway. It always turns out different in the execution. It's never what you've been really thinking.

It doesn't put you under special pressure when you have a limited audience. You don't paint before your audience and you don't paint for your public or your friends. You

> *paint for yourself and this is the most important factor. The rest completes it. What happens to the painting after it leaves you? Anything can happen to it.*

Existing conditions force the contemporary artist to cultivate this attitude of apparent detachment from the subsequent fate of his work. Being essentially without a choice in these matters, he cannot allow himself to "care" too much. Yet artists are too close to their feelings to maintain such distance consistently, without at least an occasional break. They may assert that it all matters very little, but the feeling often comes through that given a situation where meaningful choices could be found, they would indeed care a great deal:

> *It's immaterial to me who buys it. Naturally, if I had the choice I would have preferences, but it's not a serious matter because in most cases I don't know who buys them. It's just some anonymous person. I find out the name from my dealer, but this doesn't mean anything to me, that is, unless it's some person who is publicly known—maybe a big collector or some such person. I then have an idea of who the person is, but that's all. I usually don't know.*

> *I think the old patron was lost around the eighteenth century, and after that you had no more patrons—just irresponsible purchasers of paintings. That is, if someone buys a painting, he is not a patron—he's just a customer. I've sold hundreds of paintings and I don't know where they are or who has them. They've disappeared. There are so many customers that you can't keep track or control of them.*

> *Sure I have some interest in who buys it and where it ends up, but for purely pedestrian reasons. Once the thing is made up and I've settled in my mind what I think about it or what it's worth as a thing, then it's not too important. It goes out of the studio and I'm fairly indifferent. Of course I'm still interested though.*

> *The important thing is that if a man buys your painting, it means he's putting up $500 or $1,000 or whatever it is; he's putting this up and this is a token of his faith. If he*

doesn't understand the painting and he puts up so much money, well, that's his tough luck—it's just too bad for him. I think there's a very real sort of relationship—even though I don't know the guy. He's anonymous but he's real. I can't see the situation as intolerable. I always thought it was awful and terrible, but I always thought it was tolerable.

I'm obviously on the side of the person who has some feeling for my work. I think for a composer's music to be locked up in a safe wouldn't be helping much, that is, if you believe a composer is good for mankind. The same holds for the artist. When your paintings get into the wrong hands, then it's curtains down. But you can't let it get you.

Others are even less successful in detaching themselves from this aspect of their situation. They reveal more clearly the human suffering involved and how deeply they experience the consequences of the mass "acceptance" which is their lot:

I would like to feel that the people who are buying it would have concern for it or really feel for it, but I won't refuse to sell to people I don't particularly respect. There is conflict, however. You're really giving part of yourself away, and after they're gone you sort of have a lost feeling. But I guess I'd rather sell than keep it.

I want to sell and I do, but it does matter who buys. If I feel that a man buys because he loves the work, it means something to me. On the other hand, if somebody goes out and pays his money and buys the work, that's it. I've been accused of trying to control the situation for my work, but I've never really tried to control it. What I've always wanted was some pleasure in the act of the sale, some human satisfaction—not just material satisfaction.

Look. We don't paint masterpieces every day. It may take twenty pictures to arrive at one good picture. The other twenty pictures may be good, but they aren't it. We know the difference. I may have worked ten years to evolve the one picture that is "it." I feel a protective influence that I must exert on that picture. And I don't feel I'm robbing anyone by selling him the second best. I think it's good, but in a different sense than the particular one which contributes to helping your image survive. We have children. These are children, if you want, and there are certain children I want to protect. It seems to be a perfectly normal thing and I want the buyer to like the picture first of all.

Some painters heal this breach by selectively withholding certain deeply prized works from public sale. Others make gifts of their important works. Most refuse to make block sales. Beyond this, however, it is difficult to manage or dictate sales, or to control the fate of a painting after the commercial transaction has been completed:

Now that I'm older I am concerned about where my paintings go. Certain pictures I prefer certain strata of collectors to have. I'm involved just enough with posterity that I want to know where my better pictures are going. Just for the sake of selling, I wouldn't really sell. I've refused to sell pictures, for example, in blocks, because I knew that they would go into a warehouse. I don't care particularly if a buyer gets my message. If he doesn't get it now, he'll get it ten years from now, that is, if he has contact with it. My concern is the very cold fact that if he doesn't get the message, will he give the picture to a museum or will he stick it in a warehouse? That's the practical concern.

I'm pleased if somebody I think has a real eye and a good collection buys a picture of mine for the right reasons, but generally I don't care. There are certain pictures that I won't give up because they are key pictures. There aren't too many of those, however. It would disturb me quite a bit if all my pictures went into a vault for investment. But regardless, most of them are likely to be seen some of the time at least.

Sure it matters. For example, at a recent exhibition someone told me, "Hey, I just sold three paintings." And I thought "Fine." It was fine for him. A few days later I heard that one collector had bought them—a man who was evidently going everywhere and buying up things sight unseen—and was putting them in storage vaults. He was buying them practically unseen, although he did it on the word of his scouts. These things aren't bought blindfolded; somebody looks at them and he makes the judgment. The point is that my reaction to that kind of buying is very negative, and I think that others probably think the way I do. I just wouldn't sell that way. If the Museum of Modern Art had bought them then it would have been different.

Given these negative reactions, it is surprising when even an isolated respondent values the collector, and what prompts his positive remarks is not readily apparent, since he is situated so similarly to all others. Such views are far out of step with those of close colleagues:

I'm amazed at the number of buyers who seem to be so deeply involved in the feelings of what I'm doing. To become so involved and so responsive—it's somewhat new for me and so different from the forties.

I think that to some people maybe it is chic, but I think that with the people who are really involved—young collectors, for example—this is a passion. It's changed their lives. I've seen the people who have bought paintings and it's a different kind of collector. It used to be that Rockefeller or Barr at the Museum said, "We ought to have one of those guys in there," and so they'd buy something. In recent years a generation of self-made men, who have made a little money, have responded to works, have bought the works, and it's changed their lives. It's a different attitude toward the work than that of the original inherited-money collector who was involved in a do-good relationship and bought the painting to uplift. Today's collector is engaged in self-uplift; he can't live without it.

The only other positive note is struck by artists intimately associated with a specific collector. Their sweeping denunciations of collectors as a breed have already been recorded, but we must remind the reader that they are willing to impute creditable motives to individuals:

> *I sold a lot of paintings to A.R.; I sold about seventy paint-*
> *ings to him. But first of all, he knew me for years before*
> *he bought most of them. He bought a few things at first,*
> *and he hung them around his house. Some he donated to*
> *museums and other places. Some he saved and put away*
> *some place. He buys a lot of other people's work, too. But*
> *with him, it isn't a blanket kind of approval. He thinks about*
> *those things before he does it.*

> *I remember when D.F.K. bought a picture of X's for $8,000.*
> *Well, that really changed the whole scene. X was alive*
> *and painting and people were collecting him, but the paint-*
> *ing could've been gotten for less. He really wanted to pay*
> *$8,000 for the painting to make the mark and he did it.*
> *I don't mean he wanted to pay $8,000 to make himself look*
> *grand. He wanted to give that picture that much importance.*

Even the following broad group assessment (by a non-Jewish artist) must stand as highly personalized unless it can be supported by data not available to us:

> *The rich Anglo-Saxons aren't interested in buying paintings*
> *—at least not very much. They have to have a foundation.*
> *With the Jews it's a personal thing. That's been my experi-*
> *ence—they take more of a personal interest in things—*
> *which is very good for everybody's morale. There's this guy*
> *who collects paintings and so does his wife. Suddenly the*
> *son comes down and is buying paintings. He's a friend of the*
> *artist and he thinks they're pretty terrific. It's a traditional*
> *thing with them. The more Anglo-Saxon types like B.Z.—*
> *well, it's pretty abstract for them. They do it like a good deed.*
> *You have to have a foundation, you have to have a big*
> *museum, and it all has to mean something for society. It*
> *isn't just like they liked the paintings. It's like they're obli-*
> *gated somehow to buy those paintings—like because they're*
> *the leaders of the country. My paintings sell mostly to people*
> *of Jewish stock. I know that's a fact.*

Most typically then, the collector's relationship to art is regarded as shallow, as being no more than another example of conspicuous consumption or of crass financial speculation. He is considered an accumulator who lacks artistically acceptable motives:

> *Some guy came in the other day. First he went around and looked at the other artists and followed them around. He demolished them one after the other. And then he came back and looked at my things. Since I was there personally he was a little more restrained. He was a buyer who handles large lots of paintings. He said that he couldn't like my things because I would have to have at least thirty similar things—they'd have to be done; he also told me I shouldn't be so insecure. Then later I realized the only reason the fellow came in was because he had money.*

> *I think it's really everybody wanting in on culture. You see, there's more leisure time, there's more money, and there's more ennui; it seems as if suddenly you want to buy a picture rather than a Cadillac. Museums are filled with their daughters who are given some kind of a life by doing Junior Council stuff.*

> *I think that the consumption of art in America—and I use the word consumption advisedly—is not much different from the consumption of automobiles, refrigerators, jet planes to Europe, and so on. We are living in an affluent society—a society in which culture with a capital C, and in quotes, has become a symbol for those who can afford it. I think that the reasons most people buy art, are willing to pay high prices for it, is that they can afford to part with the money without straining. And the fact is that when the stock market dropped some time ago, sales dropped off. Most people only buy art as a luxury, not as a necessity.*

> *Institutions buy art for what is known as prestige advertising—public relations. They have so much money it is difficult for them to put it into so-called direct advertising. They have to put it into something which then gives their product an aura of public works. I think this is the main motivating*

factor. Of course, there are other contributing factors: their wives come from Wellesley or Radcliffe, or they themselves have gone to Harvard or Yale. They've taken some superficial cultural survey courses which give them the feeling that if they buy art they are also developing their cultural sensibilities. But they won't do without a mink coat or a car or all the things they consider necessities. They won't buy a second-hand car in order to buy art. You can't call this stuff cultural activity.

VIEWERS

Painter attitudes toward the third group, that is, the mass Viewing Audience, compared to those experienced vis-à-vis the collector, extend over a much wider spectrum. This becomes especially obvious when we study positive reactions. Some of our artists feel that while the viewing public has no real devotion to art, the level of its taste and appreciation is slowly rising. The gallery- and museum-going boom, in conjunction with university and adult education, is regarded —but with many reservations—by a number of our respondents to be of at least some didactic value:

Well, I think that there's a fantastic interest. I mean if you just step up some Saturday to some of those galleries, there are some numbers of people that pour out of those galleries. It's phenomenal. There must be some kind of awareness of painting and all that. Yet I don't think that it's all so good. The people are interested in art and the artist is obliging them by coming down to meet them. There's nothing wrong with it. Sooner or later somebody's going to benefit from all of this. If you go around to the shows, if you like painting and all that—pretty soon you discover you don't like this one anymore, you liked that one in the past—you like this guy better—this person is not so good anymore, and pretty soon your level becomes . . . once you get the idea, you begin to have a higher and higher level of appreciation. You grow up to these things.

I guess I have contempt for the general public, but as I

get older, I have less and less contempt, or rather, I will shut up more now instead of wasting my energy trying to convert what can't be changed. Taste may be better, but the general public does not have a heightened feeling. They are just better educated and so they know better what to look for. I mean, you probably get more about modern art at Radcliffe than you did fifty years ago, but I doubt if the passions of these girls or women are any deeper or heightened. The people have better taste, but no greater appreciation.

I think that there are a greater number of people that are showing an interest in art, but not for the right reasons. There is just too much art. There's too much of everything. They cannot choose safely, as they are too insecure to feel safe in their choices. So they lean on the choices of the museums, or on the taste of a prominent critic, or the taste of a prominent collector, for instance, and this is a denial of vision and their own sensibility.

I have no real feelings about the public. I think it's wonderful that the attendance in museums and galleries is as high as it is. I think that it's wonderful that the public is as free to express itself about a painting as it is. Now I say this because there was a time when this was not so. It wasn't within one's particular range to assume that he knew about these things. He had a completely different attitude. You can walk up to a stranger today on 42nd Street and ask a stranger what he thinks of modern painting, and boy, he will tell you, and he's never even thought of it.

I think what I have noticed is an awareness in the public taste at any rate. I mean they mostly don't like what is going on, but they know what is going on. This is also different than it was, whether I like it or not.

I think that the creative impulse is never going to be close. to public understanding or insight at the given moment. I think there's a great gap there between what needs to be mined and what can be understood after. And there's always going to be a great gap between the conscience of the artist and his public appearance, his ideas, performance, and the attitude he wants to present. The public isn't going to understand that so quickly. On the other hand, the public isn't so dumb or isn't as dumb as all that. They catch on pretty quick and they know what's good pretty much right away. But there is this gap between visual understanding and verbal understanding, and this is a major problem for the visual artist.

Notwithstanding this mild optimism, negative reactions still far outnumber the positive, and our respondents make any number of blunt damning statements as they discuss the Viewer:

Among ourselves we might say—no, I withdraw that. I would say that I publicly avow that the public is stupid. I make no bones about it.

The modern art audience is really a spineless and recumbent mass of people.

Most people don't understand what they're looking at, they don't understand what they are talking about, and they don't understand what they think they're interested in.

There's a falseness in this picturization of artists. First they're considered disingenuous and finally they are seen as very sophisticated. By that time you have a flock of people who also wish to enjoy this sophistication. But it's hard. It is still the stupid audience.

When I hear certain people talk about this abstract this or that, it's like they are talking about mink coats or something. There may be some acceptance deep down, but I still think they feel the same way now as they used to—they still think, "My three-year-old could do it."

When a man looks at a painting and says, "My child can do it," he is saying that the child is inferior to him; there's no question but that he can do it. That's the appreciation, if you like; he enjoys the idea that he can do it, too.

And even for those people who can't afford to buy it, the

simple interest in having names of artists and styles on one's finger tips can become a social asset. I don't think it has anything to do with basic culture.

To be quite sincere, I am slightly contemptuous of the public. I think in a way an artist should produce for a smaller unit of people he respects. But to be accepted by large audiences is fame and so that is something everybody wants, too.

I don't think it is valuable for people to think they are appreciating art when they are bored and think they are doing something good for their souls. I think they are sort of brainwashed into thinking they should like it and so they like it. I think that I prefer people to really enjoy themselves. I don't know. Maybe they do enjoy themselves. I don't know. I don't want to sound too snobbish about it, but I don't know what they really get out of it.

I think people are accepting a great deal more now because they're under enormous propaganda pressure and they are brainwashed.

If you follow history, you will find that the situation was always the same, except that this kind of audience is more blatant. It's more naked in its attitudes. I don't think that basically things were that much different when the church and the nobility were the patrons. It's just that the diffuse public is primarily middle class, and to me, there's nothing more horrible than the middle class. That's the only change, really. The middle class is now in charge. That gives a pretty clear picture of my attitude, doesn't it?

Yet for all the severity of their comments, artists still convey an air of detached amusement or bemusement as they discuss the vices of the non-buyer. At odd moments an individual might decry the absence of a truly appreciative viewing audience:

Artists need more than just an audience; otherwise we'd be pleased with the hordes of viewers and buyers that confront us today. I think that the painter does suffer more than

people in other fields. He has a much less literate audience.
He doesn't have a painter's audience.

But most of this man's colleagues are more dispassionate. They do
not take the viewing audience too seriously and consequently are
less disappointed by it. They observe the teeming crowds at galleries
and museums with a mixture of contempt and tolerance; they express disapproval and cling quixotically to a bit of hope for the
future. Even the most disdainful artist does not treat the viewer
with the total severity with which he unsparingly treats the collector.

This is because most artists feel relatively remote and distant
from anonymous viewers. They may group the viewer with the collector while assessing the motivations behind their art "interest":

They are docile conformists who can't resist the blandish-
ments and pressures of today's push toward attaining social
standing by demonstrating an active interest in things cultural.

Beyond that, however, they make fewer demands on the viewer.
They feel that meaningful art appreciation cannot be achieved by
a mass audience, so there is no reason to expect a properly responsive
reaction from it. More importantly, however, artists see the actions
of this mass audience as having little direct effect on their lives or
the fate of their work.

This is the nub of the artist's quarrel with the collector. He
may treat viewers with any number of feelings as he observes them
"playing at being interested in art." But theirs is felt to be a world
of fantasy, and when necessary their pretensions to knowledgeability
can be exposed. For buyers the case is different. They make decisions
about artists by dealing with their work in a direct, controlling, and
judgmental manner. They operate under the guise of connoisseur-
ship; it implies a higher claim to appreciation and understanding.
This causes the artist to demand a higher level of involvement with
art from the collector, who, however, is seen as a man entangled
with matters extraneous to the work. Therefore, while both the collector and the viewer are harshly criticized, the viewer's incapacity
is judged as considerably less reprehensible than the collector's. The
collector's actions impinge directly on the artist, confronting him

with frustration, disappointment, or despair. An artist's contact with buyers may be minimal, but the latter's actions have tangible consequences for him and his work, especially where strong buyer demand develops for particular styles which the artist may be outgrowing, or where particular styles find little acceptance:

If you don't develop as a human being, you cannot improve your art. If your art stays the same, I don't believe you are a real artist. It must move. It must go. It must change. If it doesn't change, you are dead. If the market demands that you stay the same, or if you produce ten paintings for a certain client who wants the same thing, you are already denying your organic life as an artist, and this is the primary thing, to keep that organic life going.

Once a signature is recognized as the *signature, they want more of the same. Experiments are not allowed at that time. A collector would be shocked if suddenly he couldn't recognize the handwriting anymore. He's invested thousands and thousands in that signature. But I've refused to sell at those times, and I needed the money, too—very badly. But I've refused to sell under those conditions because I think it is bad, and I think it works out badly for the artist in the long run.*

CRITICS

The artist's relationship to his fourth public, the Critics, is even more complex and overshadows all others, both in its intensity and probable importance. Artists are involved in a serious tug-of-war with critics—a hip and thigh struggle which reflects the desire of each to be the ultimate arbiter of "good art." The artist may be tempted to shrug them off: "The art world doesn't extend beyond other artists. There is no real place in it for the critic." "I do not think that the average artist—the kind I respect—respects the average critic. So therefore what the average critic has to say isn't going to affect the work of the artist." Quiet reflection quickly modifies such reactions. The final, sober consensus is that critics are a weighty factor in the art world, that their responses are more influential in determining art futures than those of all other groups combined. This is an agreed-upon fact of artistic life, no matter how the individual artist delineates it. Whatever aspect of the art world comes up for consideration, the influence of the critic can be felt.

Artists note that a power hierarchy exists among critics, but there is no general agreement as to the relative position each holds. The art writers and reviewers of *Art News, Life,* the *New Yorker,* the *New York Times,* and *Time* are among those to whom positions of prime importance are most frequently assigned. Additionally, there are certain affiliated and unaffiliated individuals, such as Alfred Barr, John Canaday, Clement Greenberg, Thomas Hess, Harold Rosenberg, and Meyer Schapiro. Each publication and each critic is viewed in a highly personalized manner, with no perfectly consistent pattern emerging (although the *New York Times* draws more than its share of brickbats). As a group, however, critics are resented because of their excessive "taste-making" powers. This is not simply a matter of economics, although artists generally recognize that the critic can and does influence art sales:

> *Each critic has got a lot of collectors in his grasp, and if he sounds the word, if he says somebody is good, really good—well, he certainly wouldn't have to worry financially for the next year.*

> *Now he rhapsodizes over them. He hangs them in his dining room. Ten years ago he wouldn't even look at them. But that taste isn't his. There are exceptions, but if in all New York you can show me a half-dozen collectors who are really involved with painting and not following the choices of a few critics, well . . . they're cowed and intimidated and this isn't so hot.*

> *I've been told the* New Yorker *reviews have a very important influence on actual sales. As a matter of fact, one very important dealer has told me that the* New Yorker *is the most important force in influencing sales. The* New York Times *may be the most important in influencing opinion. But prob-*

> *ably Alfred Barr is about* it. *If* he *buys, if* he *is enthusiastic about any young artist, then immediately other museums begin to follow, and you get on the museum circuit.*

> *I personally think the patronage in this country is pretty bad. I think they make all the wrong choices. They are over-anxious to be led by their noses. They are not able to make up their own minds. They have taste-makers and opinion-makers. Like I read in the* Times *that Canaday said some good things about a gallery, and then the next Sunday he said that Monday the artist had gone to the gallery to pick up his mail and the gallery was closed, but people were already waiting outside, already wanting to go in and see the show. The show was sold out. Canaday had already prepared these people, in a sense.*

Even more disturbing to the artist is the critic's ability to structure his public image: "Certain critics, whether right or wrong in their judgment, are able to capture the hearts of people by fixing certain images into neat phrases. They transform the public mind and give it the channel in which to think." Artists see this "brainwashing" power as overwhelming, and even those who view critics with moderation are troubled by it:

> *I have no specific argument against the critics. It's just that they keep you boxed in, in relation to the wide world, under the guise of presenting you properly. They present you, and the world believes. The thing about the Pollock story is that he had no proper public image. They called him all kinds of names—the dripper and this and that. What does that mean? The average guy still figures this guy is a painter, but what the hell is he after that?*

Painters and sculptors see "reaching the public domain, not the domain of *Time* magazine," as their main task, and the critic is experienced as a potent obstacle to that end—a personal obstacle whose objectivity is often doubted: "Everyone has judgments about the reviewers in the *New York Times* or *Art News*. A lot of that stuff is whether people like *you* or if somebody wants to take up *with you*." As the sheer bulk of art work increases, reaching an audience becomes more difficult, and resentment of the critic who "legislates and decides what is worthy of the public" correspondingly increases. Artists feel that he has grown from being a critic to being an "all-powerful judge who rates people howsoever he chooses. They know their opinions are highly regarded; they then decide whether so and so is an artist. I don't think that that's what a critic should be."

There are occasional attempts to discount the critic by suggesting that his views are really not his own:

> *I think that what has happened is that I and some of my colleagues have imposed our ideas of what art is on some of these authorities. We rammed it down their throats and thereby won an important victory over the authorities. We wanted to be accepted by them, but on our own terms. Now I think they understand a lot better. In fact, I think the whole problem is to keep ahead of them. They catch on very quickly.*

One artist even suggests that the art world is now so large that critical authority carries little weight: "If there's some kind of ability, it will be recognized by at least one segment of the art world in America. The art world in America is very large and diverse and nobody is so powerful that he can make or break somebody that has ability." Others counter that: "While I don't think they can break anybody, I think that neglect can cause you to wither, and I've known some very worthy artists that just didn't make it early enough." Some despair:

> *Americans live under a dictatorship—brutal and bloodthirsty. Those people who buy, even more those who influence the buyers, are being brutal. They're not intellectuals and they're not sensitive, and they call the shots.*

> *I think a very few people who have authority and power commit themselves, identify with something for either the right or the wrong reasons, and then they give the armies the nod to follow.*

> *Critics have a lot of power because they are published, and one doesn't like to read an unfavorable opinion in a widely*

> *circulated journal. But if one were really rational about it,
> it would be as if your cleaning woman had said it. It shouldn't
> mean too much, because a lot of them are very dumb about it.*

This last, almost contemptuous rejection of the critic is different
in quality from the rejection of the other segments of the "public."
The sense of disappointment and underlying ambivalence is far
clearer here; for the reality is—the artist needs the critic in a more
profound sense than he needs the friend, the collector, or the viewing
public, at least at certain stages of his evolution. As one of our
better-known painters points out, the artist is "self-appointed." He
has a belief in his work and considers himself an artist—which is
sufficient to keep him working. But now and then he needs some
confirmation of himself, at least in the process of developing. He
may gain it from his peers and teachers at the outset, but eventually
he needs a response from the knowledgeable world; it is the art critic
who, despite all reservations and disappointments, represents this
knowledgeable "world-at-large":

> *I would put it this way—I'm putting myself back to that
> earliest period—if you had asked us what we would like,
> I think we would have said we would like to be accepted
> in the art world and be recognized as artists by people in
> positions of authority, for example, a critic or a museum
> director. There were questions as to whether we were artists
> or not, since an artist is self-appointed. You then have to be
> recognized as being an artist.*

> *I can only speak for myself. I want to be accepted by people
> who feel as I do and whose opinion I respect. They have
> to be willing to accept me as an artist, to recognize me as
> an artist. Probably a critic or a museum director. Some such
> authority. A person in the position of authority.*

In view of this felt need, the artist finds it depressing that "art
criticism has become so remote and regimented. Critics are beginning
to depend on their sub-critics . . . you know, they have talent scouts
who do the initial sorting . . . and you have a whole pecking
order of questionables developing this way. Human equations are
forgotten."

The persistent need for a positive personal response is demonstrated by a very successful painter when he recalls that: "Two months ago I made a good painting. The day I finished that painting I called up W.Y. and I said, 'Hey, I've just painted a painting.' I called up on another pretext. I really wanted to announce that I had painted a *good* painting." As an artist, he needs no reassurance; as a human being, beset by typical doubts and insecurities, he looks to a respected authority for some kind of confirmation.

No wonder then that the artist is ambivalent about the critic who publicly does so much to define him and his work; since this definition is subjective, some uncertainty must always exist for the painter. He then must struggle to keep the person and the artist in himself separate. He acknowledges that critical comment can influence him as a person; he dare not let it affect him as an artist: "In fact, this is the acid test for the painter. Can he be left unshaken by even the most knowledgeable criticism, regardless of its source? The critic may be able to tell us what we've done, but he can never tell us what to do. That would be our finish." "The proof of your ability is to survive and withstand any kind of shattering criticism and continue working. You can be vulnerable as a person, but not in your work."

The artist thus recognizes his dependence on the art critic, even if for most it is only on this human level. Dependency fosters ambivalence, and where the stakes are so high the pitch can sometimes be extreme. To know that your position may depend on someone's subjective and possibly fickle judgment is not easy to stomach, but this is the way it is:

> *An artist's reputation is objectively established when the people who are in the art world, whose opinions are highly regarded, decide that so and so is an artist. Then they rate him in whatever way they choose. This is then the opinion which will be held by the whole culture.*

The critic clearly represents the most important of all artist-public relationships, both from a practical point of view and in terms of meaning for the artist. On a very concrete level, critics are in a position of decisive influence in fixing the artist's position, particularly in relation to other publics—the collectors and the viewers. He serves as the interpreter and the judge of the artist and his works. Equally important to the painter, however, is that to him the critic is, like the dealer, a needed representative of the world-at-large. This role holds especially for the period when an artist still requires support and his peers no longer supply enough of it. The critic is then the most powerful segment of the artist's general public, significantly shaping the external realities of his life—against which his inner self can never be too fully protected.

7

Museums and Dealers

The past two or three years have witnessed a proliferation of galleries selling paintings "by the yard" and suggesting to the would-be buyer that he should purchase paintings as an investment. The surest way to make millions!

Well, this is a crude approach. It may serve the interests of some galleries, but does it serve the purpose of art? Does it satisfy the artist, even though he may be starving? Are these galleries selling paintings or paints? All this follows the bankers' childish line: "With a dollar open a special account. Feel and act like an executive."

Those methods are like neon lights to attract naive buyers from all over the country, to attract poor butterflies.

Now, does this help the public? Does it *serve the interests of art?* Does it promote good and earnest painting?

There is a fallacy in confusing art with investment. If the reason for owning a work of art is only money, why not treasury bonds? It may be safer. A painter who "sells" at, say, $12,000 one day may well, through changing fashion, sell at much less a few years later. Examples abound of sudden excitement over young painters who are heralded with the drums of publicity but who produce too much too fast and eventually lose "public appeal." Anything of this kind is an affront to art as well as to the taste of the public which may be unaware of certain factors but which has enough sense to distinguish between the genuine and the fake.

—SAINT-EVREMOND in *Art Voices,* 1962

CREATIVITY is a fuzzy concept encircling a mysterious matter —"the *x* factor" in art—about which scientist, artist, and layman alike are necessarily vague. Although one may assign an arbitrary meaning to other words that constantly recur in discourse with or among artists (such as vision, inspiration, afflatus, sensitivity, and sensibility), we are in similar straits with them.

Partly because of this terminological burden, for which no lighter substitute has yet been devised, not even the logical positivists have been able to scientize aesthetics. The vocabulary of art, when translated into non-art, produces nothing referential; it violates all the laws of general semantics. Hence, art criticism is notoriously impressionistic, and the "scientific" study of artists continues to be inconclusive. The great fog that hovers above "creativity," "art," and "artist" contributes directly to a commonplace Romantic conception which etherealizes all of them.

Yet it should be clear that there is nothing ethereal about the artist who, like his work, merely looks otherworldly by reason of his temporary dislocation from other segments of society. The highly organized artist could be called disorganized only so long as he was (and in some measure, still is) differently organized. Before the anomalies of his social situation came into being, when he belonged to his guild as other craftsmen belonged to theirs, the ethereal illusion —with its overtones of sublimity and diabolism—did not prevail.

A sober look at the fine artist, as "his world" moves toward the so-called "real world," completely dispels that illusion. There are now many new points at which these two spheres intersect, and a few where they nearly concenter; people immersed in one are still not wholly comfortable in the other, but lately they find that it takes less effort to glide back and forth between studio and marketplace, or Tenth Street and Madison Avenue. No self-respecting artist openly endorses commercialism, although of those we interviewed several were willing to accuse others of succumbing to its blandishments.

Sometimes the roles are reversed: a dealer upholds artistic purity and denounces painters for worshipping Mammon. Recently John

Crosby, the syndicated columnist, quoted Raymond Cordier, director of a Paris gallery, as follows:

> *Bad business is good for painters because it brings them back to true values. Twenty or thirty years ago a painter was living among the poor people and he was anti-bourgeois and he didn't want to be integrated with the bourgeois because it made him anti-artistic. Twenty-five years ago a painter was anti-conformist . . . Now the artist paints only to make money. He wants to buy a new car, to marry the banker's daughter, to get his picture in the papers. His aim is to be integrated with the bourgeois, to go everywhere and do everything because he has money.*

And another dealer, more temperate than his colleague, is also pleased with a bad season he has just had. George Bernier of l'Oeil Gallery tells Crosby :"I'm sure it's a healthy adjustment, provided it doesn't go on too long and provided it doesn't hurt the painters too much. I don't think the wives of artists ought to be wearing Dior dresses. On the other hand, I don't think artists ought to be penniless again the way they were." [1]

The art market, with its dealers, collectors, auction houses, direct sellers, and showplaces, is no less fickle than ever; probably at this moment the purchase of a picture is as chancy as an investment in the stock market. In the early fifties Germain Seligman, a noted connoisseur, observed:

> *Within the first half of the century, public interest in art in the United States has passed through three great cycles and is today in the midst of a fourth—or has the threshold already been passed into a fifth? Around the turn of the century the Barbizon School was predominant, then the Old Masters enjoyed a revival, only to be succeeded by the Impressionists and Post-Impressionists. . . . Today the works of the twentieth-century artists with their abstract and intellectual tendencies have taken the lead. How strange it is to observe the generalization of taste, trends, and fashions across this immense country. When Troyon's cows were admired and in demand in New York, they were also at a premium in*

*Boston, St. Paul, or San Francisco. Bouguereau's sweet figures
and the martial scenes of Meissonier follow the same graph.*[2]

For the year 1949, he remarks that French primitive paintings
reached a new low, English paintings brought one-tenth of the
values of the 1920's, Dutch paintings held their own only because
of Dutch dealers and collectors, and a Courbet was practically
given away.[3]

THE GROWTH OF THE MARKET

No one has yet fathomed public taste and popular preference in
any of the arts. Who will pay how much for what—as between one
kind of art object and another—is no clearer to us than to the
economists, who are curious, and the professional intermediaries,
who would desperately like to know. The art market is volatile and
unpredictable. No doubt it always was. Dips and rises are to be
expected even though the current "cultural explosion" places a
premium on modern art. If plotted over a period of decades, our
own and those to come, the graph with zig-zag lines may conceal
a steadily upward trend. Art museums have more than doubled since
the Second World War, and their expenditures are up from 70
to 100 percent. Since 1952 the number of art galleries has also
doubled, and we are advised that Americans spend approximately
$200,000,000 a year on paintings, reproductions, and other art ma-
terials. A recent issue of *The Art Market Guide and Forecaster* states
that art prices have gone up an average of 975 percent for established
painters alone, with successful newcomers "showing gains whose
speed and magnitude dazzle the imagination." And, "Equally sen-
sational are the skyrocketing prices of sculpture . . ." [4]

Whether or not prices continue to soar, the art market—and the
art scene generally—can only get bigger. The very rich still collect
art with a passion; upper middle class people are hardly able to re-
frain from aping their betters; and now the lower middle class consumer has been reached. The end is not yet, but it may be in sight
as retail chains and giant mail order houses go into the art business.
A major turn toward the working class market occurred when Sears,
Roebuck & Co. commissioned Vincent Price, a Hollywood actor and

art collector, to seek art "throughout the United States and abroad" for shipment to central depots in Los Angeles and Chicago. George H. Struthers, vice-president in charge of merchandising, in announcing his firm's bold new policy, indicated that henceforth the Sears catalogue would picture oils, water colors, collages, etchings, drawings, and sculptures turned up by Mr. Price. They were to be offered in the below-$100 retail range especially for towns and cities outside major metropolitan areas. With this decision, fine art as a commodity for everyone had surely arrived. Some months later, *Time* magazine reported how Mr. Struthers' brainchild was working, in a story under the headline, "Bargain Debasement":

In an ornate Paris hotel room, a trio of men, all but lost in a crowd of artists and their works, peered at canvases spread before them and then at one another. "You like?" boomed the tall one with the familiar face. "I like. We'll buy the lot," said the one in the short sports coat. The third man, in a dark suit, scribbled checks. The process took about an hour, cost $5,000, and added another 100 paintings, sketches and etchings to the stockpile of something called the Vincent Price Collection, Inc.

The familiar face was Price, veteran of more than 50 films and a collector for 30 years. The short sports coat was Harry Sundheim, Jr., a Chicago businessman and also a collector. The dark suit was Lester Salkow, a Los Angeles theatrical agent who is Price's business manager. The three were buying original art for Sears, Roebuck, which will sell it to the public along with snow removers, Oxford cloth shirts, storm windows and mink coats. . . .

His [Price's] spree in Paris left the Right Bank gasping across the Seine at the Left. In the austere Berggruen Galeries the trio waltzed in, snapped up 50 lithographs. Steaming into another gallery, they flabbergasted the owner by buying up, at 33% off, all the works of an unkown Sunday painter. Within hours after their arrival in Paris, word of their vacuum-cleaner technique spread around the town, and the work began coming to them in their hotel. "They've started bringing their mothers', brothers', wives', and ex-wives' paint-

ings in now," said Price at one point. Their average rate of buying was 500 works a day.

No matter how discriminating a connoisseur might be, it is doubtful that he can buy so fast and still maintain the quality that Price genuinely wants. What was meant to be a basement bargain in art could easily become bargain debasement. But still, the public is buying. "In square old Pasadena," says Price, "3,000 people came to the Sears art show, and 180 paintings were sold in one night. They're not buying for investment; they're buying for pleasure." It's a pleasure for Sears too.[5]

The vulgar, wholesale, promiscuous, and catch-as-catch-can purchase of art leavings in Europe, followed by their profitable sale to men and women who have learned that it is chic to buy "originals" and nothing else, confirms a view recently expressed by Walter Goodman—and goes a bit beyond it: "As the *nouveaux riches* in New York these days far outnumber the *vieux riches* in Europe, a seller's market exists here for *objets d'art*. The problem is getting the merchandise. The man who can track down and obtain the most desired paintings is an important man." [6] Mr. Price is a very important man. He scours the world to obtain any painting, any sculpture, any artsy-craftsy thing that will go in Pasadena or Podunk —and nearly everything will go.

By any quantitative measure, important men serve the *haute bourgeoisie,* and very important men, the *petite bourgeoisie.* Under their aegis, the "art public" expands till its saturation becomes a realistic goal of sundry promoters. That this public is systematically deluded into mistaking paper flowers for real flowers does not dismay a considerable claque of intellectuals who like to sit on the sidelines and applaud America's coming of age. Ernest van den Haag, the acerbic culture critic, has said that he can understand how people might confuse paper flowers with real flowers, but he cannot understand how anyone could believe that the paper flowers will grow or that widespread appreciation of them leads to greater and greater refinement of aesthetic taste. Neither can we.

THE MARKET INFLUENCE ON ART STYLES

What about our artists? They would like to be far removed from all that "fouls their nest," and in a way they are:

> *After all, you don't paint before your audience. And you don't paint for your public or your friends. You paint for yourself. The rest is incidental. What happens to the painting after it leaves you—well, anything can happen.*

Among the pleasant things that can happen is to have many people see and admire your painting. In due course they come to identify it with your name, to recognize your style, and to anticipate more paintings of the same kind. If you allow yourself to be governed by such expectations, you are lost:

> *There are instances where men have stopped enlarging their vision and improving their consciousness because they thought they had found a successful way of making an object . . . but I mean, this is death for the artist. To die as an artist is not to develop as a human being. It's a twofold process: if you don't develop as a human being you cannot better your art. Your art stays the same, and therefore I believe you cease to be an artist. Art must move. It must go. It must change. If it doesn't you are dead. If the market demands that you stay the same, or if you produce ten pictures for a client who wants the same thing and gets it, you are already denying that you are real, you are denying your life as an artist—when the primary thing is to keep that life going.*

Organic development comes from inside, and it dies when arrested from outside. The artist who permits himself to be manipulated by dealers and customers into making more and more of a good thing is humanly and aesthetically atrophied. Artists believe that petrifaction is the price of prolonged repetition, and that their public presses hard for repetition. Viewers are less interested in an aesthetic experience than in "spotting" artists by their "handwriting," their "signature," their "trademark." A well-known painter explains that for some time he made large pastels, pictures that soon came to be associated with their creator's name. One day he brought "a bunch of gouaches" to his dealer, whose jaw fell upon seeing them, or rather upon noting simply that they were different. "People," the dealer exclaimed, "want your pastels, those nice big pictures." The people referred to are collectors who have invested many thousands of dollars in their artist's old manner and who will be appalled at the new one, not because they dislike it but because a considerable investment may be put in jeopardy. The economics of art requires continuous recognizability in the art object. A drastic shift in style means that familiar handwriting has suddenly become unfamiliar, unrecognizable, and possibly unsalable.

> *Personally, I've always had trouble. I've changed much too often, and in a big way. It's always been held against me. You know, with Picasso it's all right, but here they don't like it. I've been refused by dealers, by good dealers, on that basis. They want more of what I did before. And then, after a certain number of years, they look upon me as unstable. Word gets around.*

> *Dealers build up a market for one particular thing, within which a certain amount of change is permissible, but nothing radical. In the last few years I've had several radically different shows. That was held up to me quite recently by a very good gallery. The dealer said, "I like what you're doing now, but how do I know what you'll be doing next year?" . . . Yes, there are those who want new things, but they don't want them all that new.*

> *A trademark? That's a difficult thing. Yours can be very simple. Franz Kline, for instance, has a very simple trademark. He painted big black and white things bound to look like Kline. But many painters don't have a trademark that easy to discern. It takes time to establish, and then to register in the public mind. People don't take kindly to having it disestablished—or even much modified.*

It is perennially tempting to repeat a successful, widely admired formula. Leonardo warns against it in his *Notebooks*. One painter, taking the long view, forgives a moderate indulgence of this venial sin, holding it against no colleague of his "who doesn't do it too long." Monet is mentioned, and Corot, "who hit that popular style of his, grey trees, you know, and he sold everything he made." We are reminded that Corot's students produced imitations which the master touched up and signed. Thus the standard joke in France that Corot painted two thousand pictures, of which four thousand are in America.

> *And Matisse had a very popular period like that. So did Picasso. There were years when he did an awful lot of pot-boiling. When you really hit a popular vein, you are inclined to give a little bit there and do more of them than you should. And I would say that's probably par for the course.*

The problem—whether to repeat or strike off boldly in some new direction—is still acute, and, according to some artists, more acute than ever. Another problem, *whether always to do something new and different,* is universally understood to be characteristic of our time. The artist must steer a difficult course between these problems or find himself marooned on their shores.

THE MUSEUM AS A PURVEYOR OF "NOVELTY"

Many forces push the artist toward newness for its own sake. The ordinary man, seeking new sensations, is so easily jaded that change can never be rapid enough to satisfy him. And we live in a global society where extraordinarily rapid social change leaves a deep mark on every one of our institutions. Consider the art museum, which has for centuries been a stronghold of traditionalism, designed to conserve only the best work of the best artists, work that has proved itself by withstanding the test of time. Whoever steps into a museum today knows that it no longer plays just this conservative role. Museum directors buy new things and have even begun to sell them. That they are receptive to the new and will promote it is sufficiently startling. Yet "aggressively seeking the new" often more adequately describes the change.

> *The Museum called up my gallery one day and said, "Do you have any new Tobeys?" And M. said, "New Tobeys! No.*

> *We have Tobeys, but we don't have any new Tobeys. We have wonderful old Tobeys." It seems just curious, this emphasis on the new. Anything that Tobey did last February—uh-unh. They would have to be last September.*

The artist who makes this observation feels that for museums art has ceased to be enlightenment, that it has become entertainment measured by the size of crowds who have enjoyed a good show, whereas, "It used to help you to live, to elevate you . . ."

Quick visibility in the museum can exact a heavy toll:

> *Let's say I paint a painting tomorrow, and I show it in May, and someone from the museum sees it, and he's crazy for it, and they buy it. Then by September it's hanging in a public place, and it's integrated already in the public domain. Well, I go there in October and my work is assimilated, so to speak, by the world. What am I supposed to do? I mean, this is fantastic speed in which to spill one's innermost guts. Am I supposed to go back to those old guts? This is a personal problem every painter has today.*

Just today? Was it ever much different?

> *I think so. Everything used to be slower. Even the Impressionists, before they got to a museum, were visible in the galleries and they fought among each other. Now you can be visible on 57th Street and the world doesn't even know about it. People go to museums who never go to the galleries. It's a different kind of audience with a different kind of function. Your work becomes public in the sense that* Time *magazine reproduces it, and then thousands of people in barbershops get to see it. It's this unnatural speed, the too-rapid public and cultural involvement that makes things difficult.*

Museums are said to pick things up that have just a little newness in them, things that reveal slightly different techniques or slightly different materials. These things are not yet art. Their premature arrival amid much fanfare may cause them to die stillborn. Talent, when it needs careful, quiet nurture, is given immediate acclaim by museums which used to confer only an ultimate accolade. Artists tell of men who were known and shown too soon, who at age eighteen or twenty were already familiar to museum-goers, and who at thirty have failed to fulfill their early promise. Failure might have been their lot in any case, but quick exposure made it that much more probable. On the other hand, a very gifted artist can overcome this obstacle, taking it in stride like so many other problems—while attacking the new museum policy of indecent haste.

> *I think museums should be discouraged from buying too soon. They should wait until the work really ripens and comes, until it develops into art. . . . I said to a sculptor recently that I had been observing his work ever since he started, and that I had a feeling for six or eight years that his stuff was hardly art. It always interested me: I'd seen every one of his shows. It seemed to me that only in the past two years has it become art. "Until then," I told him, "you were just getting acquainted with your materials, your techniques and all." All those shows gave him a hard time from the beginning.*

And at each show you have to prove yourself all over again. "You have to win the game every year." Not so in Europe, for there "when a painter was a good painter, he was a good painter no matter what, and for life. Maybe he was doing bad paintings, but they weren't so ready to call him a has-been." In America, says a prominent sculptor, the artist who achieves early recognition is seldom allowed a fallow period, for it will soon be said of him that he is slipping or that he has fallen by the wayside.

Novelists are frequently "written out" at a relatively tender age in the United States. After the spectacular success of youth, some stop writing, some go on writing the same book, and many fall into mediocrity. Far from growing, their earliest work is also their best. All this is reason enough for the kind of pathos that attaches to such names as Sinclair Lewis, Thomas Wolfe, Ernest Hemingway, James T. Farrell, F. Scott Fitzgerald, and even our sovereign genius, William Faulkner—not to mention writers of a later generation who seem to be reliving the same sad experience. The best American novelists often shoot their bolt before (or soon after) age thirty.

Attended by publicity from then on, they dry up and wither away as serious artists. Whatever produces this pattern, it is not inherent in the craft of fiction. The greatest European novelists do develop —which makes late Mann as interesting as early Mann, late Joyce more exciting than early Joyce, old Gide still a real writer and not a desiccated shell or an echo chamber. We have to do, then, with a national literary tendency—and one which is so far not matched in the fine arts. Painters and sculptors feel that they must serve long apprenticeships, that they cannot quickly reach the proper pitch of maturity, that their growth should be organic and therefore necessarily slow. To date, whatever their other vicissitudes, in this matter American artists have been unimpeded. The accent on youth did not extend to them. It does now, as "museum people," in digging up the new, "look for new talent," which means young people.

> *Actually, I think the situation in America is kind of re-stricted to new talent, to the new name, the new thing. . . . If a youngster has something a little bit gimmicky, a little bit different, they have the machinery to promote him. They look for him. They even beat the bushes looking for him. It really works to the disadvantage of older, more mature guys.*

These are not sour grapes: our artist is prospering both critically and financially, but he is disturbed by the rapidity of change, from one gimmick and one novelty to another. He identifies "museum people" as a major instrument of this dizzy rate of change which strikes him as a direct threat to serious art:

> *You need a certain amount of time just to make the goddam thing. You can't just dash it off. It takes three months, six months, two years, six years. And, I mean, by the time I've made, let's say, five of these things, my God! the whole situation has changed. Something new has come along. In any earlier century I could have worked comfortably on these things for forty years, really developed all the possibilities, all the potentialities, and I would have felt leisurely about it, knowing that I had plenty of time. But now, by the time I work on something for two years, it's outmoded, and I've*

> *got to, you know, like develop something else. And I think that's unhealthy. It can't be reconciled with the fullest maturation of anything that happens within any of these styles.*

Even artists who see virtue in rapid change, greatly preferring it to stagnation, distinguish between natural and artificial (or contrived) change. One may simply express vitality, the other profanation:

> *That particular element has been put into the nature of our American art. I think the reason is that we are now producing a more living art than we've ever had before. In other words, the nature of painting today is quite different from what we used to call plastic art. It always went through cycles, but because it has another kind of living quality now, naturally the cycles are faster. In some cases these cycles are purposely put in motion to demoralize artists, to react against art, to offend it.*

Sound business principles call for constant change in our consumer economy; if goods lasted too long, people might stop their feverish buying, which would cause profits to dwindle and threaten the whole system. Art galleries are business enterprises and an integral part of that system; it would be foolish to expect them to be run on any other basis. More surprising is the frequency with which artists equate galleries and museums. They are coupled as institutions controlled by the profit motive, caught up together in its exigencies, and therefore given to tactics generically no different from those of business at large:

> *Museums and galleries play a very important role in shifting the focus from one thing to another. And all of a sudden now we have this whole shift into pop art and comic strips and the figure. And everybody says to me, well, I did a radio show Wednesday night on the subject "What's New?" Naturally they had a person there who started to recite all of these articles in magazines. "It appears as if such-and-such is new." So, when it came to me, I said, "Look, there's only one thing that's new as far as I'm concerned, and that's a good painting. That's always new." Of course, there always*

*is that which appears to be new. In most cases it's vulgarity.
And we have a great deal of it here on the art scene. And
we have to contend with it. I mean, there's no question, it
affects us.*

Art treated simply as a commodity can scarcely leave all artists
unscathed. A new gimmick is required every year in automobiles
to make the consumer pant after a model superficially different from
last year's. To keep the old model, which becomes obsolete months
after its purchase, is to date oneself:

*People want to know how the 1964 Buick differs from the
1963 Buick. And we too really are products of our society
in that sense. The artist likes to think he escapes it, but I
would like to know the difference between that attitude and
our own.*

Artist after artist testifies to his skepticism about the value of contemporary museums. Their "true" function, that of conserving good
art by separating it from inferior work, has been sacrificed to business and amusement or, more accurately, to the amusement business.
People go to museums in much the same spirit of passivity as they
attend movies, providing themselves with a kind of respite from their
grueling existence, "to be distracted from—not confronted by—the
human predicament":

*The museums have exhibitions that are constantly changing.
They're like moving pictures. In fact, they are moving pictures. Just stand in one place in a museum—in September,
October, November. You have a moving panorama of pictures presented to you.*

The audience is increasingly weary, surfeited, "overstimulated
by new shows every month in museums," its appetite for newness
enlarged as steadily as that of a dipsomaniac for alcohol: "You
have one drink, two drinks, then you need more and more. Just so,
the Museum of Modern Art has a show where Tinguely burns down
his sculpture. What do you mean, lastingness? What next? Will the
Museum have to be burned down? Will the aesthetically sated man
have to find his kicks in pyromania?"

Artists note a reciprocal relation between audiences bent on having new but superficial experience, and museums catering to their
needs. Curators and directors of museums are alleged to have "forced
the hands of those who do these things, that is, the artists," to have
invoked and accepted the necessity of ceaseless change. Why? "It's
just a question of money. It attracts the public. Like, over a million
people going to see the 'Mona Lisa' from a distance, behind glass,
for whole seconds before they move on, each of them paying one
dollar. Every museum is in business." Museum-goers in New York,
given their great exposure, may require special titillation, but: "Even
hidden places like the Cleveland Museum suddenly buy Klines and
Yunkers—just to make it, to be modern, to pull in the crowds."

THE IRRELEVANCY OF TASTE IN THE MUSEUM

One painter rails against the traditional museum whose worst prac-
tices, combined with new defects, make the whole institution objectionable to him. It now does violence to art, the artist, and the
audience:

> *Take the Hirschorn collection at the Guggenheim. You get
> one or two paintings or sculptures by fifty to a hundred artists.
> That gives you maybe a sociological or cultural picture of our
> time, not an aesthetic picture. You can walk around the
> Hirschorn collection and tell what's been done in sculpture
> all over the world. This is not an aesthetic experience. It
> doesn't encourage penetration into the work of one or two
> artists. Nobody can tell from looking at one Michelangelo
> or one painting by Leonardo what his work is like.*
>
> *Museum directors stand, not literally but figuratively, at
> their doors with a clock numbering the audience. They are
> naive enough to tell you that the last show brought in twenty
> thousand or forty thousand and created a great deal of
> interest in art. But they're just talking about some kind of
> entertainment.*
>
> *Now I think the proper function of the museum is to show
> the work of one artist at a time—in its entirety—or at least
> it should cover a major portion of his work. There is no*

*other way to discover the meanderings and the expeditions
this artist has made in order to create a style, a visual image.
Otherwise, with a skimpy sampling, all you get is a kind of
disharmony. . . . I think it was Paul Valéry who said museums
were an abomination. You know, you come in and there's
this polished floor; it's overheated and you have your coat,
and you don't know what to do with it. And you're tired.
It's too quiet or too noisy. Getting into the place is a problem. And then you enter a room and you see a landscape,
and at the edge of your eye is a nude, and a battle scene.
And so on. And Valéry says it's like listening to ten orchestras
playing at once. And it is. Every one of these works was
made by the artist over a long period of time; he meant it
to be contemplated and penetrated and examined by knowledgeable audiences. Our audiences are encouraged to look
around, read the notices under each picture in order to get as
much factual information as possible, and move on. It leads
to a sense of disquiet, of jumpiness—which is not what art
means or has meant or should mean.*

This bill of particulars is fairly long. Artists who have found a new
patron in the museum seem to be no fonder of it than of other
patrons currently available to them. The museum's motives are also
dubious: it is suspected not only of commercialism but of chauvinism.
A board of directors in Texas or Oklahoma may sponsor living
artists out of regional pride—to show New York, Illinois, and
California that there is nothing culturally backward about museums
which were once content to receive classical works from artistic
centers. They aspire to *be* artistic centers; patronage is a means to
that end. When the outlying districts are infected by culture-vultur-
ism, it may be said to have infected the whole country. And the whole
country bids competitively against other countries which suffer from
their own more ancient *amour propre*. "Like Frenchmen, Americans
feel that we must show the newest innovations of our boys, our
team. In order to . . . I don't know . . . put it on record that we
got there first, or something like that."

The artist who has fortified himself against all forms of extrane-
ousness is undismayed by, if not indifferent to, the cry that he really

isn't doing anything new, or that now at last he has achieved his own familiar style. For the true artist is always in a state of becoming. That state unfolds at a tempo peculiar to each artist who will never be gauged by an average rate. His next step cannot be artificially hurried or unnaturally delayed without hobbling him. The art manipulators depicted by many of our respondents are much like parents who attempt to interfere with the growth of their children, either speeding up their development or holding it back. Those eager to attain status through their children speed them up, just as overprotective parents slow theirs down. But artists are not children, and they are in no such relationship of total dependency upon the art world as children are upon their elders. So the best of them will go their own gait—with perhaps a sidelong glance at how things are (using only a kind of peripheral vision, saving the central vision for better things), deploring a situation admittedly harmful to many, but hopefully untouched by it:

> *Some painters discuss the fellow who does neckties, and gets all this attention for doing it. He doesn't upset me. It's true that he gets a lot of space and a lot of attention. And he pushes plenty of other, serious people out. I know it's going on. I hear it everywhere. The conversation about it is end-less, but I don't think my friends are bothered by it in their work.*

The museums are indicted for lending themselves to the use of gimmicks; they are charged with having become the merchandisers, rather than the custodians, of art. If so, theirs is a heavy responsibility. After all, museums decisively influence an artist's "success." A review in the *New Yorker,* a spread in *Time,* or a notice in the *New York Times* "will bring crowds to your gallery," but they come to see, not to buy. Let a museum pick you up, and: "You are immediately followed by a certain buying public which goes wherever the museum goes." Therefore, the really significant tastemakers are the curators. We ask, "How did this come about?" Answer:

> *I would ascribe their power to the fact that upper-middle class people, who make up most of the buying public, have forfeited their historic role as arbiters of taste. Through lazi-*

ness, apathy, and ignorance, they have given up the old role, handing it over to their own creations, to the museums. Do you follow me? They create a museum, and the museum does the dirty work for them. And then, if the museum certifies that something's all right, they go out and buy it. Those who support museums financially are also the biggest buyers of painting. If the Museum of Modern Art has a show, and you're in it, they say you're okay. The stamp is on you; otherwise, it isn't. That's why I say there's no truly enlightened public. We have an elite, but no free-wheeling public of any sufficient weight or dimension to consider our work seriously and then support it.

An artist who feels that "his imagination is constantly on the block" typically criticizes the museum as such, the museum in New York and the museum in Dallas, the Museum of Modern Art and the Metropolitan Museum. Then he tends to shift his fire onto curators, subcurators, and other officials who run the museum—or those who hire them, the irresponsible upper-middle class dabbling in art works. Finally, while conceding that their revitalization has done some good, he pictures museums as inherently defective because "their faults are the faults of our society." By fostering new art every season, museums lend their sanction to that "ugly contradiction in terms, art for the moment." Thus they share the general guilt, but disproportionately since "the mere fact that they are museums gives them status in the community, tremendous respect and power." How do they use these great assets? Not to make moral or aesthetic judgments, not to be like the academies of an earlier age which stubbornly upheld certain conservative standards. In our day young men need not rebel against the academicians by establishing galleries of their own. The museum as a sort of "historical storage house" is stuffed with every manifestation of every trend on a very busy scene in perpetual ferment—which it wishes to reflect as comprehensively as possible. The museum's attitude is basically reportorial. It may set out more or less descriptively to capture the cultural ethos, to exhibit it as a full and fluid, rapidly rotating kaleidoscope:

They just want to report the scene, but lots of people misinterpret what they are doing and say that they are promoting this and promoting that. I don't think they mean to promote. They simply want to show, well, everything. But you see, what happens is that buyers take advantage of their choices, and there you have a problem.

The contemporary museum is not an academy, but it is still widely assumed to have preserved many academic criteria. While the museum is palpably not limited to classical art, it is usually thought to be governed by some principle of excellence. The message that museum selections are so much a matter of reportage has not yet been communicated to large segments of the art world. An ironic consequence of this situation is that buyers continue to act as if the reporters were nothing but arbiters. They collect on the basis of choices that were not meant to be normative, made by men who, willy-nilly, became tastemakers. And the public, overwhelmed by an immense and increasing quantity of art, passively accepts as admirable those works bought under the influence of museums which only intended to tell people about "our times."

From this there follows a great confusion of tongues. Artists maintain that fashion can never be a valid touchstone of their work, and curators honestly reply that they agree. From their point of view, to hang a picture on museum walls is not to say that it is good, but that it is indicative that—good or bad—it exemplifies what some artists are doing this year, that their work heralds a new trend or brings an old one to completion. The spectator can keep up with developments in art by attending a museum and by reading his daily newspaper. In neither one is he likely to find an unequivocal judgment. Our artists feel about museums much as Patrick Heron feels about critics who shy away from evaluating the art they publicly report: that they show not only aesthetic but moral timidity. Heron writes that for these critics condemnation and praise are equally meaningless:

The attitude is that all works of art present us with "phenomena," and that these phenomena may be described, listed, categorized and their causation, psychological and physical, hazarded: they will, it is held, inevitably be interesting simply because they exist, just as fungi, curiously shaped pebbles, philodendrons, the Milky Way, or the bacteria

234

patterns on a pathologist's slide exist. I am opposed to this critical tendency for two reasons. It represents an attempt, in my view, to bypass the fundamental result of any response to art, which is, baldly, to pronounce a moral judgment. One is trying to decide how good or how bad the work is. Secondly, it so magnifies the very necessary discipline of "being open to," of "putting oneself in sympathy with . . ." that it renders it meaningless. If one has renounced altogether the right to condemn, disapprove, or in any way find fault with works of art, then one's aceptance of whatever is offered is automatic. The art-work thus becomes a mere object, the neutral manifestation of certain causal laws at work in the matter of which it consists.[7]

To be *au courant* then, is to be in the know about what's up in contemporary art, defined by one painter as "that which has been produced in the last five minutes." Disrespectful of public opinion, including that of museum people and critics who seldom express an opinion no matter what their gestures may seem to signify, he wonders how his work can mature through those consecutive small stages which flower when the pace is slow and change organic. How very different from "the Greeks who might refine the proportions of their capital, column, pediment, and so on—over a period of centuries." With us, "As soon as one artist does something, it is automatically forbidden to anyone else. Instead of adding your bit to some existing structure, you must go out and stake a claim in new territory—and build a hut." Hence the culturally induced craving for originality produces a quantity of discontinuous and mediocre art.

ANOMIE IN STYLES OF ART

This problem is exceedingly complex, and is so perceived by those implicated in it. Few indeed subscribe to any kind of devil theory. Far from conspiring to shape the way that art will go, museums are becoming passive receptors or reflectors. As for dealers and collectors, "I'm sure that occasionally you find some who try to push the type of art that they own. But I don't think that's much of a factor." Nobody important is considered to be acting wilfully: the situation, rather than any particular person, has conspired to produce a certain transvaluation of values.

These musings by an artist who grapples with the issue are most revealing. They do not attempt to fix the blame on any individual or group for something finally regarded as simply situational:

> *I could say that what I am doing is most true to myself. That's a very good thing to say. I could also say that I am doing what I feel is the most important or the most omnipotent art. Now that, of course, is a judgment which involves what everybody else is doing. There isn't another artist in the world who would agree with me on that. I know, for example, in the recent exhibitions I've had, from the gleanings of opinion I could get about them, because nobody discusses these things openly, that they most admired those things which were most peculiar to me.* It was not a question of whether they were better in any absolute sense. Very possibly we've given up thinking in those terms. . . . *There is this thing that only you do, and nobody else touches it: that's you, and a place is made for that. It gives you the place.*

Another artist, underscoring the enormous pressure to make something new, confirms our general impression. He does not suspect the motives of those who generate this pressure, for they are viewed as creatures of our time, "attempting to be very fair by presenting the thing as it is without judging it." In the absence of widely accepted aesthetic standards, they are receptive to anything which may be momentarily typical, and by that attitude unintentionally hasten the burial of all remaining standards. This anomic, literally normless condition prevails "not only in art but in everything we do." Once more, aesthetics implies ethics: abdication of one spells abandonment of the other. Consequently, "The premium on novelty does not exist for its own sake. It's not that people think tomorrow's thing will be better. They're just more interested in what's going to happen tomorrow than in what happened yesterday. . . . Nowadays, you know, we speak of a generation as ten or fifteen years at the most."

The theory, common among social scientists for a century, that *anomie* is causally related to rapid social change, could not be formulated with more compactness or precision. That artists do some-times formulate it puts them in an anomic position: they may refuse to make a value judgment.

> *Oh, those poor museums! They get it from all sides. They only do what they're expected to do, and then they get criti-cized for not being two days ahead of yesterday. It's too bad.*

Who, then, is to blame? If anyone, it is the artist himself:

> *After all, nobody comes down here from the Metropolitan Museum or the Museum of Modern Art and says, "Now next season we need a new thing. What can you do in the way of color on cloth?" . . . The most violent complaints come from people whom I respect the least. They talk about dictatorship through world fashion and the cult of novelty and all that. The artist doesn't realize that in complaining this way he puts himself in the passive role of the poor help-less little thing who has to do what somebody says. If he had half a spine in his body he just wouldn't do what he doesn't want to do. If the museum thinks that this year there has to be red and green paint on type two stainless steel, he can ignore them. Or if* Harper's Bazaar *won't photo-graph his paintings behind a model for Lord & Taylor, what's it to him? And if* Art News *happens to be on a kick where they think abstract impressionism is the thing this year, and anybody who uses a brush wider than four inches is* out, *what is it to the artist? If that's not the way he wants to work, who said he has to? Really, by confessing to the influence that all those outside things have on him, he's admitting his own mendacity. Yes, I believe that's the word: mendacity.*

Just as he is finally the sole judge of his own work, so the artist feels required to obey only the biddings of his own conscience. To the written or spoken reaction ("Oh, no, not that again," as well as "Why *not* that again?") a deaf ear must be turned. Thus, "At a show, someone will say, 'Oh, I liked your paintings of three years ago much better.' I sort of listen—and it passes over my head."

Change has its place in an experimental frame of reference. The artist who declares that several times for a year or two he went into a departure, for instance by substituting thick paint for thin paint or sized for unsized canvas, did so "to capture an image, to investigate it, to get it over with, to find out if there was more to find out about it." All this improvisation and exploration was "to perfect what I do best." What he does best, by his own lights, is a picture that comes out stained and spotted, and that, while not a replica, has an imagery and symbolism quite its own. To perfect such a picture, innumerable experiments must be performed. Methodologically, the artist resembles the scientist whose enterprise is likewise interminable. Each sets himself a technical problem and undertakes to solve it in much the same way: freely, pragmatically, by provisional hypothesis to tentative conclusion. The creative spirit, to artists as to scientists of our time, presupposes endless innovation.

Why, then, their resistance to the museum's policy of newness? Because, for all their infatuation with "the deformed term *newness*," trustees are still basically conservative: "They boost whatever is called new, or seems to be new. They do it for purposes of exploitation, for the time being. The so-called newness is not valid. It's just meant to shock, and the museum uses shock to bring a crowd. You don't make new things, in any creative sense, like that." The artist adds:

> *You haven't got shears and a little cutting knife for turning out bumptious little things in order to make curiosities. We're not talking about tricks. We're talking about the qualitative side of human existence.*

Tricksters, more lacking in sensibility than in scruples, abound on the art scene—where they play a variety of roles. The successful artist will have to deal with curators, collectors, and dealers, most of all with dealers—toward whom he is likely to feel at once scornful and respectful, contemptuous and grateful.

ACCEPTANCE OF THE ART DEALER

The artist usually appreciates having a dealer who acts as a buffer between him and the buying public, who spares him the awkwardness of having to sell his things, which "is almost like selling yourself somehow," who performs a service which would be repugnant to the artist himself and deserves to be rewarded for it. He is a kind of broker, or better, he is like a publisher engaged in antagonistic cooperation with the artist. As such, he occupies a strategic place in the "hierarchy or the bureaucracy of taste." Thus:

> *I think dealers are tastemakers in one very special sense. By being the first to exhibit your work they bring it to public attention. It's like a publisher publishes a book. What happens after that, whether it sells, whether it becomes a bestseller—that depends on public acceptance, which he does his best to foster.*

Differences are also noted. If people very much like a book, there are hardly any so poor that they cannot buy it, but few of them can afford the paintings they like best, and not even Vincent Price wants petty bourgeois America to like his latest choices better than the work of accepted masters. The clientele of a Manhattan art dealer is as small and select as that of a Manhattan book publisher is large and indiscriminate; the nature of their transactions, so similar in one way, diverges as much as the targets they aim to hit.

The publisher and the dealer have in common that, economically, they are small potatoes—at a time when corporate giants stalk all business enterprise. The college-bred youngster of an earlier age, preferably one able to live off inherited wealth, might well and sometimes did choose to settle down as a publisher or a dealer. In that capacity, as a small businessman with good family connections, treated indulgently by creditors, he could hope to exercise his taste for literature or the fine arts. Big profits in a mass market were out of the question; if we use almost any other sector of our economy as the yardstick, they still are. Yet, by comparison with the recent past, book and art profits seem huge, the market colossal, and its "growth potential" beyond measure. Mergers take place, there is even a modest flotation of public stock, new and larger galleries open, Texas oil barons buy in, an established English art house opens its lavish New York branch and raids American dealers of their star attractions: all this looks much more like the hurly-burly of big or greatly expanded business. For such business, the dealer cannot be quite the type of man he was.*

One artist knows an ex-publisher turned art dealer who fits the old mold better than the new:

> *This man was in Buffalo. Then he came to New York, gave up publishing, and got the idea of starting a gallery. He's quite remarkable, what with all the commercial pressures, because he retains a certain freshness. He feels as if he can manipulate and stimulate cultural activities, and that his gallery will be some sort of outlet for that. He's started publishing poets again, he's interested in the theater, he*

* Writing in a popular weekly, Katherine Kuh makes some apposite observations: That so many dealers have recently invested in new quarters could augur well for America's escalating art business. As an interested bystander, I have long been troubled by soaring and often irrational prices, particularly where works of the last hundred years are concerned. But Frank Lloyd of the new Marlborough-Gerson Gallery . . . claims that "the surface has not yet been scratched," that possibilities for the New York art market are virtually unlimited. To be sure, he added that most art dealing at present adheres to old-fashioned nineteenth-century traditions. He advocates drastically modernized methods that will keep pace with up-to-date international merchandising techniques. If we judge his advice by the success of two galleries in London and the one in Rome he was instrumental in founding, we can only conclude that Mr. Lloyd is right, but I am skeptical.

For no matter how hard-headed we are, *art is not merchandise*. True, we buy and sell it; true, scarcity becomes an economic factor, but final judgments rest on history's decisions, and obviously history must rely on time. Art does not, as a rule, wear out. It peters out, if it cannot stand up to the demands of passing years. Moreover, time is never static; what we reject today, we applaud tomorrow. At the start of the century, Turner's watercolors brought formidable prices; forty years later they could be had for a pittance, and now again they are astronomically high. Our sights change as our attitudes change.

In the long run, I suspect, art dealing must remain a personal matter, above all in relation to the work of living artists. For, since paintings and sculpture are not assembly-line objects, they are ill-adapted to merchandising methods that reflect the psychology of mass production. Ideally, artist and dealer are more than business partners. The greatest dealers have always recognized creative work early and backed it with the full stamp of their own convictions. The man who selects the art must almost of necessity be the man who sells it. How can a slickly trained sales staff operate on a level of total commitment? All the advantageous financial contracts in the world do not compensate for the loss of a personal relationship between artist and dealer. We are constrained to add that precisely this relationship, to the extent that it ever existed, is rapidly disappearing. Miss Kuh's attitude, while surely laudable, also seems to us to be more than a little wishful.[8]

sponsors foreign films. Actually, it's all a little old-fashioned, and I don't know if it really works out—though with the acceleration of his income, his taste has improved: you can eat marvelous lobster down at his place.

Jibes aside, the artist has some fellow-feeling for a minority of dealers—men of taste not totally dedicated to their own economic aggrandizement. One painter recounts another unusual case:

A dealer came here from California. I had a picture around that I had been trying to talk myself into liking for years. I mean, it's a little thing. I'd keep it up for a while, then take it down, and say to myself, "You know, that's not bad." Three days later, I'd say, "It still stinks." Well, he came on one of the days I didn't like it. I was embarrassed, but he kept raving about it. And he took it. So you see, dealers can have some standing. I mean, after all, without my Californian that painting would never have gone out into the world. After all, he's not entirely devoid of taste. . . . Maybe it is good. Anyway, the artist never really knows whether something he's done is good . . . and maybe he shouldn't.

Among the many aspersions artists cast at dealers, there is an occasional tribute, like one to the dealer "who has never suggested whether I change or not change," who would not "dare to advise me whether I was underproducing or overproducing," and would not dare "out of self-respect." This dealer is praised for showing work which she herself admires while refusing to show work offensive to her just because it might make money:

My dealer has never even hinted at what she would like me to do or objected to anything that I have done. I expect that if I had gone off on a wild tangent, if I had suddenly begun to do something radically different, she might dislike it very much—not for the difference, but as a matter of taste. If so, she'd tell me she didn't want to show it, and I wouldn't want her to show it. This is the understanding I believe we have.

There is also reference to a Venezuelan art dealer who allegedly has a keen mind, responds to art, and is therefore "absolutely amazing," and though very wealthy, does a lot for real art. In summary: "You'd never believe he was a dealer!"

We do not find many instances of altruism in these data, but one account by an artist, who sells well, of how she came to switch galleries—after three of them in the chic midtown area put out feelers to her—does seem to afford a case in point:

> *I was having lunch one day with my dealer, discussing galleries. I hadn't given much thought to the matter till she began talking about it. She said, "Well, I don't have to tell you again that I think you're the greatest artist in this direction. I would hate to lose you, but if you go over to that gallery, you'll be the only artist there in this direction. You could be pushed individually." She said, "Here there are several others in this direction, and the untrained eye can't tell one from another. So when I'm showing the work, people will ask, 'Which do you like better?' I have to say I like them all." So, after we talked about it, I accepted an invitation from the S. gallery.*

Such solicitude is so exceptional that no one else reports anything like it.

SOCIAL AND ECONOMIC NECESSITY OF THE DEALER

Mostly, as we have already suggested, the artist is thankful to his dealer simply for providing him with protection: "I had a wealthy widow in here one day asking, 'How much is this and this?' And I said, 'Get the hell out! Out! Out!! I don't care anything about you.'" By forfeiting 40 percent of his price to a dealer, the artist is spared "those god-awful types trooping around" his studio, "nagging and niggling about deals and all that." He tells us that we have no idea how unpleasant it is to have to do business, "to have every person who might or might not buy a sculpture come into the studio and spread out the deal." We did not encounter a single artist who wants to be his own dealer. The gallery is a convenient place to show one's work, and those who run it are most useful for "the dirty work they do." The artist is happy to delegate a most important role to the dealer: that of financial and personal representative to the buying public. Partly it is a matter of conserving time and energy: "If I had to be strongly concerned with selling my pictures, I wouldn't have time to make them—" and, "I'd be dividing myself into too many energy packages." To sell oneself is unbecoming and inefficient:

> *A good art dealer has the kind of personality that will work for his artist in a way that the artist can't work for himself. The average artist isn't able to call up critics, or museum people, or big collectors and say, "You've got to come down and see my most recent thing. I think it's for you." But a dealer who's on the ball will do just that.*

The same sentiment is expressed in somewhat different terms:

> *How can anyone talk about himself? I mean: "Oh, those yellows are gorgeous! Look how it moves. I mean, Jesus, that picture is so moving." A dealer doesn't always talk like that. He may not say, "Those yellows are gorgeous," but he has his pitch. How could it be the same as mine? I mean, maybe he thinks that picture stinks, but knows how to sell it. I couldn't care less . . .*

The role difference is viewed as a character difference. No painter or sculptor likes to think of himself as temperamentally suited to salesmanship, least of all when it is required for the promotion of his own work. If, therefore, he wishes to deprecate another artist, nothing cuts deeper than to say, for instance, that so-and-so is "really quite good at this sort of thing," that he is "terribly shrewd" or fundamentally "a businessman." To have the dealer's aptitudes is somehow to diminish oneself as an artist. Should you admit to having them in some slight degree, as an artist you recoil from their use: "Actually, there's no reason why I couldn't send out postcards and say, 'Come and see twenty new pictures in my enormous studio.' But somehow that isn't what I want to do." For doing it, the dealer and his gallery are a great convenience.

The impersonal character of this convenience troubles a few of our artists. A painter, well past middle age, observing the "mechanized and rationalized" relationship he now has with men of business not even personally known to him, remembers Paris in his youth: "It was rather a small world. It was very concentrated. You would sit down with a specific group of five or six dealers, all well acquainted with you and your friends. That's all there was to it." The number of people involved in art today is so great as to preclude intimacy; the quantity of interaction transforms its quality, and now and then produces some bewilderment:

> *I think the whole thing is in such confusion. There are so many painters, so many dealers, so many galleries, so much in the marketplace that the real meaning of it has gone. It's all collapsed.*

But for every artist who laments this dehumanization there are several who hail it. They feel relieved of the strain that is set up within and between any two people required to act warm and personal while engaged in cold cash transactions. These artists were glad to be shielded from the public; they were even happier to be shielded from their dealers: "My dealer is a nice man. He's been very good to me. He does his job very well. And I never see him." Is he pleased with this arrangement? "I'm glad. Very glad. I'm so happy. I have no telephone or anything. It's the first time in my life that I've had it so good." How so good?

> *Look, I don't even know where my pictures are. Sometimes a couple drops in from God knows where and tells me my pictures are in the gallery, but it's just gossip. And then if something is sold, so I get a check. I tell you, it's a delightful situation. When one has such a dealer, one can reach this stage, the perfect condition for an artist to be in.*

Nor is the dealer always so highly valued for his role as buffer:

> *I think it works the other way around. The client in America is so conscious that he must have a prestige product that he needs the dealer to convince him that it's kosher. It's the dealer who convinces the client. He doesn't protect the artist so much from the client; his role is to give weight to what he sells—which means that a well-known dealer can sell many*

> *bad things that a poorer dealer can't. But protecting the artist: that's a minor factor. None of us likes to have clients coming in and rummaging around. . . . Some woman called up the other day. She asked to see small pictures and wanted to come over here. Well, I called the dealer, and he said he'd come over. He knew the woman, he knew her house. He'd pick the pictures out and take them over to my gallery, and show them to her there. So this is protecting me, and I like that. That's good. But then, that's not a major problem at all. I mean, nobody, not even De Kooning, sells pictures so fast that his painting time will be taken away by a string of people outside his door. No, I think it's a very minor point.*

No unqualified blessing is ever bestowed by artists on dealers. The most generous assessment is coupled with a touch of contempt, and most assessments are far from generous.

RESENTMENT OF DEALERS

But, "even a bad dealer is better than none." Narrowly defined, a good dealer goes about his business, which is money grubbing, as unpretentiously as possible. He does his dirty work and keeps his distance.

Artists are undeniably testy on the subject of dealers. Why? What are their concrete grievances? Do they "constantly have fights with dealers," and are they "always switching galleries," as an esteemed painter heatedly contends? And if so, is it for the reason he advances, that no gallery really offers the artist what he wants? If not, our man wants to know, why do even very successful artists at the "top galleries" keep looking for better ones?

Many artists feel that they are lifting the lid of corruption just a little to let us glimpse a hideous world they know too well. In their eyes many dealers are: irresponsible ("they don't handle the person correctly"); actually cruel ("they'll pick up artists and drop them"); filled with *réssentiment* ("unconsciously they hate artists. Lots of them are frustrated artists who can't stand productive people, and they take their revenge on us"); exploitative ("they take

advantage of artists, but what's worse, they take advantage of ig-
noramuses who come to them for advice"); meretricious ("gimmicks
are their stock-in-trade"). They are, above all, powerful agents of
"a sick system and a sick society which no artist by himself has
the strength to lick."

Dealers and clients, at their worst, reinforce one another:

> *The kind of audience we have here is based on nothing
> but prestige. These are people who want to buy pictures by
> big-name artists from a certain stable. And another kind buys
> because they think they are going to have a real little gold
> mine. Before very long a little Picasso will be discovered.
> He may be misshapen, the poor slob, but he will be found . . .*

Patrons used to be churchmen and noblemen. They had nothing
to do with intermediaries, "secondary men," agents, now called
dealers, who do not proceed, for the most part, either from their own
likes and dislikes, if any, or those of their artistically illiterate customers. Their common concern is with exploitable art—from which
mutual benefits may be derived.

One reason for the great proliferation of galleries in New York
(and in the hinterlands) is that they meet a new demand from
people who have suddenly come into money and need to spend it for
tax write-off purposes. A corps of financial experts advises them
on how to invest in art and helps to generate demand. That the
relationship is characterized by socio-cultural homogeneity becomes
most apparent when we examine the supply side and discover that
dealers may be motivated to set up in business for reasons indistinguishable from those which prompt their clients to buy:

> *Mostly they're not hard-hearted businessmen but crazy busi-
> nesswomen who run tax-loss galleries because their psycho-
> analysts said that they'd be happy doing it. And some of our
> major galleries are under those hands. Of course, a few com-
> mercial galleries are real hard business concerns, and they're
> the best, I think, for artists. But it's a very mixed-up field.
> It's full of people who aren't really art dealers. I would say
> nine out of ten galleries are phony. They have no commit-
> ment. They come and go like the wind. They're tax fronts.
> Now I would say this is a very unhealthy situation.*

Worse than the villainous dealer, who merely cheats artists out of their money, is the manipulative dealer who, like too many curators, tries to dictate to artists about their work. Many say that the tentacles of control are put out by nearly every gallery in the city. Why? "Because dealers feel their lives are at stake." Money may gratify the artist, but to the dealer it is, and must be, everything. Dealers are accused of thinking that they can get good art by heaping financial rewards on the artist. "Then, they feel . . . have the audacity to feel, that they can direct the artist, choose which pieces to show, advise him to keep producing more of the stuff that sells, to show off, to have too many shows."

A young painter, already considered distinguished for his innovations, expresses delight that the critics have begun to murmur about him for being too varied: "They can't follow me from one moment to the next. I think that's great." At this early stage in his life as an artist, it strikes him that his gallery dealer leads a procession of critics and purchasers who emulate museum officials, all admonishing him: "Whoa! Take it easy. No more changes. Consolidate your work. We've just gotten a big order from Such-and-Such Museum for a picture like such-and-such you did." So we come full circle once again to the pressure and counterpressure, emanating mostly from museums but funneled very often through galleries and their personnel:

> *So you're praised for something new and original. That means you get a painting to do, and you change the color or shift the elements around. But it's the same picture. You just make variations on a single theme. That's your patent, and once you get it you're supposed to protect it. You have a vested interest.*

Such quotations, and there are many, take us some distance toward the clarification of an apparent paradox: that artists, at one and the same time, complain of being pressured to repeat themselves and of being pressured not to repeat themselves. The contradiction is resolved as they in turn are absolved of being mere malcontents, if the constraint toward newness is superficial—more a matter of appearance than reality, actually a disguise for doing the same old thing. Then indeed we have to do with coloristic and stylistic sleight of hand under cover of what one respondent calls "aural jugglery." And the artist's sense that he is being driven two ways to the same arid terminus becomes much more intelligible.

Are the dealers all that important? One answer is: "For the moment, more than any other group, they control the art world. But they haven't always, and they won't always." Another:

> *Today they are playing, I believe, an over-important role. In other words, it's almost become as if they write the obituary and then sit around like pallbearers waiting for somebody to paint it for them. . . . Their advertising is so intense! I think, for instance, this whole business of Pop Art, and everything connected with it, was completely planned in the galleries. Even the name was dreamed up in advance. These few gallery people sat down and thought about it and brought in this comic strip and these particular elements, and promoted it and gave it a tremendous amount of publicity. . . . I think a lot of this happens on account of the constant shifting of attention from one gallery to another. A gallery comes on the scene with a certain importance, and in one year it can drop way down the ladder. So naturally, when that happens, the dealer tries to cook up something to get back up again.*

Fads artificially induced to make money for gallery owners who wish to establish, sustain, or recoup their position do have detrimental effects—at least on good second-rate artists, if not on their betters. These are artists who before the fad "were good in terms of what they were doing, men like so-and-so, who were doing their kind of work, which was never the best, but they were doing it very, very well." What happened? "Well, as soon as this new situation developed they weren't able to do what they had been doing half as effectively as before. It was true for every one of those painters." "Those painters" are not of the first magnitude, but they are mature and serious and not to be lightly dismissed. If even they can be injured by the arbitrary rules of fad and fashion, how much more vulnerable are the young and the inexperienced. A lady painter in her thirties, also scandalized by the promotion of Pop Art, angrily avers that: "If I were a young artist beginning now, looking at that stuff, I would say, 'I don't want to do it. If that's what it is, I don't

want to be an artist,' and I'd go on to something else." She emphasizes that art is now in an amorphous period of transition and, consequently, that artists are unsure of themselves. The masters will not
be troubled by this openness, but those below and those still outside
who may have the potential to move up and in could be deterred
from doing so. At these levels the dealers' gimmickry is disastrous.

An anecdotal insight:

> *Well, I'll tell you, I've an Italian friend who works at the
> ABC Gallery, and she told me people come into the place,
> and in the course of working there she discovered this word
> "crap." She said, "What does this word, crap, mean?" So
> we told her. She said, "Everybody who comes in to see the
> show says, 'This is crap and that is crap.'" But then, on the
> other hand, I asked her (she also works in an Italian gallery),
> "When you get back to Italy, are you going to handle this
> crap?" and she shot back, "Yes, I'm going to handle it!"
> So, it's something. It's a business. And they all say the same
> thing, so I guess it's true: if it's junk and somebody buys it,
> why not sell it? Like the thing is set up by these people
> who are so calloused about it, and certain artists will produce
> for this kind of thing because they get momentary success
> for it, they make some kind of money, they're fawned over
> for a few days. Certain people need that.*

Certain people need that and will be attracted to it, but others are
repelled, and if not yet launched in the fine arts they may be irre-
trievably lost. It is not inconceivable that some of the worst will be
attracted and some of the best will not. In that case, worrisome
inferences must be drawn by everyone concerned with discovering
and fostering creativity.

Do the number and variety of galleries in New York City mitigate
their harshness? No one in our group is impressed by the number
and few admit the variety. The gross number of galleries in New
York is a matter of dispute: some artists venture the round figure
four hundred, but most scoff at the estimate. Characteristically,
"There may be that number, but I'd hardly call any of them
galleries." Or, "When you cite that figure, it really means very little.
They don't do anything for their artists, nor their artists for them."

And, qualitatively, "I mean, when there were forty galleries they did much more than these four hundred." A painter in his eighties, but still going strong, remembers that when he got started there were only two or three galleries, ". . . quite undistinguished, you know, but they had nothing to do with contemporary art." Presently, one or two more, notably Stieglitz's, came along, and they had off-shoots manned by "people without any social background whatever," who, by displaying current work, led to our own speculative and inflationary era.

Sculptors have a special problem:

> *If you think there are so many galleries in New York, remember first of all that not all of them show sculpture. That eliminates a whole group. Then you take those that remain: if you have any objective vision about your own work and about the galleries, you don't just march into any one. There are some that don't handle Americans, some that don't handle contemporaries. Pretty soon you work down to a group of perhaps fifteen galleries in the whole city. So you look them over, and you decide that out of that group there may be five that can use a guy like you. For one reason or another, some of them may have too many sculptors already. . . . Now it's tougher for a sculptor, but I think no artist has more than five galleries that are really right for him, and—it's almost impossible to achieve, of course—but they should come to him. He shouldn't have to go to them.*

Perhaps he shouldn't have to, but as things stand he does have to—and therein lies much of his trouble.

8

Women Artists: A New Force

There have been thousands of women painters, but only the men have been remembered; it would be unkind to make a comprehensive list of famous women painters. Even the greatest central situation of Christianity, as of life—the relation of the mother to her child—which appeals so strongly to a woman's heart, has never received memorable rendering at a woman's hand. In sculpture, also, it is scarcely necessary to add, the great names are all men, from Phidias to Donatello, from Michelangelo to Bourdelle. That there have been two or three women whose names deserve honorable mention is the most that can be said.

—HAVELOCK ELLIS, 1929

WOMEN, who in the United States outnumber men, are still sociologically a "minority group." Despite the triumphs of feminism, theirs is generally a subordinate status. They are virtually excluded from the national power structure insofar as it is comprised of government, business, and the military.[1] In our sphere of inquiry, i.e., the visual arts, they have also, until very recently, been conspicuous by their absence. There have been women, but—with rare if shining exceptions—none on the distaff side for whom greatness could be claimed. Since at least half the world's population consists of women, some of whom have taken to art, their persistent lack of distinction raises interesting questions. We have no reason to believe that aesthetic sensitivity and other native endowments which constitute "talent" are not distributed as widely in one sex as another. Yet woman's lack of high achievement in art is universal; it is not just a peculiarity of Western culture. Havelock Ellis has pointed out that:

> Primitive women have in their hands all the industries, and, in consequence, the rudiments of most of the arts. But when we get beyond the rudiments the position begins to change, and when we reach fully differentiated arts, even among savages, we find that they are almost exclusively in the hands of men.[2]

These and similar assertions have never been seriously challenged. The most aggressive proponent of "female superiority," Ashley Montagu,[3] has attested to their accuracy even while rationalizing them. Over the years our modern civilization has produced, at best, a "woman artist of the century" and little more. One can point to Angelica Kauffmann in the eighteenth century, Rosa Bonheur in the nineteenth century, Mary Cassatt in the nineteenth and twentieth centuries, and Georgia O'Keeffe or Kaethe Kollwitz in the twentieth century. Beyond this handful, which could be enlarged but not by much, there are the thousands of women who have worked at painting and, at least until the present generation, have contributed little of true distinction.

The change in women's position in the art world which can now be perceived, is on the other hand, quite striking. While as yet we cannot assess the importance of contemporary women artists with any real perspective, there are indications of a radical upward swing. It is suddenly evident that several female painters and sculptresses of consequence have been unveiled in the past decade—a fact which seems to have taken well-informed observers by surprise. For example, while writing about the emerging generation of successful American painters in 1956, Rudi Blesh was constrained to comment: "One of them, remarkably enough, is a woman: Joan Mitchell. Rosa Bonheur and Mary Cassatt must surely be turning in their graves with joy." [4] If Blesh were writing his book today, not quite a decade later, it is unlikely that finding successful and talented women painters would impress him as remarkable; a casual survey of the current art scene shows that they are achieving "permanent" status. To mention only some of the more important: Elaine de Kooning, Helen Frankenthaler, Grace Hartigan, Joan Mitchell, and Louise Nevelson.

This improvement runs counter to the present trend for professional women. Despite the presumed impetus of World War II and their generally emancipated state, women have steadily lost ground in all the professions during the past quarter-century: "Indeed, the proportion of women in college back in 1939—four women to six men—was higher than it is now. In those days, too, a larger proportion of B.A.'s, M.A.'s and Ph.D.'s went to women." [5] In contrast, steadily larger numbers of women are "making it" as artists. Not a few now receive acceptance and even acclaim from dealers, curators, critics, and collectors. They are increasingly important as practitioners and producers, and not simply as custodians (their "proper" station in the past). So much is beyond question.

The change does not mean that everything has become rosy for women. Indeed, this new development has stirred up something of a hornet's nest in the art world. A previously all-male preserve has been unexpectedly invaded and the statutory occupants are uncertain in their response. The "intruders," finding themselves in alien territory and in an unfamiliar role, have been equally uncertain and provisional in setting up codes of conduct for themselves. It then comes as no real surprise that more emotion was generated among our respondents by "sex" questions than by any other single topic. Men expressed themselves with feeling, and at times with vehemence, about the woman artist. The reticence that caused some to be nearly tongue-tied in discussions of the Negro (see Chapter Nine) was completely absent.

THE REASONS FOR FEMALE "INFERIORITY"

It has always been difficult in Western society to consider woman's social role objectively. Some see her as exploited, subjugated, disadvantaged, and generally lacking opportunities for fulfillment except through the procreative process; others see her as the "vital force" which controls society and its life lines. Very little moderation is found in these judgments of woman's presumed frustrations and aggressions. It may be impossible to establish "the truth," but in art, regardless of where the fault lies, one thing is abundantly clear: historically, the greatest musicians, composers, sculptors, writers, and painters have been men.

Numerous attempts at explaining woman's relative lack of attainment in the arts have been made. Pertinent—and impertinent—theories have followed biological, psychological, and sociological lines; of these, the biological is easiest to deal with—and to dispose of. In the past, many learned men propounded views which advanced "biological inferiority" as a primary factor. Havelock Ellis, for example:

> *If we turn to the pure artistic impulses, as manifested in the higher stages of culture, we find that the supremacy of men in painting is unquestionable. Even among school children boys are found to show more aptitude for drawing, notwithstanding the greater diligence of girls. . . .*[6]

Ellis was suggesting, in this passage, that boys have greater artistic potential than girls because of their biological inheritance. This pronouncement on childhood talent was based chiefly on several provocative but hardly scientific studies carried out by numerous "researchers" at the turn of the century. Ellis did not accept their implications without qualification, but he felt them to be approximations of the truth.

To Ellis, a notorious assertion by P. J. Mobius that the art impulse is in the nature of a male secondary sexual characteristic, was also partially acceptable.[7] And so on. Today these ideas strike us as simply outlandish, but they were widely entertained not so long ago. Theories of "biological inferiority" are at last in poor repute, but when less than a century ago John Stuart Mill delivered his famous defense of women, *The Subjection of Women*,[8] it burst like a bombshell, exposing, if not exploding, Victorian prejudice.

When our respondents speak of biological factors, they do not refer to inheritance; rather they are concerned with adequate "levels of energy." Some feel that in this matter the woman is slightly disadvantaged, for example, by her menstrual cycle. But they offer this possibility for the most part with tentativeness, and almost always in conjunction with a variety of other factors which are viewed as distractions:

> *The menstrual cycle is certainly sufficient to cut down on the continuity of thought, the continuity of energy.*

> *You can't ignore the menstrual cycle. It's going to cut things down for the woman. Also, being a wife and a mother is important. You'll notice that most of the better painters are not hampered by these problems. If you look around you'll see that women artists are not raising large families or supporting their husbands.*

An occasional woman might concede a comparative weakness: "I probably get tired quicker than a man. It takes a lot of muscle to do the frames and I sometimes wish I was stronger." But other women demur. They grant the male's greater muscular strength but cannot see it as particularly relevant in painting or sculpting.

Many male artists also resist giving priority to physiological explanations: "Are you kidding? Have you seen L.'s work? Maybe they haven't got the muscles, but there's vitality. Maybe they can't keep it up for so long, but so what?" They consider that the woman is probably subject to a greater number of distractions, while according physical factors a position of reduced importance:

> *I think that the male artist will find it easier to work harder every day, and he will also have a compulsion to work longer*

> *hours, not necessarily with more passion though, but he will find it easier to sustain interest in his ideas. Women are apt to get dispersed more quickly and that's a great problem.*

One woman pointedly summarized her situation and that of sister artists:

> *They [men] don't have more than the "normal" conflicts about being artists. But we are always in conflict about our capacities to be women, our attitudes toward our children and toward our husbands; the energy we have to have as artists and how this influences our everyday lives.*

She obviously places greater stress on role conflict than on physique, and in this she concurs with most writers who give major consideration to social and psychological factors that heighten the tension surrounding a woman's domestic and professional life.

In contrast with Ellis, for example, Freud rejects Mobius' biological hypotheses: "I do not support Mobius in the view he has put forward . . . that the biological contrast between the intellectual work and sexual activity explains the 'physiological mental weakness' of women. On the contrary, I think that the undoubted fact of the intellectual inferiority of so many women can be traced to that inhibition of thought necessitated by sexual suppression." [9] Montagu specifies three additional factors which, in his opinion, interfere with woman's achievement. They help to round out the problems by which she is continually beset:

> *Among the principal reasons why women do not have as many achievements to their credit as men are the following: (1) for the greater part of their history most fields of achievement have been closed to them; (2) in fields in which women were admitted they were not permitted to enter on an equal footing with men; (3) or, having been admitted, they were not encouraged to excel, were actively discouraged, or were not noticed at all.*[10]

In a word, Montagu means that the "ruling powers" (men) are basically to blame for woman's poor showing.

MALE CHAUVINISM

Some male artists (especially the older ones) seem content to perpetuate these immemorial relationships. They are oblivious to or will not recognize recent shifts: "I've always had the attitude that men were better artists than women. There are more men geniuses, and so in that sense painting has to be more of a masculine thing, if anything." Such complacency is not shared by all older artists, but most of them are willing to defend their "superiority" with vigor. These hard-bitten males steadfastly refuse to give the present revolutionary turn of events official recognition. Mainly they deny its reality by doggedly claiming that "things haven't changed," that the position of the female painter is "no different now than it was in the past." But they do not voice these conclusions wholeheartedly; tacit recognition of the female's changing status creeps into their *obiter dicta:*

> *No, I don't think there are more women painters, but a few have become well known recently. There might be a few better ones now, possibly. You know, I doubt it.*

> *There were probably more, even then there were probably many more women artists; since things didn't get around so much then, they just didn't get heard of. Not that it really mattered.*

> *I don't think there are more women artists now. I think there were always a lot of women who were painting, that is, as far back as my memory goes, which is well over forty years. There used to be as many women and they got into it for the same reason—they all had a flair. But considering the opportunities today, there doesn't seem to be a larger percentage of women and I don't think they are any more accomplished now than before.*

Other assessments of the female by these older men are equally negative. They direct a good deal of their "ire" toward what they see as her abrogation of the only "proper" role, which is motherhood. They avoid coming to grips with her talents and capabilities;

instead they make vague and often tangential objections, or hew to the cliché that "procreating is enough creating for them" and "they should be willing to let it go at that." Two of our most celebrated, elderly, and remorselessly male artists, while unable to deny the enhanced status of women, make their feelings abundantly clear. Unfortunately, the intensity of these feelings render their reliability and validity as opinions more than somewhat suspect:

> *I think it's practically hopeless for a woman to be an artist. After all, men can't have babies. If male artists could have babies, I'm sure most wouldn't go to the trouble of being painters. Why should they? And I think a woman who's trying to be an artist is sort of dividing herself. My feeling is that they should create at home.*

> *Women? Oh heavens. I've noticed a tremendous number of them painting, including a vast majority of bad ones. As far as her having a bad time is concerned, as far as her having a tougher time, I don't think so. I doubt if it's so. If she's a mother, maybe she shouldn't paint; for God's sake, who asked her to do it? She's told by a psychiatrist that she should paint for therapeutic reasons. She's told that if she dabbles in paint it'll be good for her relationships with her children and all that, which I think is pretty silly.*

Reactions of male artists to the female, then, are not only often unreasonable but also are typically divided along generational lines. Younger men, although they have their own unfavorable and harsh judgments to render, seem to make this broadside gesture of rejection only when their professional contacts stretch far across generational boundaries. Then they accept for themselves the attitudes of a much older generation. Otherwise they are more likely to "acknowledge" the female presence in their occupational universe, along with the right of any woman to pursue art as a life work. On occasion they will even credit her achievements. Still intensely critical of her, their complaints are more likely to focus on specific aspects of personality, behavior, and work. The older artist seems to have difficulty in attuning himself to feminine independence, to the association of women and professionalism. To that extent, he cannot extend recognition to her as a rival; the younger artist can do that much.

It would nevertheless be unfair to leave the impression that all older artists are so rigid and biased in their attitude toward women. Individuals rise above their generation's prejudice and attempt to deliver reasonably fair judgments. Even here, however, the road is treacherous. The best they can offer are "objective" appraisals, and the convoluted paths that these fair-minded men must take are painful to behold. That this should be so provides some hint of how much opposition, both overt and covert, the female is still likely to encounter from senior artists who are, after all, members of the "teaching generation":

> *Now, I have no rules that she should do anything. I have no prejudice against her for being a woman. There may not be women who are the greatest painters, but I can name some who are better than some men. But there are a lot more women, relatively, and some are good and some are bad. There are some women artists whose work interests me more than the work of some men artists, but when you get involved in a general proposition, then of course you can say that there are no great women artists, and well, you can prove that there are great men artists.*

> *Now, there are several good woman artists. Without analyzing my likes or dislikes, and they are strong, and forgetting my dislikes, that is, just accepting the quality, the seriousness of it—although I may disagree with what they are doing —and some of it is very dubious, I would say offhand that there are about six women I know of whom I would respect. The most interesting students in my classes are often the girls. And once I went visiting the XYZ University art department. And I stepped in front of a painting and asked who made it. A voice piped out of black stockings when I looked around. It was a woman—a girl, and it happens all the time.*

But willy-nilly, and in one way or another, male artists are coming to recognize that the present generation of successful painters includes women who hold their own not by imitation but as a result of having evolved unique and personal approaches worthy of critical recognition.

PREJUDICE AGAINST FEMALE ARTISTS

Yet when the woman artist still complains that it is difficult for her to gain a foothold in the art world, she's not simply being paranoid. For all her achievements, she must be prepared to deal with bias, prejudice, or outright hostility—and it emanates from many sources. At least one well-known and successful modern female painter felt compelled for some time to exhibit under an assumed male name. She thought, probably with justification, that as a woman she would not receive anything like the same treatment, the same objective reception automatically accorded to men. Shades of Currer Bell, George Sand, and George Eliot! Some women deny being sensitive to all of this, but they recognize that it exists; many are extremely thin-skinned about it:

> *I've never had any self-consciousness about being a woman artist, but many men have. Certain dealers, for example, A.Z., have said that they would never take a woman artist, and women artists are considered by museum directors as a separate deal. But I know that some women painters can be easily insulted, especially if anyone should say, "As a woman artist, what do you think?" They'll even walk out of a party or some such thing.*

That certain gallery owners still openly refuse to show or represent the female painter is a well-known "trade secret." This action is rationalized in a variety of ways, all easily refuted. Some of our respondents interpret it at the level of artistic evaluation: "I think many gallery owners wouldn't take women at all. I think they've decided that it's impossible for a woman to be a great artist." Some put it on a purely economic basis: "If I were a gallery owner or dealer, I wouldn't feel necessarily that a woman artist would be harder to handle. But she would be harder to sell; she would be harder to promote." This argument might carry some weight if it were not well understood that the "tastes" of most collectors are molded by others, including art dealers and gallery owners. Many collectors reveal anti-female biases in their buying patterns, which include the price they are willing to pay for a woman's work, but this too is a posture they have learned to assume.

One artist, whose observations may strike closer to home, guesses that "some dealers just don't like women." Since they do not find it politic to express that feeling openly, many dealers rationalize their prejudice by seeing women as "difficult to deal with." One put it this way: "The women I have known have been difficult in dealer relationships. Whether they are more difficult than men, I don't know. I've known some pretty difficult men in gallery relationships too. But I know there are a lot of dealers who do not like women painters and give that as a reason. How valid it is, I don't know." Museum directors are apparently guilty of the same reactions as gallery owners, although it is not as easy, from our data, to establish this feeling as fact.

Under these conditions we hear one famous woman artist say diffidently: "Women artists have a difficult time getting accepted. They don't get the same prices or get shown or get bought. But that's just in the world of making a living and that's not why anyone becomes a painter." Her point is valid, yet one could hardly expect the same kind of indifference from those women who are still struggling for recognition. Still, most of them do manage to maintain a professional perspective:

> *I think that if you get hung up on how we're treated in the marketplace, you lose sight of our whole purpose and involvement. I mean at times everybody has a gripe about everything. Lots of things are unfair, depending on what is important to people at the time. I'm not unrealistic, but you're not an artist to make money and be treated nice, al-thought it's helpful in the long run.*

But since artists themselves are the most influential "tastemakers," it is the reaction of her peers which, at least initially, has the greatest impact on the female painter. Since men still effectively dominate the art world, their reactions become most important. And here a woman has special problems. The feelings of older artists toward her are predominantly negative; younger men may profess greater tolerance and acceptance, but there are still no "male artists in shining armor" to grant her or her ventures unqualified support or passionate endorsement.

Under these circumstances it is not surprising that she finds it difficult to survive as an artist. If she wishes to exist in the art world as it is presently constituted, she must make one of two choices: she can passively accept the treatment accorded her, or she can aggressively resist and struggle with and against it. But to dramatize the perverseness of her situation, one male painter complains:

> *Let's just say that I can't think of any woman artist that I would be interested in, either as a person or as a woman. I think they're all too cranky and unreasonable. Or if they're reasonable, they are so damn reasonable that I can't stand them. Why are they that way? They're that way because they are that way. They just can't be different, I guess.*

Thus she is damned if she does and damned if she doesn't, and it is the rare male who can see the irrationality of it all. Oldsters are quick to condemn her for always imitating men, but they do not see how little latitude they give her to develop naturally. They may suggest that "real" women have their own art styles, and that if they only stuck to them everything would be fine, but they also make it clear that they view "feminine" styles as inferior to their own.

Criticisms of the female for being excessively "reasonable and compliant" remain rare; accusations of masculinity and aggressiveness are the norm. Men frequently characterize their female counterparts, with varying degrees of resentment and understanding, as hostile, competitive, and overly assertive:

> *They have to pay a price in femininity. They become more aggressive. Successful women artists tend to be castrators. I would say so, definitely.*

> *Some of them are very masculine, practically a masculine protest, especially some of the people who are abstract expressionists.*

> *I think most women seem to think in terms of being a man. And therefore they think that in order to be a painter, they*

have to do it bigger and better and more. That doesn't necessarily make better art.

The fact that most artists are males affects the women. One of the dangers they run then is wearing their balls around their necks in order to prove they aren't women. You know, overpainting and being too masculine in their painting just to prove they're not women. This affects their painting at times because they seem to be leaning over backward to be unfeminine.

You see, most women try to imitate the characteristics of a man, and I think that's very bad. They're trying to be something that they're not. There's a difference of temperament involved. It's a question of competition, which is a pity, because a number of them are very talented painters, women painters, and you can't even tell. It seems as if they refuse to be themselves.

It's hard to think that women artists are women and that they really aren't men. If you see them, they're terribly aggressive and not female; they try to act tough and it's hard for them to be tender. I wouldn't be certain that this is completely fair, but there's an awful lot of evidence to go on.

And on they go. They may qualify and hedge, and sometimes they are quite as critical of themselves, but their attempts to soften harsh judgments are rather halfhearted:

There can be a great deal of self-centeredness. There can be a certain fantasy about their importance, or they can put on masks and mannerisms of very great efficiency and direct action. I think that's enough for you to get the idea.

I would say that most of them are very aggressive. I would say so about most of them, but certainly not all of them. Most of them are really pushers though, you just can't get away from it. They're really pushers. They have themselves a wheelbarrow and they're pushing it in front of them all the time. Pushing through, breaking through, going right on through. I don't know whether it is because this is the way they are or what the world has done to them. Some of them have never been out in the world and I don't really know if they've ever been invited. They take their work with them everywhere, and at any time they will say, "Here it is and let's have a show." But I suppose many men do the same thing.

It is beyond our competence and our data to judge the accuracy or objectivity of these pronouncements. Our own observations would lead us to be much more generous in characterizing the female artist as a person, but only an occasional comment from male respondents is less severe than those quoted above. Truly favorable remarks could be numbered on one hand. An eminent artist, considered something of a maverick in the art world, tried to be moderate as he reflected on women artists. However, since he began by admitting his preconception that *all* women are highly competitive, and therefore aggressive, his contribution did little to alter an essentially negative image; his sympathy with women's difficulties was less than overwhelming, although he did try to be disinterested:

I think it is probably true to a great degree because, you know, they fight terrific pressures from other women who say, "Oh really, you want to be a big mother?" So it's like the same when they do work. They work with great vengeance, like "I am a female." But they all seem like females. They're like women. I mean, they're not like a man to me, even if I'm not attracted to them physically. So what? They've had affairs and they want to get married. They are just like any other women.

At the same time, however, he stands out among our male artists because he strives to maintain some measure of reason. He experiences women artists as human beings, normally perplexed by having more than their share of difficulties.

One thoughtful male artist, while concurring in the judgment that female artists are excessively assertive, showed equal interest (no one else did) in colleagues who are so easily put on the defensive by them. He conceded that the world of art has always been a "male stronghold," but his subsequent attempts to explain male reluctance to admit the female as only a matter of habit and custom rang a little hollow. Although we may not be inclined to accept his analysis of a very complex situation, he at least makes no plea for innate male superiority. He even accepts the idea that women will eventually win through to serious artistic expression, against all odds and in the face of all interested parties:

> *As for women, they* are *aggressive. But it's hard for the male world to accept the infringement of the female world. It has gone on for ages and suddenly there is this phenomenon of the woman sticking her head in. In spite of it, there is no reason why there shouldn't be a female Rembrandt or Leonardo.*

The unequivocal assertion that women not only have talent but their potential for realizing it is as great as a man's, is in this context both bold and rare. Only one other interviewee was willing to take so strong a stand. One of our soberest and most guarded male respondents bewilderedly and fatalistically conceded that: "Some women are very good. What can you do? They're fantastically good artists." This concession to the female was unique. The man who made it was also willing to interpret feminine behavior at a much less malevolent level; here again he stood alone. His perceptions were exactly those of his confrères, but he drew opposite inferences from them:

> *Well, I think there have always been women painters, but I think today there are probably many more serious ones, because they seem to have incomes. If they didn't have an income, I don't think they could be too serious. That's because I think it's much harder for a woman to have people pay attention to her. If she makes it, she's either very rich or she's dynamic. The ones I meet are unusual, as women go. They are more alive or something; they're more intense, more dynamic. Even more than the men are. Women artists either have money or they can get their hands on it. A man can be a slob or something; he doesn't have to be anything special. The women seem to be. The ones that are just coming around are more alert, are more intense, and are even more determined.*

THE ROLE CONFLICT OF THE FEMALE ARTIST

Only one other male defected from the faultfinders; he refused to contribute to the steady salvo of carping. Instead, he offered a reasoned view of some aspects of the problems and conflicts with which the woman must contend. He also was the only respondent to compare the situations of the two sexes without introducing extraneous considerations. This man's views are of special interest because they demonstrate how a person who has worked through his own conflicts can be more understanding of problems that beset others, even those of the opposite sex. This man, over the years, has had to make a series of difficult decisions concerning his own family life and work. His verdicts were always in favor of art, but each determination was complicated, and in "working through" his own conflicts he apparently secured a deeper apprehension of the complexities surrounding everyone's life. His insight into his own struggles seems to have made it easier for him to empathize with women. He has been able to establish an emotional and intellectual distance from the problem of female artists that is unmatched by any of his colleagues:

> I've got those conflicts between being a father and a husband and being an artist, but I'm not involved with them to the extent that I would be if I were a woman and I had a husband and I had children. It's much easier for me to say, "To hell with my children." I had an argument with my wife once. She wanted me to come home and do something. And I got annoyed. And I said, "Look, you forget one thing, and that is that I'm first of all an artist." And I told her this cold turkey. So you can see what I mean. I wouldn't talk this way, I am sure, if I were a mother. As a father it's easier for me to talk this way, and play this role, you know, which I play as an artist, and put the father role and the husband role in a second-rate position. But it would be harder if I were a woman, particularly in regard to children. If I were a woman, I could tell my husband to go jump, but I don't think if I were a woman it would be so easy for me to react that way to my children.

Without embroiling ourselves in such problematic concepts as "the maternal instinct" and "mother-love," we may say that mothers are usually closest to, and therefore more emotionally involved with, their children. That male artists with families are good fathers as often as not hardly contradicts the point our respondent wishes to make.

His observations bring the dual conflict confronting the female artist into clearer focus. Thus far we have centered our discussion on her difficulties in relating to the art world. We have seen her striving for acceptance in a hostile and rejecting environment, and in her struggles often making accommodations which are irksome and unpleasant. This process generates a vicious circle, a situation in which rejection induces objectionable behavior which results in further rejection, and so on.

The second dilemma facing a gifted woman in the visual arts is more formidable and troublesome. It centers on the role conflict occasioned by being an artist as well as a wife and mother. Each role constantly demands a personal involvement and dedication seldom required in other occupations or activities. Allocating and distributing a limited amount of energy into these channels is a major source of internal struggle which cannot be resolved by mere persistence or action. It calls for a "working through" of needs and motivations which is difficult for even the most introspective and insightful individual. This conflict becomes the female artist's principal stumbling block. The attendant ambivalence is necessarily deep-seated and not easily clarified. Emotions are engaged which become difficult to sort and channelize, and they are the emotions most likely to impinge on a woman's effectiveness.

Returning for a moment to her status struggles within the art world, it is evident that here she needs little assistance in "coping." While things are made difficult for a female, her techniques for mastering external blocks are very adequate, even if they are not always admirable. Fine artists of the distaff side represent themselves articulately and effectively. Given the hostility and rejection to which they are sometimes subjected, it surprised us how little defensiveness and aggressiveness they displayed in our interviews. Correlations between what they say in an interview and their actual behavior are uncertain, but we are able to record that these women were calm and matter-of-fact, even in responding to strong criticism of their manners and morals. They were seldom provoked to a high pitch; their comments lacked the bite and sting we had been led to expect. Only on rare occasions did real bitterness and resentment seep through. Thus if the woman artist is occasionally abrasive and aggressive as charged, she can also be on her good behavior when not scandalously provoked.

Our female respondents seemingly accept their more advanced status without much ado. They believe that their artistic potential has always been as great as men's and that recent social changes have freed them to develop their talents more fully now as compared to the past: "Women are as creative, as capable of anything that men are. It may be more difficult for them, but that's all. I think that the rest is tradition." And from another celebrated female painter: "Women weren't allowed to explore their own province and now they are. I suppose it's as simple as that."

One woman even displayed unusual optimism as she surveyed the present situation:

> For one thing, more women are freer to do what they want. The other thing is that there are more people who take painting for what it is, rather than who did it. Now it's less being a woman painter and more being a painter. I mean I think the people who really look at, want, and get my pictures, don't say, "This is a lady painter." They just say, "I bought this and I like it."

This perception of the present market situation is not very common. Most women feel that they *are* singled out. But there is pervasive certainty that they have arrived as a potent force in the arts, although they are aware of not having reached the pinnacles: "We still haven't produced a De Kooning, and the best male artists are still better than the best women artists. But give us time. We've still only been around for a little while. Give us time."

They respond to specific judgments as might be expected: some are granted, some are denied, others are "explained." Since women are most commonly taxed for their "masculinity" and "aggressiveness," it is to these phenomena that they address most of their rejoinders. The most typical responses moved the question onto an intellectual plane—and away from themselves. They turned to discussions of instincts and impulses characteristic of *mankind:* "I think aggression is a normal human component. It doesn't mean anything bad, and I'm not talking about hostility. I'm not aware whether it's aggression that makes art or art is what I will. I think it's a matter of will, but there are many who would disagree."

When confronted directly with charges of "personal aggressiveness" so often made against the woman painter, they reject the stereotype. They do not see themselves as masculine, any more than they see male artists as "feminine":

> *I have not found the old stereotypes to be true. I know many women artists and I'd say I know two who have real stature. One of them is a real woman and the other has real problems. But she'd have them whether she was an artist or not. In fact, if you go through history you'll see that most women artists are very feminine looking; most of them get married and many of them have children. Many of them are even pretty sexy dames.*

Although they are used to parrying these questions, some of them are still provoked into emotionally charged responses: "I know. I'll show them. I'm not worried about them. Any artist who says that is a bad artist. I never heard it from a good artist." But then with a flash of ironic humor: "I'll make them feel very sick one day. You see, I know *one* very aggressive female artist." Following this momentary burst of feeling, she delivered a rather convincing discourse on the relationship of "masculinity-femininity" and art:

> *You can't really say that. They're not all aggressive. I know that there is an army of women artists. Many of them are wonderful people and capable. Further, art is a feminine thing. It's feminine in a sense that even a man has to have. It's not the gross strength of the masculine cult. There is a lot of tenderness in being an artist and in being susceptible to things. And this is what you mean by freshness and sensitivity, which is so required. So there is no difference, except that a man who is crudely masculine—I don't think he'd be a good artist. I don't think that a man who is crudely mas-*

> *culine could be intelligent either. But I don't think we're completely feminine. You know, there's aggressiveness in painting, so we all have some feminine qualities without being fairies. I think a man can have feminine qualities without being effeminate. Not in the least. A man can be tender. The same holds true for women. A woman can't be a man in that crude sense and still be an artist. We all have some qualities of both in us.*

While capable of explosive outbursts, then, women manage to keep their feelings about sexual discrimination pretty well in hand. The inequalities of their position obviously rankle; yet they are usually able to "smile" about them. While admitting their resentment, they want to keep it from becoming a personal issue: "I don't think there's any use in saying that a woman artist will get less money than some men artists for a painting. The most marvelous artist in the world could get less money than some, uh, buckeyes. So why make it male or female? The prices don't go that way." They treat painter-dealer relationships in much the same manner: "I suppose it depends on the artist, but actually, for the most part, it seems to be the opposite for women. Women have hung on for so long that they're aware of the problems involved at the galleries. So they don't give a hang and they are more patient. They have to be."

This, then, is their characteristic mode of response and reaction, at least in these interviews. There is some intellectualizing, some evasion, some denial, and a good deal of forthrightness. Even disdainful charges that their work is unoriginal and imitative—the most devastating criticism that can be leveled at an artist—seldom produce more than an amused smile and a shrug of the shoulders. The struggle may be wearisome and unpleasant, but they generally manage a grim detachment which suggests their recognition of a reality which is not likely to change soon, which is in many ways quite painful, but which at the same time is not overwhelming. As is so often the case where there is no great internal conflict, real pressures which come primarily from the outside do not arouse intolerable anxieties. The treatment accorded women is so obvious and blatant that they can marshal their defenses and, with some support from changing social circumstances, persist vigorously with their artistic interests. This battle between themselves and the external world is experienced now as more of an affront and a nuisance than a deterrent.

THE COSTS OF ROLE CONFLICTS

Whatever discomfort the female artist may experience with entrenched prejudice in the art world looms inconsequential when compared with those acute inner conflicts that stem from assuming the dual role of artist and wife-and-mother. It is always hard to play the role of independent professional woman while having parallel desires for complete acceptance and fulfillment as a female. Avoidance of either role solves little; the defenses needed to achieve a choice take their toll of the talented woman's energy and so remain as constantly limiting factors. Denial is of no help. The energy she expends to bridge the gap between divergent roles, or in rationalizing the absence of one or the other, is what really stirs up the greatest amount of uncertainty and confusion in the woman painter. One of our most alert and introspective female respondents gave a comprehensive picture of the emotional drain that role conflicts entail; a very articulate woman, she still had to grope as she explored and attempted to clarify the situation that she, as a painter who is also a wife and mother, faces:

> *You want to understand something about the woman artist, something which I feel very strongly about, and which I couldn't let on to myself until very, very recently. I couldn't admit it before, but now I have to admit these feelings. I can't explain them in exact detail, but there is a lot of feeling of depression, and this is carried over into my real life. Of course it is. I'm not pretending to be—I couldn't be—I'm not a gentle and passive woman. I want to be and sometimes I can be very calm and very sweet and almost gentle, but as a rule I'm not. It's not aggression either. It's a will to conquer and to understand, to be part of a living process; to make things by myself and to make things work by myself. There's a consciousness of myself as a being which*

*is not secondary, but which is quite primary. I think that I
share the same problems that other women artists have, but
I am very fortunate that my husband is a creative man and
understands my needs, understands my silences, and so on.
This is a desperate situation for most women. The creative
push makes normal relations and normal relating so difficult.*

In further discussion this woman touches a characteristic conflict.
All women artists in our group describe their more or less painful
coming to grips with the role problem, or report behavior which
clearly derives from the same conflict—though perhaps it is experienced in a less conscious or articulate way:

*After I got married, I sort of stopped painting, that is, in a
real way. It was horrible, but I just couldn't somehow paint.
Of course, that was my problem. I didn't really stop, but I
was just grinding things out and terribly slowly at that. I
worked all the time. I never had doubts about being an artist.
I just had an awfully hard time getting going.*

And despite her present eminence in the art world, this block persisted over a period of many years. From another important woman
artist:

*One thing I feel about painting and maybe all the arts,
although I couldn't speak for any other, but if you have a
family—you know painting and having children aren't unrelated—they're both very creative activities. It's very true that
they are a very difficult combination, because unless you're
a very heroic woman and can think more about yourself—
after all, ego is very involved with painting—it would be
very difficult. It was certainly very difficult for me. As soon
as I had a child, it was hard to think about painting in the
same way. For a long time I didn't paint anything. I almost
was paralyzed; I just couldn't. As soon as there is a house-
hold, there are lots of thriving egos and you're certainly
not the ego that counts the most, especially if you're the
mother. And that's what may account for the complications
the woman artist finds herself in.*

273

Other women speak in the same vein:

> *I studied some and then immediately established myself in a studio. I painted and, as I say, I was successful in the sense that I was seen as a very promising young painter. And I got married. Then there was a period, quite a long period, of no activity really. I always painted. I mean always and very hard. But it didn't . . . I didn't show very much, except occasionally in a group show. I didn't have a show until last year, actually, again. That's quite some time.*

> *The trouble is that I have wishes to deny one and the other all the time. I often have wishes never to paint again and just be female, or just be a woman who does nothing else or who has no profession. But if I try to do that for a day or two, or if I try to do nothing, I'm constantly—I guess I think too much. I just can't be that. It's not the way I am. I know that as a conscious being I need to be both. I suppose that in that sense I should consider myself to be very lucky.*

> *To be very specific, I am married and I am very much involved in my marriage. I like it. I also love housekeeping. You were in our house—well, I did it. The woman makes the house work. I do the same with the studio. I also like being and looking like and feeling like a woman. I have my hair set and I read* Vogue. *I like lunches once in a while. It isn't as if I decided to be a painter and so I gave up being a female, although I know a couple of female painters who have. At the same time, I want my pictures to be rated with any other man or woman, so that at times I have to compartmentalize facets of my days and weeks and say, "I'm not going to do this and I'm going to do that." That's where it's more difficult for a woman, because a man can be a husband, hunter, or whatever, and pursue the things he wants to pursue. For a woman to pursue the things she wants to pursue and still be a woman—well, it's a much more complicated business.*

These women thus see the family as an institution which makes great emotional demands. They recognize that routine domestic responsibilities are in the "external world" and can theoretically be turned over to mother surrogates. With adequate financial resources, the maternal care of children can be surrendered to others. But these aids cannot do away with emotional entanglement and the psychic drain that it imposes. Successful artists must be egocentric in a way which makes family involvement very complicated, especially for women. As one happily married woman artist still felt obliged to state: "But marriage and family, as far as I have seen, have a great deal to do with why so many women often have trouble. Even when you have money and someone takes care of the house and of your children and so on, the involvement is such that—you know, it's very much like the involvement you have to have with your work."

This is an inherent difficulty which no amount of external acceptance can resolve. Talent, conviction, and persistence are perhaps sufficient as the basic qualities necessary to insure some degree of fulfillment as an artist, but only as an artist. If a woman has them, she can continue her artistic pursuits even in the face of active resistance. External support and approbation are always helpful, but only if the environment is totally destructive of the individual's self-esteem can it destroy the felt need of pursuing art as a life work. But an existence as a *man* or as a *woman* can only be carved out if there is appropriate response from the environment. In our own culture the "approved" role of the woman has taken traditional forms; deviating from them, she is not likely to evoke a response conducive to the developing sense of a feminine self. Further, social pressures and cultural influences are so weighty from the very beginning of her life that deviation from the norm will of necessity induce varying amounts of inner conflict.

Despite the sexual revolution of our time, in America girls are supposed to be more docile and conforming than boys. This makes it more difficult for women to develop the necessary "ego," the self-contained and self-directed orientation toward life and work that they need as artists. To the extent that they do cultivate these qualities, they run the risk of being regarded as unfeminine. Thus the current conflict about being a woman versus being an artist has its developmental precursor in the individual woman artist's earliest years, which deepens the conflict and heightens the level of threat that it represents. Presumably, if the woman could have avoided earlier feminine role pressures, her present role difficulties would be markedly reduced. As it is, the current conflict becomes quite formidable for most women. Marriage and motherhood deflect needed energy from their work; yet not having them involves a drastic renunciation—one which can hardly be shrugged off as casually as the lack of material comforts or other gratifications and rewards. As Simone de Beauvoir has said: "In so far as a woman wishes to be a woman, her independent status gives rise to an inferiority complex; on the other hand, her femininity makes her doubtful of her professional future." [11]

The evaluation of critics we respect suggests that there is some relationship between the attenuation of this conflict and the level of recognition secured as an artist. Those of our female respondents who appear to have worked the conflict through, regardless of how they have "resolved" it, appear to have secured the greatest recognition. These are all women who discuss their conflicts with clarity and consistency, without heavy emotional loadings which would reflect defensive behavior, and yet with sufficient feeling to indicate that they have grappled with the problem, refusing to evade or merely intellectualize it. On the pessimistic side, however, the full resolution of built-in role conflict can never be attained. It waits on elimination by larger forces than any one person can muster.

In these respects there is no doubt that the man enjoys many advantages over the woman. His professional pursuits will not only be encouraged, but as he achieves, his opportunities for fulfillment *as a man* are likely to increase. His maleness will probably be reinforced by his successes. He is likely to be applauded for the total involvement of his energy and capabilities in a profession, and none of this seriously precludes other satisfactions for him, surely not those that derive from having a wife and family. As one of our artists indicated: "He can have these and still be independent. You've never heard of a man sitting at a desk or clerking so that his wife could be an artist, but it's true of a lot of women." Another points out how the male has no minute-by-minute responsibility at home, as is the case with most women:

> *I may feel some conflict about the proper husband and artist role, but I have more freedom than a woman does in the same situation. Her situation is so much worse. For instance, I can say, "Well, look, I'm going to see a show tonight. So long." But my wife's stuck, although she doesn't seem to mind it. She gave up painting when she married me. She thinks of picking it up in the future, but you know, it'll be hard.*

And further:

> *Among the artists I know who married artists, the only ones who continued painting seriously were more aggressive as females than other women: the "artist-dash-wives," that is, not "artist's wives." I mean those who have kept up their work along with their husbands. There are not too many of them, but of those that I know, perhaps a half dozen, they are all castrating women. The marriages work out okay because that's the way both of them want it. And there are usually no kids.*

Since time is precious to the artist, protracted family (especially parental) responsibilities can be a problem. If this is true for the man, it is even more true for the woman. Everyday obligations, mundane activities, taking a child to a movie, demonstrating concern for his health, his education, or even his clothes: all this may be viewed as an annoyance and a distraction. One artist declared that the simple matter of choosing a rug for his living room meant trouble for him; he was interested in the rug but resented the "drag" that picking it out placed on his time. It is thus evident that only in special, and no doubt rare, marital situations could a woman persist wholeheartedly with her work as a painter and still deal adequately with her everyday family responsibilities. It may take the "heroic woman," whatever this implies, to carry it off, as well as a partner who fully understands, endorses, and supports his wife's artistic needs and is not threatened by them. Whatever qualities her husband must possess, they are not limited to men in particular professions; husbands of women artists in our sample are professional painters, academic and literary people, as well as businessmen. It was interesting to hear each woman explain why "this type" of man was so important. To them, the work involvements of the male partner were secondary; rather, he should be the kind of husband who relates in a truly "accepting and non-competitive manner, who can see me as a separate person."

Crucial differences in feeling are associated with the woman artist's two main problems: a certain disinclination by others to accept her as an artist, and her own role conflicts. The first produces anger and aggression overlying a basic frustration, which, however, induces no overwhelming sense of impotence. On the contrary, it may increase the woman's determination to meet a challenge—"Something can be done about it." The prevailing mood is optimistic, for from her point of view a bad situation has vastly improved, and there is no reason why it should not continue to do so. By contrast, a feeling of futility often surrounds the second problem, which is experienced as a conflict with no foreseeable resolution.

9

The Negro Artist

"They live such ramshackle lives," said Simple, leaning on the bar.

"Who?" I said, leaning too.

"Most Negroes," stated Simple.

"Why do you say most *Negroes?*" I asked.

"Because I don't know anythin about most white
folks," declared Simple, "and there is many Negroes that live ramshackle lives . . ."

"But thousands of other Harlem husbands live decent lives, too, work hard, help their wives keep
the budget, and pay their rent. So I still wonder
why you say *most* Negroes lead ramshackle lives.
Why not say *some?*"

"*Some* is so many they become *most,*" said Simple.
"I am not faulting them. Most Negroes lead ramshackle lives because they got ramshackle jobs,
live in ramshackle places, and has ramshackle
hopes. That is why they is picketing City Hall
and such mansions today—to get better jobs, live
in better houses, and have some kind of little small
leeway to dream about what it might maybe be
like when we get away from these ramshackle
times in this ramshackle city in this ramshackle
world."

—LANGSTON HUGHES, 1963

I T IS significant that on close interrogation—and with all good will—our artists were unable to identify a single top-flight Negro painter or sculptor now at work in the United States. They did not dismiss the question casually or treat it cavalierly. Rather, when asked, those respondents who were completely free and spontaneous grew hesitant and even offered their comments grudgingly. Each searched with evident effort to bring someone to mind who could be given real accolades. Eventually most of them produced a name, and then felt compelled to limit its acceptability. Clearly, many would have felt more comfortable reporting that they knew accomplished Negro painters; that none exists was a unanimous judgment, rendered after much thought and with great reluctance. Those names that were called to mind reflected personal acquaintanceships rather than critical assessments.

Our overall impression is corroborated by the fact that there was absolutely no overlap in the names they gave. The only variations in opinion were those that dealt with causes and with projections of the future; evaluations of the present were in complete accord.

Considering that the Negro comprises more than 10 percent of our population, chance alone should have produced one individual with talent (which admittedly is not sufficient in and of itself), an artist who persisted and eventually achieved meaningful approval. In other fields, where their entry has been actively resisted, where the training is expensive and extends over long periods of time (for example, in grand opera), certain Negro performers have done exceedingly well. The same is true for creative writing. In composing classical music, William L. Dawson and William Grant Still have gained professional acceptance. And there is no need to detail the Negro's contributions to the entertainment world as actor, dancer, and jazz musician. There are several modern Negro poets who have justly received plaudits. But Negroes continue to be absent from the ranks of well-considered fine artists. Negroes who paint and sculpt can be named, but they do not have "acceptance" as first-line artists.

The absence of well-known or highly regarded Negroes in their milieu is viewed with self-conscious concern by our artists. One very well-known painter highlights this feeling:

> *I don't like to put myself on the record for that; on that sub-*
> *ject I don't like to step on anybody's toes, especially since*
> *I know some Negro artists pretty well.*

This underlines how charged the race issue has become even for
artists. This man had spoken bluntly and directly on a variety of
controversial issues, yet here he had qualms. He went on:

> *If I had to tell you confidentially, I'd be glad to give you*
> *my opinion. I would say that the art world leans over back-*
> *wards in order to encourage Negro painters and to give them*
> *opportunities. There have been a few who have done quite*
> *good work, but I can't say that there's anything brilliant. I*
> *think it is safe to say that the American Negro does not*
> *figure at all in the art world. There are a few Negro artists*
> *who are quite good, but none of them are very brilliant.*

There would be little disagreement on the above from our other
respondents. Their observations are in the same vein:

> *I knew B.H. for many years and he was a close friend. I used*
> *to go to his studio and apartment a lot. He was always*
> *showing me drawings of sensitivity and insight and inventive-*
> *ness, and I felt he was going to be one of our greatest*
> *painters. But he never moved up and he has never gone*
> *beyond that. He still does the same thing.*

> *Well, there are a few Negro artists, starting with J.J., but*
> *they haven't had a reputation. They aren't that famous. I*
> *don't know why, but the way they paint is very dull.*

> *I have wondered why there aren't more Negro artists. But*
> *it seems that the Negro artists I know today are the same*
> *Negro artists they were a long time ago.*

> *I don't know. I know two or three Negro painters, but*
> *they are awful painters. But I have a feeling that if I knew*
> *a lot of Negro painters, I might possibly be able to say I*
> *knew a good one.*

> *I only know personally a few Negro artists and I haven't*

been able to get any picture of the quality of art as practiced by the American Negro. You'd better ask museum people about that. My window looks out on a little corner of the art world. Well, okay, I don't know what might be at the bottom or root of this, but I don't know any really good Negro artists.

This applies not only to the present in America, but also to the past. Historically, talented Negroes have appeared throughout the last century, and occasionally they have received a measure of recognition and acceptance. Margaret Butcher, in a sympathetic treatment of the Negro in American culture, points this out while emphasizing the extreme difficulties he has encountered:

> *The task of the early Negro artist was to prove to a skeptical world that the Negro could be an artist. That world did not know that the African had been a capable artist in his native culture and that, independent of European culture, he had built up his own techniques and traditions. It had the notion that for a Negro to aspire to the fine arts was ridiculous. Before 1865, any Negro man or woman with artistic talent and ambition confronted an almost impassable barrier. Yet, in a long period of trying apprenticeship, several Negro artists surmounted the artificial obstacles with sufficient success to disprove but not dispel the prevailing prejudice.*[1]

She also cites specific cases in which individuals did gain a degree of appreciation for their work, including placement in several important museums. But the achievement and recognition missing now and in the past imply that a body of work was created and that many men contributed to it. One must question why, in that tradition, no Negro artist has attained much standing, despite his undeniable share of artistic potential. The almost total oppression the Negro suffered during the eighteenth and nineteenth centuries in America has been well documented; that he produced no great visual art under those conditions is self-explanatory. The question must be why, when his opportunities are so much greater, have his contributions to art failed to keep pace with his attainments in music, the dance, and literature?

The present limited achievement of Negro painters clearly does not reflect racial bias among artists. On the contrary, their social conscience and general orientation are such that they would be gratified to have the Negro "make it." But the painters have an even stronger artistic conscience by whose standards Negro art has failed to measure up. The verdict rendered may seem harsh, but it is an evaluation, not just a feeling—one made so consistently that it deserves careful hearing. Some artists do not despair of the future: "I think there's going to be a breakthrough, and it's going to be quite astonishing. I mean I really expect something—just as something happened in jazz. I really think that something is going to happen."

But others do not share this feeling: "I'm a little dubious about their being on the verge of anything. I know the line, but I'm dubious. There's too much involved in background for them right now." They see too many talented Negroes fall by the wayside. Of those they know, few if any seem to them to hold much promise: "I've had Negro students who were very good. But only one of them is likely to become a painter. And all the other Negro students have turned to teaching school." This observation might tempt one to conclude that they founder on economic shoals, that they lack necessary financial backing. This is not supported by the evidence. Some who have financial resources give up and others continue to paint; some who lack the needed funds still are willing to undergo all manner of hardship in their efforts to pursue an art "career." Evidently talent and persistence by themselves will not produce great painting.

THE NEGRO'S DILEMMA

The Negro painter has always suffered more than his share of rebuffs and rejections; for example, he previously was not shown by reputable galleries. This situation has changed. With today's inflated market, many galleries are mercenary enough to exhibit anyone who has a chance of being sold. Cooperatives formed by younger artists take in Negro members. Opportunities have opened in art at least as much as in most other fields. Richard Bardolph, in *The Negro Vanguard,* overdraws the picture as he gives his buoyant view of the Negro's situation in art:

> *Indeed, the sheer number of younger artists—exhibiting a notable vigor, wide stylistic variety, and a growing preference for non-racial themes—is perhaps even more newsworthy than are the achievements of those whom we have cited as examples. The group has in recent years found ready opportunities for one-man shows, for gallery affiliations, and for entering competitions . . .*[2]

This idyllic picture is not remotely related to the reality of either the Negro or the white painter, but there is evidence of markedly increased opportunity. Bardolph introduces his cheerful statement with a list of Negro artists who, in his opinion, are on their way to well-deserved recognition. Except for an occasional name known as early as the thirties, not one has thus far gained meaningful acceptance. It is too early to close the books on these people since they are still working, but hopes for their success are not high.

If the picture of available opportunities has any substance—and it seems to—there is even more reason for pessimism. If the few known Negro painters and sculptors began their work thirty or forty years ago, when conditions were almost impossible, then improved opportunities have had no discernible effect. There are artists from other minority groups who began to work well after World War II, with no greater talent or opportunity, who have already received critical acclaim. It would be easy to dismiss this comparison as further proof that our most submerged and deprived minority is totally victimized. Yet we know of important figures in the art world who have tried and failed to bring a Negro protégé to success.

When we consider contemporary art styles, the problem deepens. As one artist puts it:

> *Now that I've often thought of. Why in the United States in the last twenty years are there so few Negro painters and sculptors? It would seem to me that the particular kind of art that is being done these days . . . the kind of exuberance*

> *and spontaneity and so on . . . is the kind of thing which*
> *we assume in today's art and which the Negro seems to*
> *have. So why a Negro hasn't gone into it, I don't know.*
> *It's a mystery to me.*

If the average oppressed Negro is correctly seen at this moment as a person who still expresses feelings more easily than he performs intellectual tasks, it should be easier for him to function within the modern art world than it was at other times when more formalized academic requirements prevailed. But regardless of the causes, his work fails to meet exacting critical standards. Since lack of native endowment is ruled out by people who know Negro artists, we need to look for psychological, social, and cultural factors to explain this state of affairs.

Our artists developed several interesting hypotheses, along with the expectable and more obvious explanations, as they attempted to fathom the Negro's relative artistic stalemate. Their ideas may be placed in four inter-connected groupings that all relate to one major theme—the Negro's miserable position in American society. We treat them separately only for convenience.

The ideas most frequently expressed have to do with Negro impoverishment—both economic and socio-cultural. They explore this condition as it influences the Negro's educational experiences and his artistic endeavors. The second cluster of ideas refers to the historical effects of forcible separation from an integrated cultural heritage, unaccompanied by any substitute or replacement of consequence. The third deals with certain motivational factors presumably operating inside the Negro painter, and the way in which they influence the content, and ultimately effect the quality, of his productions. The fourth group of speculations deals with the personality of the Negro artist, especially as it turns on specific family relationships branching out from the total pattern of American society.

ECONOMIC AND SOCIO-CULTURAL POVERTY

The largest number of suggestions focus on economics. These responses were to be expected, but they fail to provide new insights

—which in no way minimizes the grim reality of the Negro's past and present economic privation. He has always been employed to a vastly disproportionate extent in unstable, poorly paid positions. Through years of presumed progress, his relative economic status (vis-à-vis the white man) has remained static or actually deteriorated. In 1949 the income of the median Negro family was $1,650 as compared to $3,232 for the median white family.[3] In 1953 it was reported that:

> *The money income gap between the white and Negro populations is closing for the urban populations but shows the usual differentials in the rural populations. "Half as much" continues to represent the relative family income of the Negro group when compared with the white.*[4]

In 1962, Kretch, Crutchfield, and Ballachey, using United States government surveys, showed that in 1959, 41.2 percent of all occupations fell into semi-skilled and unskilled categories, and in 1961, 45 percent of all family incomes fell under $4,000.[5] Since the occupational level of the average Negro is mostly that of these two lowest categories, with their poor pay, it is simple to estimate just how little comparative improvement he has enjoyed. If anything the gap has widened, and not only for lower class Negroes. It holds even for the middle class. When E. Franklin Frazier's book, *Black Bourgeoisie,* was reissued in 1962, the author explicitly stated that he saw no need to revise its contents. In 1955 he had asserted that the Negro middle class held an inconsequential economic position in the United States, and he felt that nothing had happened in the intervening years to change its status.[6]

To postulate, then, that the poverty of the Negro has been a critical factor affecting every aspect of his existence is to take a reasonable, indeed an unassailable, position. It is thus not surprising that so many artists' initial observations were along these lines. They gave greatest recognition to the Negro's limited resources and his unfavorable market position. They also emphasized how psychologically exhausting the struggle to surmount these obstacles must be for him:

> *He's more liable to become a writer because a ream of*

paper and several pencils are an awful lot cheaper than about an acre of canvas and all of that expensive chemical paint. You know, one thing that people don't realize is how much it costs to paint a painting. To buy a good piece of linen and enough paint to cover it . . . I've known painters many a time to sell a painting for less than it cost them to paint it.

Yes, I doubt if anyone could indicate a good Negro painter. You can suggest that the reason is that since they are the most submerged part of American society, they just haven't been exposed to the necessary stimuli. To me that seems like a rationalization. To me . . . it's energy. You have to compete to achieve simple status if you're a Negro. All one's energy is used up to achieve this little thing. It absorbs everything else. You're so low that everything goes into getting up.

I still think it's money—security, wives and children. And I see that they have to pay double for everything. They couldn't rent this place and I know it for a fact. The girl across the street is a Negro, and when she came they doubled the rent on her—and in a slum neighborhood like this. It's money.

Yet the fact is that many Negroes are painting, and regardless of the source they do find material means to continue their work. Whether it be from scholarships, family or mate, or by dint of their own outside work efforts, and regardless of how much more "expensive" life may be for them, many Negroes can "afford" to pursue their painting (in the purely economic sense); quite a few of them are motivated to do so. Further, their financial lot does not differ materially from that of their white counterparts. Thus economic reasons, plausible as they may seem, cannot stand by themselves when closely scrutinized.

Other comments in this area follow anticipated lines. They direct attention to, and deplore, the Negro's inadequate educational opportunities, his limited exposure to art at home and in the community, the traditional resistances to high culture found in lower class families, and so on. They also emphasize the relationship between these disadvantages and his low socio-economic status. All of this is indisputable, but it does not get to the core of the problem. Other ethnic groups can point to individuals with similarly meager backgrounds who become artists of stature. The Negro's difficulties may be twice compounded when compared with those of others, but their immediate relevance to his frustration as an artist is not easily demonstrated. Greater support for this hypothesis might have been mustered under earlier, more extreme conditions; paucity of money, education, and "culture" were not barriers to the current generation of successful painters.

THE INFLUENCE OF HISTORY

After these stereotyped responses, our artists made other and perhaps more helpful proposals. They attempted to assess the effect of the sharp break in the Negro's cultural traditions on his present situation as an artist. A disastrous disruption obviously took place during the period when the Negro was brought to this country as a slave and then found himself blocked from practicing his craft skills on cotton and rice plantations. This predicament was ably sketched by one of our painters:

> *The Negro came to this country from areas with rich plastic art traditions. But within a generation the memory of this was wiped out, because he was not granted free time on the plantation to pursue his native crafts. Either he was working for the plantation owner or he was eating or sleeping. And by the time the new generation was born, even the memory of that artistic tradition was gone.*

Or, as summed up by Margaret Butcher:

> *We will never know, and cannot estimate, how much technical African skill was blotted out in America. The hardships of cotton- and rice-field labor, the crudities of the hoe, the ax, and the plow, certainly reduced the typical Negro hand to a gnarled stump incapable of fine craftsmanship even if artistic incentives, materials, and patterns had been available.*[7]

The importance of this gulf between present-day Negro painters and their original artistic heritage is hard to evaluate, but it cannot be dismissed. The less so when we consider how effectively the Negro uses his musical and verbal talents today. Those talents were in many ways enhanced by life on the plantation. When the Negro was deprived of his craft outlets, he turned to song, verse, and story for expression and relief. The intolerable conditions in the compounds and at work may have been made more bearable by songs and chants, and they were utilized to the maximum.

That the Negro has by now made a rich contribution in these areas is generally accepted; that he has given relatively little to the visual arts is also fairly clear. Yet there is no reason to assume that his graphic and plastic ability is less pronounced. Seeing fine art (at any rate, its creation) as an aspect of culture that in America has thus far eluded the Negro is more realistic. His music and literature not only come from himself, but he has always had, so to speak, "permission" to use them. In fact, though with some condescension, he has even been encouraged to do so. The same does not apply to fine art.

Yet how much the hiatus in graphic expression during the period of slavery can be directly related to the Negro's present art failures, a century or more later, is regarded by many as problematic. Frazier, for instance, has suggested that the African heritage of the Negro is no longer a pertinent force on the American scene. One of our artists agreed:

> *That kind of reasoning doesn't make any sense to me because by the time R.F. was born—he was a guy I went to school with—his father was a professional person and so on. He is about as related to Africa as . . . I mean, I am a Jew, at least I was told I was and people act as if I am, but anybody who would make a story out of that . . . It may be sensible, it may be possible, but I don't know that it really is. African art was related to a religious life and a village life and things like that, and we don't have them anymore.*

Another respondent suggested that the graphic arts have deteriorated even in Africa: "The work of those people was terrific, but they seemed to stop doing it. Nobody seems to know why. Apparently there's some connection with their contact with our civilization. But why that should stop their creative work I don't know. Maybe the missionaries convinced them that they shouldn't make any fetishes." This may sound flippant, but it is conceivable that the thoroughly disruptive circumstances of their contact with our civilization robbed both the African and the American Negro of the context within which their art was embedded. Confronted in America for so long with a demoralizing, raw, and painful reality must have had more than a temporarily numbing effect.

But this need not be an irreversible phenomenon. One artist reported on a recent experiment in one of the world's most backward and deprived Negro nations. In 1944 an attempt was made in Haiti to encourage interest and work in art. Our respondent felt that this effort had led to an "artistic renaissance of amazing importance. It gives you an idea of what tremendous talent lies in people, if given a chance." Taking this argument one step further, he assumed that as the Negro bettered himself and had greater opportunities to engage in artistic activity, he would eventually move into the front rank of Western art. But even with high optimism, so bewildering are the Negro's present difficulties that this artist hedged his forecast with a final qualification: "Certain groups, either racially or nationally, have tended to concentrate their creative energies in one area more than others. It builds up historically and just keeps rolling that way." This comment suggests that since the Negro has gained eminence in music and literature, his momentum will carry him along further in those areas, and therefore he is less likely to move into fine art.

The fallacy in this argument is that a significant number of Negroes show artistic talent and demonstrate an unflagging interest in painting and sculpting. The purely historical argument is thus insufficient, although it is not irrelevant. Our speculations lead us to believe that while discontinuity was initially a factor of some importance, there are more immediate problems which now interfere with the Negro's development as an artist.

PSYCHOLOGICAL PROBLEMS

Artists are convinced that an important part of the Negro's predicament lies in his inescapable preoccupation with himself as a Negro.

They see that he is unable to separate his existence as a member of an oppressed group from his art. He is unable to transcend his immediate life and enter competently into artistic developments of broader, let alone universal, significance. Painting, more than other art forms, seems to require liberation from specific aspects of experience. This need may have become more acute in the last three decades as art moved away from figurative content and "messages." Religious and social themes were of course used validly by great artists of the past. Today, extraneous preoccupations, commitments, and allegiances which compete for his dedication seem to prevent the painter from gaining mastery of his talent. By being so inevitably preoccupied with himself as a Negro, the Negro painter finds himself in an at least momentarily insoluble situation.

Surrounded by a brutal reality, it is virtually impossible for him to forget that he is a Negro. The reality is too much with him; it confronts him wherever he goes, relentlessly imposed on him by the ingroup and the outgroup. He cannot realistically escape it. To "transcend" this state would entail the massive use of denial, a psychological defense which is incompatible with the honesty, directness, and openness to experience which are prerequisites for any creative artist. To do so would entail avoiding just that reality which is continuously with him. But when he fails to utilize this defense, the harrowing truth of his social situation demands that he deal with it at all times.

Faced with this dilemma, two possible solutions present themselves. The Negro may try to dissociate part of himself while he paints, a reaction which will impoverish and limit his painting, because in this process he also cuts off a vital part of his emotional life. Alternatively, he can depict his Negro experience—and protest. He then uses his painting to resolve conscious conflicts and concerns; but in his intense preoccupation with content, he ends with stereotyped forms of expression. Because he is intensely involved with a single truth, the many levels of truth which are present in great art fail to materialize. As long as the Negro is caught up in this vicious circle his art will suffer: "As long as the Negro paints as a Negro he is doomed to disappointment." This is not a dilemma of the Negro's choosing; it is the consequence of his extreme social subordination.

In this connection, one artist raises a pertinent point. Immersed in problems of station and status, the Negro has had forced upon him a special concern about color. This refers not only to his darkness, but also to color shading within his group. The importance of color variance is impressed upon him as soon as he is capable of noting it. Perhaps conscious preoccupation with color coming too soon interferes with its spontaneous use. Our respondent also speculates that this was a major bogey for the female artist. He attributes the present proliferation of gifted women painters (considered more fully in Chapter Eight) to a new conception of woman's role, and consequently to a new pattern in her upbringing. Women are reared today with much less emphasis on homemaking and the attendant interest in "things going together," colors matching, and so on. This, in conjunction with their other new freedoms, permits them to deal with color spontaneously and "naively," which "frees" them as painters; previously few of them could rise above "commercial art." The Negro, still color-bound, may be inhibited from using his talent with the innocence and spontaneity that are called for.

Returning to our main theme: pressures in American society are such that the Negro at present finds it impossible to divorce his personal identity from his sense of belonging to a particular group. To go even further, his group identity is constantly forced on him, and he must make an heroic effort to evolve a separate and independent image in a society which so relentlessly deals with him through stereotypes. The most crucial characteristics of the successful artist are his sense of self, of separateness and intactness. Should he fail to attain this level of maturity and individuation (a failure which is increasingly common in our culture, even among whites), his development as an artist will be stunted.

It is of passing interest that Negro painters who have managed to gain some recognition in the past were often expatriates (for example, Henry Tanner, Richmond Barthe, E. Simms Campbell, Ollie Harrington, and William H. Johnson). By leaving the country they sought to define their identities in terms more differentiated than color. James Baldwin has written: "I left America because I doubted my ability to survive the fury of the color problem here. I wanted to prevent myself from becoming *merely* a Negro; or, even, merely a Negro writer." [8] Existence in America was intolerable because discrimination made it impossible to escape a stereo-typic group identity. In leaving the country, however, Negro artists often discovered that the problem had become internalized. Again quoting Baldwin:

> *"You can take the child out of the country," my elders were fond of saying, "but you can't take the country out of the child." They were speaking of their own antecedents, I supposed; it didn't anyway, seem possible that they could be warning me; I took myself out of the country and went to Paris. It was there I discovered that the old folks knew what they had been talking about.*[9]

If he stays within the United States, the Negro's choice lies between adopting a "white" identity or fitting into the white stereotype of a Negro. There is little chance for him to develop and define himself simply as a "man." Erik Erikson describes the outcome:

> *But what if the "milieu" is determined to let live only at the expense of a permanent loss of identity?*
>
> *Consider, for example, the chances for a continuity of identity in the American Negro child. I know a colored boy who, like our boys, listens every night to Red Rider. Then he sits up in bed, imagining that he is Red Rider. But the moment comes when he sees himself galloping after some masked offenders and suddenly notices that in his fantasy Red Rider is a colored man. He stops his fantasy. While a small child, this boy was extremely expressive, both in his pleasures and in his sorrows. Today he is calm and always smiles; his language is soft and blurred; nobody can hurry him or worry him—or please him. White people like him.*[10]

Confirmation of Erikson's assessment can be found elsewhere. In 1949, Charles E. Thompson prepared a modified set of Thematic Apperception Test cards with Negroes, rather than whites, in the pictorial material. It was assumed that identification would be easier when the stimulus material more nearly reflected the "culture" of the individual. Clinical practice did not support this hypothesis. As Erikson suggested, when the Negro was confronted with a reminder of his condition, instead of developing more fantasy, as had been anticipated, he was more restricted. He was stifled rather than encouraged and freed.[11]

Thus when the Negro begins to paint, he fails to move in the direction that his artistic sense might normally take him; he is too strongly moved by his external involvements. This is the judgment made by our personally accepting but aesthetically critical artists. They have a sympathetic understanding of many difficulties experienced by the Negro painter, but they are impatient with him as an artist. These artists resent the dissipation of real talent. These rather caustic comments are typical:

> *They are very boring to me. I mean that kind of thing. When they paint, they seem to use it. A lot of the ones who are terrible use it as vehicles for their racial suffering, so that becomes very boring. I don't mean that the idea, the whole business of racial suffering is boring, but the way they do it is very dull. They use certain kinds of painting clichés. They get so hung up on the story that they don't devote any time to painting. After all, painting is about painting, too. You know, you have to fix color, you have to put it down in a certain way; you have to leave this, color this. Those are the problems you should deal with in painting.*

A very keen and sensitive artist, after a passionate defense of the Negro in which she detailed his disadvantages and expressed her high hopes for his future, still concluded by saying:

> *And another thing is that when they do become artists, they have a tendency to lean over backward, to be a little slick, to make up to the stereotyped kind of thing. They become commercial artists or just slick artists. This is terrible to say, you know, as if there is some absolute way of telling, but I do think that this is the way it is.*

These are not impulsive statements; they are made by people interested in seeing the Negro succeed. They are also the observations of those who cannot permit themselves to temporize in their judgments of art. Other members of our group, while perhaps more circumspect and guarded in their discussions, picture things in the same way:

You can construct a theory that where there's no hope of acceptance . . . a Negro sees he would be doing good to get a good factory job; he gets floor-sweeping or cleaning out the toilets or something, the very worst you can get. If he can hope to be an automatic lathe operator, that would be a great promotion, and so it may be that the aspiration to be an artist is too high. To move into the middle class and be accepted into the cultured world, if not as a social equal per se, as a producer of socially admired work like painting, to be taken into that society is not easy. And so it's my idea that if there's nothing operating against them because they are Negroes, they will come up against the same problems as everyone else. And what is the normal problem for any man, they take as a special problem for them, because they are Negroes and they have special problems about it. It gets into their work, too.

Well, there are a lot of Negro painters. I go over to the Cedar Bar, to the roots of things, and see them. I think a lot of them have talent, but I think they have lots of problems; many more problems than most, because I think they're more confused about being an artist. They're not willing to do the same thing like their white counterpart. I think they want more attention or something. I think they do all the right things, but they have some problems outside of all that. Maybe people don't encourage them. Maybe they're very good. I don't know.

The Negro in America is a very different kind of man or person from the Negro in Africa. The Negro in Africa had a background of primitive compulsions or impulsions which are still clear so far and were expressed particularly plastically. Modeling or sculpturing or carving. The Negro in America . . . I don't think it's anything to do with painting, but so far they haven't exploited anything of interest. So far they haven't done anything that I've seen that's worth looking at.

THE BURDEN OF PERSONALITY

This continuing insistence on the Negro's inadequacy as an artist involves no disparagement of his natural gifts. Artists view the Negro's relative failure in art as symptomatic of his total condition and not as an inherent quality of "negritude." But while they ascribe primacy to his social environment and history, they see a basic fault transmitted to and now lying within the Negro artist himself. Artists suggest, directly and indirectly, that the Negro who attempts to paint lacks requisite personality characteristics for success. They make these generalizations with different samplings of Negro painters in mind, so that the overlapping of judgments appears significant:

> *They are Negro and they have problems. Now this guy applied for membership in the cooperative gallery and this is a bitchy proposition to get. A dozen artists will vote on the eligibility of another artist they never heard of before, and about twenty-nine times out of thirty, it's thumbs down. And it isn't always on the criteria of quality. It's simple, sad, true. But this guy did get accepted. Now, maybe it was a kind of reverse bias, because I didn't think he was that good. But he was good enough and he got in. In a cooperative thing everyone has obligations. You have to put money in, you have to spend time, go to meetings, and you have to be involved in problems of advertising, paying the printer, the landlord, buying new light bulbs, and so on. He seemed not to want to bother with these things. Nobody said anything to him, but he finally fell behind in everything and then quit.*

> *I think you have to have a lot of vitality to be an artist, and American Negro men who want to be artists are, by and large, a very sad crew. They are the results of a matriarchy.*

These blunt characterizations sound so like the stereotyped charges commonly leveled at the Negro that at first one might be inclined to dismiss them as such. But while other artists are less plain-spoken, they make similar points. The proposition then must be either that these painters share common prejudices or that there is some validity to their observations. The latter possibility merits further scrutiny.

For a Negro child, the specific tone and quality of relationships with key adults in his life assume paramount importance. Family histories, while they embody social conditions, may, in all their particularity, have a more immediate bearing on the individual Negro artist and his plight. The potential circularity of this argument is evident, since social pressures contrive to influence the conduct of Negro parents, and so on. But since our data indicate that parent-child interaction is relevant to artistic achievement, such a hypothesis must hold for the Negro artist as well.

There is no single Negro personality. Negroes come from a range of backgrounds and, as they have varying opportunities and experiences, differences appear among them. But certain possibly debilitating factors, not found to the same degree in other groups, cut across the boundaries of all Negro families. Their common preoccupation with color has already been discussed. Group-oriented reactions, especially as they reveal and reflect an individual sense of isolation and confusion about identity, may be added. Two more generalized items must be considered: the structure of interactions found in typical Negro families, and the social patterns that result therefrom.

One striking feature of our artists' families, it will be recalled, was their exceptional state of intactness. Parents seemed to show a genuine desire for their children to achieve self-fulfillment. At first the mother appears to have provided her young child with "unlimited" acceptance. Then the budding artist developed a relationship with his father (or a male substitute) who was usually concerned with creative activity. This paternal figure was gratified by artistic expression and accomplishment and supported exploration, satisfaction of curiosity, and the quest for knowledge; without being competitive or threatening, he approved the child's aspirations. The mother provided her child's emotional foundation; the male encouraged the child to utilize his strength and pointed the direction in which it might best be expressed. If there was pressure on the child for performance, it was for the child's benefit, not the parents'. The child could then develop with a strong sense of worthwhileness, a capacity to act, and the indispensable inner assurance that his actions would be accepted as meaningful.

We know that it is imprudent to deal with stereotypes and averages when pondering the development of so deviant a group as these artists. Yet a particular subculture (even a contraculture) may be examined in terms of its particular kind of deviation. The pertinent literature suggests that certain characteristic Negro family structures exist, and their organization is such that fruitful artistic development is unlikely to evolve from them.

Sociologists have identified several different Negro family patterns, using geographic, economic, vocational, and educational criteria, but they all have certain common features. In each case the mother is the dominant force within the home; the male is subordinate regardless of his accomplishments in the outside world. While there is a corresponding phenomenon in contemporary white culture, often described as "Momism," the typical Negro family cannot be adequately tied to that concept, since quite different historical and social factors are involved. It is also significant that Negro family structures, more than most, are molded by brutally coercive external pressures greater than those which would cause them to evolve spontaneously under changing social conditions.

We are too close to a host of social changes to assess their possible consequences for the Negro, although it is reasonable to assume that if there are genuine shifts in his position (and what else can the Negro Revolution mean?), eventual alterations in Negro parental roles and attitudes will follow. But until that time, Frazier's assessment of the Negro family structure still seems authentic:

> *The important position of the mother in the Negro family in the United States has developed out of the exigencies of life in the new environment. In the absence of institutional controls, the relationship between mother and child has become the essential bond in the family, and the woman's economic position has developed in her those qualities which are associated with a "matriarchal" organization.*[12]

This matriarchal role originated on the plantations where, for basically biological reasons, only the mother was a consistently available figure. The plantation owner reinforced this pattern by acknowledging the importance of the mother-child relationship; he rarely separated a mother from her child. The father's role received little consideration and he was moved about at will; consequently the father became a shadowy and unpredictable figure. The Negro family has evolved with a present and predictable mother as contrasted with an undependable and seldom available father. This has been a prevailing pattern since the Civil War, one variously reinforced by social and economic conditions.

Today there are large numbers of Negro families where the woman is the actual or nominal head. This ascendancy often results from her more favorable position in our economy as a consistent provider. The male, because of his weak social and vocational situation, has dealt with his subordination in a variety of ways, but few of these engender confidence in him or in the stability of his role. His influence in the family is largely determined by the needs of the woman: "Because of the precarious hold which women of this class have on men, their attitudes alternate between one of subordination to secure affection and one of domination because of their greater economic security than their spouses." [13] In this type of family, "Negro babies often receive sensual satisfactions which provide them with enough oral and sensory surplus for a lifetime, as clearly betrayed in the way they move, laugh, talk, sing." [14] These always come from the mother or her substitute (usually some member of the extended family).

This pattern is most characteristic of the lower class family (which includes the greatest number of Negro families). Unfortunately for the Negro child, his emotional stimulation comes to him under the stress of tremendous economic and social uncertainty. It is also cut off quite sharply as soon as the adults can demand independent behavior from him, and while adjusting to these new circumstances his support is at a minimum. Interested male concern is almost never available. This constellation, practically devoid of a guiding male figure, is not likely to encourage the growth of artistic talent.

While this is the commonest pattern—and it corresponds to the stereotype held by so many—other patterns have emerged through the years. Of these, the one most typical can be seen wherever a

Negro father gains recognition at home by acquiring some material wealth which he applies to improving the family's social position. In this case mother and father work together on a cooperative and "democratic" basis, although it is the mother who makes "decisions." Responsibilities are divided equally, but the motivations behind family cooperation are troublesome. They do not reflect healthy compatibility as much as they represent complementary interests in social mobility: "To be respectable and to 'get up' in the world are two of the main ambitions . . . ." [15] Here the child often fails to receive even the initial stimulation noted before. The mother is too concerned with cleanliness, propriety, and adherence to white standards. These parents make strict, although not necessarily harsh, demands on their children for early accomplishment and achievement; they often make heavy sacrifices so that their children can receive advanced training and education. Unfortunately, little of this is for the child; it is all enacted in the service of mobility. There is an attempt to live out personal frustrations through the child, who is perceived as an extension or a reflection of the parents.

The negative effects on a child systematically reared in accordance with this newer pattern of parental behavior are dramatic. Children of ability are immobilized by the weight of the many demands made on them. Demands are inherent in whatever the child receives, and separateness of parent and child cannot realistically develop. Since implicit demands are present from the outset, the parent-child relationship takes on an aggressive coloration; not even a warm symbiosis can develop. Confidence and an individuated identity, so greatly needed by the artist, have even less room for growth in this situation than under the consistently deprived conditions of lower class life. At least the child of that life, when he does manage to achieve against enormous odds, can experience his accomplishment as his own, as an individual who has wrested his chances for success from stubborn and resistant circumstances. The child of a mobile Negro family has few outlets for constructive opposition; he can preserve his separateness by resisting external pressure through passive negativism—thus forgoing realistic outlets—or he can submit to parental pressure. He then "succeeds" on parental terms and surrenders his individual identity.

The picture drawn by Frazier of the Negro upper class family makes it abundantly clear why no superlative painter emerges from that setting:

> *Since the Black Bourgeoisie live largely in a world of make-believe, the masks which they wear to play their sorry roles conceal the feelings of inferiority and of insecurity and the frustrations that haunt their inner lives. . . . Despite their attempts to escape from real identification with the masses of Negroes, they cannot escape the mark of oppression any more than their less-favored kinsmen. In attempting to escape identification with the black masses, they have developed a self-hatred . . .[16]*

In this stratum, the preoccupation with race, even more than status, destroys free interchange between parent and child. The parent hopes that his child will not suffer humiliations similar to his own just because of his color. He gives his child advantages so that he will not have to be a "Negro"; at worst, he invests his child with an obsession about, as well as a hatred of, himself and his color. This then becomes the most hamstrung of all Negro groups. Not only are self-defeating preoccupations systematically fostered; so is the denial of reality. As a result, both parents and children are pathetically unhappy. The male, regardless of his material success, is a cowed and subordinate figure in the family. Mother represents "her" family in the world, whether she works or not, and there is so much concern for material emblems of attainment that family relationships tend to be unidimensional, with a minimum of normal emotional interaction.

With minor variations, investigators agree on these Negro family patterns. None of them, allowing for the reasonable degree of deviation expected from any group norm, contains the elements which have been found to lead to the most effective use of artistic talent. Considering the family patterns of successful artists, the Negro is deprived in all respects. "Fathers" who "encourage" activity in the arts are almost completely absent, except insofar as they are "remote" idols (for example, Richard Wright and James Baldwin) —and even these have arrived on the scene only recently.

Independently, and on the basis of his psychoanalytic investigations, Erikson has outlined the three types of Negro identities which emerge from prevailing family and community experiences; he also shows how influential the white majority is in the process of molding the Negro's experience of himself. The three types of identity which Erikson differentiates evolve within the setting of the peculiar white-Negro relationship: (1) mammy's oral-sensual 'honey-child'—tender, expressive, rhythmical; (2) the evil identity of the dirty, anal-sadistic, phallic-rapist 'nigger'; and (3) the clean, anal-compulsive, restrained, friendly, but always sad 'white man's Negro.'" [17] Various combinations of these three patterns are also found. Erikson demonstrates how the Negro is imprisoned by each of these identifications, both from within and from without, thus markedly reducing his opportunities for establishing a healthier and more integrated identity: "The Negro, of course, is only the most flagrant case of an American minority which by the pressure of tradition and the limitation of opportunity is forced to identify with its own evil identity fragments, thus jeopardizing whatever participation in an American identity it might have earned." [18]

Negro and white alike act on the basis of these stereotypes, often without questioning their correctness or appropriateness. Americans have been described as suffering from confused identities—the fine flower of their polyglot and variegated cultural heritage. In the case of the American Negro, the identity confusion has been thrust upon him, and he is still struggling to separate himself from its inroads. He is not likely to accomplish this task until society permits him a different (and more differentiated) public image, and eventually a more independent personal image. Indeed, the process is probably underway. Bleak though the present situation seems, it should be remembered that almost three centuries elapsed before white American artists produced a really distinctive style, something all their own. Despite the Negro's limited accomplishments, his future in visual art is certainly not without promise.

ADDENDUM

Our thesis that the talented Negro will emerge as an *artist* when he begins to function within a separate, "non-aligned" identity and to express his individual aesthetic responses, receives affirmation in a

recent *Art News* article, published after the completion of this manuscript. There Charles Childs lavishly praises the work of Romare
Bearden, an abstractionist who has now turned ". . . to images of
his native Harlem for a spectacular group of new collages." Bearden's stand and stance as an artist intrigue us:

> *I create social images within the work so far as the human
> condition is social. I create social identities so far as the
> subjects are Negro, but I have not created protest images
> [emphasis added] because the world within the collage, if it
> is authentic, retains the right to speak for itself.*[19]

As a Negro-American artist, Bearden's credo is simply, "I am a man
concerned with truth . . ." who has developed "along lines that were
extremely personal," and he elaborates:

> *What this meant, of course, was my desire to have my ex-
> pression individually understood. Subject matter, I find, is of
> no importance, except of course when it means a great deal
> to an artist who can transform it into something personal . . .
> something universal. If subjects were just a matter of race
> and identity, then one could not have affinities with anything
> other than one's own culture.*[20]

Here is an articulate statement from a promising painter, which
supports the hypotheses developed in this chapter.

10

The Artist: Inside or Outside?

The fact of the matter is that I have almost reached the end as a citizen and as a writer. And so have all the writers and artists (including the noisiest of opportunists) who, like myself, had joined the Party twenty or thirty years ago and went through the millstones of reality. . . .

Up to now, here at home, all of us, good, bad, and indifferent, have done well and lived well. We were generously cared for from the day our first slim book of verse was published to the solemn moment when we were given a national funeral. Take myself as an example: unlike so many of my fellow citizens, I have no material worries to speak of and the daily routine of life does not tire me out so much as the great majority of others. . . . We live comfortably since enough money can buy almost everything. . . .

Some of us hold high orders of merit and we are assured every day that, together with the working class, we are the pillars of our society. In other words, we are systematically corrupted by those in power, and we know it.

In return, we are expected to perform. And we do, in various ways and with varying degrees of intellectual dishonesty.

—ANONYMOUS CZECHOSLOVAKIAN AUTHOR, 1964

. . . a proud art which is no one's servant, posing all its problems from within.

—EDGAR WIND, 1964

I N THE folk and feudal past, status tended to be ascribed at birth and could not be achieved thereafter. Originally kinship determined one's position, and later on, in a more differentiated society, one's occupation. For approximately eleven hundred years of European civilization, throughout the Middle Ages, cottagers usually begat cottagers and noblemen sired noblemen, even as tinsmiths were the sons and fathers of tinsmiths. Vocational choice hardly existed outside the Church, where celibacy acted as a bar to legitimate succession.

As the feudal order dissolved, fixed estates, or *stande,* gave way to permeable classes. One important consequence of this revolutionary transformation has been (and is) a certain state of occupational uncertainty. Theoretically, in any of its many manifestations, the class system implies that individual ability will supersede hereditary descent. The system is open, if never in fact wide open or absolutely porous: a child of the humblest origins may legally aspire to anything. What he may realistically hope to attain is another matter about which his society will give him little guidance.

For most of us in contemporary society there is no general expectation that we will follow in our fathers' footsteps. How can the farmer train his son when there is no need for farmers? The typographer whose union used to make special provision for his offspring can only hope that he will survive the onslaught of automation. So with the industrial operative and the white-collar worker. Vocational choice, recently expanded to include a thousand possibilities, is currently contracting as one traditional occupation after another disappears. This circumstance has produced feverish competition among the young, even the very young, in America. At almost every level of our society, youth is aware of the need for academic distinction through more and more schooling, deliberately undertaken at an earlier and earlier age as part of a great rat race. We are approaching a state of affairs in which virtually all employment will require years of technical training; goals will have to be set well before adolescence as job-anxiety mounts in intensity and duration. The drivenness of this generation is merely a prelude to what we may now expect.

Aspiring artists enjoy no immunity to all these forces. How they will respond remains to be seen, but clearly, in some sense their difficulties will be compounded. Meanwhile, by comparison, the life history of any practicing artist takes on a stately quality.

MAKING DO

Not that it was ever easy. Artists rarely come out of artists' homes as artisans did out of artisans' homes. For none of them was there any way of knowing what the artist's life was like, and some declare, perhaps with a touch of disingenuousness, that knowing would have deflected them from that life:

> *I had no conception of what it meant to be an artist. Looking back on it now, I think that was all to the good. I never even gave a thought to how I was going to live or how I was going to sustain myself, how I was going to endure. I suppose at that time one didn't think of those things. I just knew I wanted to paint. If I had known more, it might have had a completely different effect on me. This way, you see, I've been very fortunate. I'm stuck with painting. I didn't prepare myself for—or even think of—anything else.*

What else was there? "I suppose I'd only have been qualified for good hard work. I didn't like that idea too much." To be sure, as an art student he had done the "good hard work" which would be so much more difficult to come by today. "I have two sisters in Detroit. So I used to go up there summers and hire in on the automobile industry and make as much money as possible and go back to school in the fall. . . . I guess I felt that I could always go out and work if necessary."

The pragmatic attitude so much in evidence among college students—causing them to exasperate many of their teachers by asking before they embark on any field of study, "What can we do with it?"—rarely appeared among fledgling artists of an earlier day. However, we would be greatly surprised if that attitude did not prevail in the late 1960's. Even a decade or two ago, one had to be insouciant to want to be an artist: "I never, never asked myself, 'How will I get along?' I just felt it would be interesting to be an artist. I thought, 'I will get along somehow.' "

Given strong incentive, the tradition of working one's way through school is well established in this country, above all as a vehicle of upward mobility for the slum child. The art student often worked his way through art school, but not in order to earn a certificate as his guarantee of economic well-being. He could not have assumed that youthful hardships were simply a passport to the affluence which his training would automatically confer. On the contrary, hardship would be his natural condition, and it would be tolerable as long as he had other fish to fry, other goals for which to strive. Those goals were incompatible with the personal commitment most people in our society make—to an ever higher standard of living. Getting through school on part-time work merely presaged the next, perhaps interminable stage: getting through life on part-time work. Why? "Well, I just made up my mind that nothing would stop me, certainly no concern like how would I feed myself."

One artist with a quasi-proletarian background who achieved rapid recognition once he took seriously to painting, reminisces about his salad days with a touch of gaiety:

> *I had had a few shows, but my future was really unsettled. I was still growing. Well, I used to have a little station wagon, and I would advertise in the daily papers. I could make fifty or sixty bucks, you know, packing and delivering. Once I took a steady job as delivery boy for two weeks. It was marvelous. Then my prospects began to improve, but instead of dropping the job completely, I parceled each day of the week out to another artist. I had, say, Monday, Al had Tuesday, Bob had Wednesday. I used to rob this store of paint, canvas, and a few other objects. I would come in with a big coat, and during the day I'd put the stuff in my bathroom. Now the owner of that establishment is my art supply dealer. I give him thousands of dollars' worth of business. I guess that's a curious morality to come by . . .*

The *bonhomie,* the mutual aid (sharing good fortune when he needed it less), the touch of ruthlessness, its lavish overcompensation, a "curious morality" that puts art above conventional honesty but preserves and extends the old ethical bookkeeping: these are typical traits, however atypical the case may be.

Few artists feel the need to steal supplies, but many have had to scrape hard to find enough money to buy them. We are told, for example, that Franz Kline's famous trademark, his use of black and white pigments, derived originally from the fact that colored paints cost so much more than black and white—and he used what he could afford. To set up as an artist, and to keep going, invariably means taking on odd jobs. The painter just quoted, who periodically worked and briefly stooped to petty larceny, had other expedients at his disposal. Every so often he would sell a picture; there would be an occasional windfall from his mother-in-law, whose meager income consisted of an army pension; and he had yet another source:

> *My dealer. He considered himself, I don't know, Jesus Christ or somebody. He called up people and said, 'So-and-So's starving. Give him some money.' And in those days some-body would come through with $75 or I'd get $25 in the mail. It was fantastic.*

Not so long ago, but it seems to her light years away, an artist recalls her unemployability shortly after graduation from college: "Even if I had had a Master's degree, I wouldn't have been able to get a job as an artist in the city. The students I know now, with only a Bachelor's, can get a job. Today it's worth something. *They* have at least that. We didn't." What did she do? "A million different things"—of which waiting on table in a coffee shop, decorating little cards, and selling expensive bridal attire stand out in her memory.

Artists who got started in the thirties are inclined to say that the specter of poverty and privation has always been with them. One conjures up the old days by remarking that: "There couldn't have been a worse time in the history of the world—except maybe during the Peasant Wars or something like that. It certainly was grim. And I've always had economic problems. Until recently." His family, he explains, had no money and gave him none. Indeed, like many others we interviewed, he contributed from adolescence on to his parents' support.

To subsist at a later stage, artists mention, *inter alia,* jobs they hold or have held: settlement house worker, draftsman, secretary, housepainter, carpenter, clerk, handyman, jazz musician, truck driver, file clerk, industrial operative—and many more. The artist who, with luck, will eventually live off his work, is almost certainly destined to live for long stretches off his wits. To live does not mean to make a handsome living or to be envious of those who do, but to get by, to survive, to possess material objects without being possessed by them. "I was getting a good salary for ten years. And I lived then just as I do now. I don't have much furniture. I really don't care for it. There are not many things I want in this world before I die." We find it instructive to visit the handful of painters and sculptors who earn big money in their own unostentatious homes; almost anyone else in their income bracket would exhibit more evidence of conspicuous consumption. A famous painter speaks for many when he points out that even Rockefeller can only wear one suit at a time.

Meanwhile, there is the problem of laying hands on enough money to buy that suit. Asked what would be best for an artist to do just to keep going, he most readily answers: a private income, or something easy and mindless, or a rich wife, or: "The best thing I can do is to work as little as possible and make as much money. That's what I was always looking for, but I never really found it." The majority of artists, goaded by necessity, seek temporary employment in fields farthest removed from their own, in which they are free from any emotional investment. Some few are dedicated art teachers who continue to instruct the young even when there is no economic necessity to do so. Many others teach art only as long as money remains a problem. At the first opportunity, for various reasons, they abandon it. Teaching takes time and energy away from the area in which it should be concentrated—a theme repeatedly stated and seldom qualified. That there may be another element in this attitude is suggested by an artist who also found employment as a factory worker:

> *Over and over again I was told by other artists that I was lucky to have another field which bore no relation to art. You see,* they envied me because I didn't have to give all my ideas away to students in order to earn my living.

While asserting, "The main difficulty was that I wanted to paint myself, and teaching took so much out of me that I resented it, and I wasn't really willing to give my all to it," another painter who taught art in a junior high school sounds much like frustrated school-teachers in general—with the difference that she had an alternative and took it:

> *It was very tough. It was impossible. The kids would come in at eight o'clock in the morning, and then another class would come in, and another class. And I'd have to go wash up after them. And then, I didn't know how permissive to be. There's a sort of standing philosophy of art education that lets them express themselves. On the other hand, I wasn't as sure that a little formal instruction wouldn't be effective, too. And it was just sort of like keeping them busy, getting through the art periods. I gave that up pretty fast.*

Artists reverse Poor Richard's famous aphorism: they do not say that time is money, that it is needed and should be used without stint to make more, but rather that money is time, that with enough money there will be time to work—and the work's the thing.

> *Money means time—and that's all it means to me. Most of us, if we can live in a poor way completely from our paint-ing, prefer that to a much higher standard of living and loss of time.*

> *All that's gone now, but in my day the cost of living in Paris was infinitely lower than here. The first few years there I worked as a housepainter. Then I began to sell, and sell enough to get by, and I was quite satisfied just to get by. And then in '36, Pierre Matisse, an American dealer, gave me a modest contract, and I almost managed the next three years off that. But the only time I ever really made a living from art was in Paris.*

> *I'm used to rough living. I always figure I'm going to get some money soon. I sell paintings not very often, and they pay, but it isn't like a steady thing. And then I'm involved in this little gallery uptown, and I sell some paintings there,*

> *but all the money has to go back into the gallery. It's very*
> *insecure . . . Now, one year I didn't make any money was*
> *1957. It was very tough for about four months because*
> *we had just had the baby, and I had some money saved up,*
> *and suddenly it ran out. For about three months we barely*
> *scraped by. About that time my wife went out to work. She*
> *has a little job, makes about seventy dollars a week. So, with*
> *my paintings and all, we manage, but she makes most of the*
> *money, more than I do.*

Working wives, and those who simply budget the family resources with great care, are often indispensable. Otherwise, an economic level which by decent middle class standards is still woefully inadequate cannot be reached. And to the artist, as he views his situation, that level may be high enough—provided it affords him the time that he needs for his work. He is not inclined to do other things for the sake of a higher standard of living; he *is* inclined to doubt that a good artist can be "really clever at doing other things like real estate," and if he is, let him abandon art.

THE PERILS OF SUBSIDIZED ART

Devoted to his work, with a passion for it that quenches any residual thirst he might have for conventional status earned in the usual way, an American artist is a person who does not fit into the system—until he is made to fit. Much of the present interest in subsidies for the artist, at a time when art is being upgraded, turns on the need to domesticate anyone who enters the Establishment. There is a general sense that he must not be wild, shabby, poor—or uncontrollable. Although his pecuniary plight may be real enough, he is chary of the Establishment's efforts to alleviate it. The artist suspects that he cannot be guided solely by economic self-interest and remain an artist. To think otherwise would be to overlook the lessons of a lifetime.

Artists over fifty had direct exposure to federal subsidy in the WPA Arts Program; all were in or close to it, and their juniors have heard them discuss the few pros and the many cons with which they now view that experience. The older men and women also recall how many of their number were attracted to Mexico in the thirties, for in that country artists were supported by a benevolent government which required them to engage in what one calls "mural turpitude." Above all, there is the sobering case of artists in uniform, as Max Eastman dubbed them long ago, artists who, if they will only accede to the wishes of their bureaucratic superiors in a totalitarian state, can enjoy power, fame, and riches. Such "artists" are the darlings of every regime behind the Iron Curtain. Yet few indeed are those, well-fixed or poverty-stricken, who envy them. With this example and their own recent past to consider, even the knowledge of better examples (in England, Holland, Canada, France, and Italy) is insufficient to sway them from general opposition to federal or other governmental support.

The Arts Council in England, while regarded as somewhat stuffy, is universally applauded for showing no discrimination in the help it offers: "All you have to do in England is pop your head above water as an artist, and you're given a life preserver. English artists are supported like no other artists in the world." There is also abundant praise for Holland where, our artists agree, an enviable system has been devised. One explains:

> *It functions wonderfully. A board determines if an artist has professional standing. Other artists make the decision. That's very important. It's not done by the mayor or the board of aldermen, but by other artists. The man who's designated receives a monthly salary to produce art. Also, the government gives him commissions, and as his earnings go up the subsidy is withdrawn, but it's there to fall back on when he's not earning. This is really a great thing.*

France comes in for considerable praise. The French government provides specific services for artists, for instance, by providing free space for exhibitions and by facilitating the shipment of art works, reducing cost and insuring safety. Such help any enlightened government could presumably supply. Italy at present fills the bill, as it did under monarchical rule, and signally failed to do during the prolonged Fascist abberation. A Sardinian-American artist looks back to his youth with gratitude to the old Italian government which, early in this century, set out to encourage a revival of the arts. Though of peasant origins, he was able to secure a state scholarship, went to design school, and learned painting in "a sort of Italian Bauhaus." While he is skeptical of its formal training, it got him started and for that he is as thankful as many young American artists are to their government for being able to school themselves with funds provided by the G.I. Bill of Rights.

In a few cases (notably that of a highly esteemed artist who calls himself an anarchist and means it), the whole idea of government assistance is categorically rejected. More often, artists concede that though there is something to be said for the idea, there is very much to be said against it. Some doubt that subsidies have ever operated to benefit the best artists: "During the time that Delacroix and Ingres were having artistic difficulties, Ingres and Ingres' followers were supported by the government. Delacroix and his followers were not. I'm sure that Ingres was a lesser artist, and certainly Ingres' followers were less important than Delacroix's."

Grants and prizes—and the manifest inequity of their distribution —are held up as proof that help today, whether private or public, is already caught up in problems that would only be magnified by a really ambitious program: "The Guggenheim Foundation has hardly ever given a grant to a good artist. They usually give the grant for reasons that have very little to do with artistic ability or artistic adventurousness." Artists are apprehensive that, to get a grant or a commission right now, they must be doing work that has "recognizable limits." Such work does not need further support, but the adventurous, unfamiliar, and probably more durable work is least likely to enjoy foundation support. Horse-trading is an additional and equally deplorable factor. Local politics already come into play. Hence: "If you give Iowa a grant, then you must give one to California—which is very democratic. It just doesn't apply to the world of art, that's all." Prizes conferred by juries are subject to similar regional or distributive criteria, and to attendant cries of favoritism. One artist says he has known jurors to decide on winners at the Biennale in Venice as follows: "We must give one to Japan this year because we've got to keep her friendly to the United Nations." Or, "We've got to show our peaceful intentions this year by giving one to Poland." All this jockeying occurs on a relatively small scale. Our artists fear that its abuse would expand and multiply

315

if the federal government mounted a large-scale program. Not that they should be deprived of access to money, "but better to put numbers in a hat and pick them out," or simply reward everybody in the same manner—two procedures our government would never accept —than to hand out subsidies on the choice of a jury.　.

Asked why, if the British have been so successful with their Arts Council, we could not follow suit and do likewise in this country, a sculptor points to our factionalism, our sectionalism, and our size. Then he invokes national character, reminding us that there is a certain decency about the English who, for example, did not create a black market in (or after) the Second World War. We had our shady dealers, France was "a rat trap," Italy no better—while the English patiently queued up for food, clothing, transportation, and the like. The National Health Act and public works also go smoothly in England, while we seem to be unprepared for either. Even though he is aggrieved as a sculptor over the fact that, despite the museums' great wealth, "there are a hundred times more painting shows than sculpture shows because shipping costs are fabulous," and that if the shows were subsidized or if the government simply paid insurance premiums, it would be helpful—still, "I'm against this kind of thing."

Artists welcome every effort to encourage the arts, but they contend that in our country it always boomerangs. They expect that a federal program would inevitably fall into the wrong hands, that the result would be an official art with its own heavily laden gravy train—onto which artists could clamber only by perverting their style. The net effect would be to discourage creativity. "An arrangement where an artist could do a couple of pictures a month, say, bring them in, and pick up his paycheck would be ideal. It would be marvelous. But we could never have that here."

Nobody denies that the prospect of a steady income is attractive, and nobody is dazzled by it. A painter who sees many complexities in the problem ("It explodes in about twenty different directions," he says, "and you can't follow any one argument to the bitter end") nevertheless underscores the danger of economic coercion if an artist accepts a subsidy and refuses to abide by fixed political or academic "lines." The backer can always threaten to withdraw his support unless artists toe his line. And what does that do to the free-wheeler who loves and needs his independence, who scorns the aesthetics of "political people" who want to make his kind of art, not theirs?

The balance sheet never really balances. Finally it all goes up in acid:

> *Actually, we have men right now who turn out castrated Ivory Soap monuments for the government. You know, like in post offices. Terrible stuff! But there's a clique that's really being subsidized—and they are a closed group. Ostensibly you get some kind of competition or bidding, but nobody knows about it except the members of this little club, and they just share out the wealth among themselves. So you do have a subsidy of a very special small segment of the art world. The peculiar thing is that this segment has no influence. It doesn't* exist—*but the government supports it. Otherwise, I'm sure the whole group would disappear. As artists, they're dead. As babies at the nipple of Mother Government, they're on nourishment just because somehow they're there. They get hold of the teat. They just flourish and thrive and become wealthy—and I'm not exaggerating—really wealthy on the money put into their production.*

The twin pressures of democracy and bureaucracy are said already to bedevil American art more than most people suspect. There is invisible sponsorship at this moment, advantageous for the few who enjoy its material benefits, a matter of indifference to the many, but deleterious to art as such. Shows selected "by the government, for the government, through the government," of which artists have had a strong foretaste during the Eisenhower and Kennedy administrations, leave them with the feeling that Washington would only aggravate a bad situation. The aggrandizement of American culture in Europe, through occasional exhibitions of "our art" by an official agency like the United States Information Service, does not seem to them to bode well for anyone concerned. Lack of taste, outright vulgarity, rank incompetence, blatant philistinism, or blind endorsement of bad art that momentarily looks like *le denier cri:* these are some of the expletives flung at those who have put these shows on the road. Fundamentally: "Art is not something that can be *organized*. Why try?"

Those who do not assume that government sponsorship is or would be harmful to art tend to believe that in any case it could not be beneficial. They see art as a separate department of contemporary civilization which no one can squelch *or* bring artificially to life: "Let's say that Kennedy was for the artist. I think that's fine. Let's say Eisenhower didn't give a damn. I think that's fine, too—because it really doesn't matter one way or the other." There is also "the philosophy of in spite of" to which many artists subscribe. Thus:

> *Personally I'm against the fostering of art in superficial ways. I think that art in this kind of world should assert itself, like in spite of . . . which is its real drama, its real takeoff. It insists on rearing its head, you know, in spite of . . .*

It will therefore serve no useful purpose synthetically to organize, socialize, or otherwise institutionalize art.

Official support means committees, and committees need chairmen, who are by definition unsatisfactory. Any chairman would be the wrong one. "A lot of people would say, 'Put M.J. in charge of the thing.' Somebody would have to head it up, maybe K., or God help us, F.J. How fair do you think they would be?" And again, "I mean, you might start out with the best guy in the world. Suppose you put H.R. in charge, and even he has his limitations, but then, who would come after him?" Officials may turn to art with the best of intentions. with some integrity, even with a degree of competence. All to no avail, for they will be thwarted by the curse of bureaucracy, and a kind of perverted academy will emerge. But doesn't an academy accord well with "the philosophy of in spite of"? An exceptionally cosmopolitan American painter doubts it:

> *Of course, academies in France were always good because everybody fought against them. The idea was to make an academy and then to break it. But that wouldn't be our pattern. Here we'd just have a political muddle which would propably injure the arts even if it did benefit a handful of artists. I'm afraid anything of that sort in America is doomed to failure.*

There is something about our culture, perhaps its immaturity, that alerts the artist to dangers inherent even in good impulses somehow gone wrong. French art, "like French perfume and French cognac," is understood to be "good stuff" because it comes to us as a natural emanation of the national culture. We whose art has earned its creators an international reputation lag far behind Western Europe in our capacity to handle that art and deal with those creators. It is for this reason more than any other that apparently beneficent offers of practical assistance are suspect. Our artists take bureaucracy—by the very nature of the beast—to be as endless as any of Kafka's labyrinths. They have many pungent epithets with which to characterize it in the abstract—almost always adding that American bureaucracy is still worse. British Councils are described as conservative, but "they allow you a hearing you're not likely to get in official quarters over here," and so on and on.

The new benevolence may be better than outright hostility. "It's better than burning pictures," and hounding artists as in the Soviet Union. "But, with us, things are never given in a disinterested spirit. A director's got to be appointed. He has to ask for some kind of commission to justify himself. The painter who contributes to make this set-up more pleasant, more tolerable, would be better received than the artist who is daring, who really creates something."

The implication throughout is that we are a culturally under-developed people, not yet ready for the delicate response to art which may come in time. A painter, acutely aware of "how terrible it is to have no money and want to do something that takes most of your time and energy," remarks wistfully "how nice it would be" if there were a permanent fund out of which a little money would be dispensed to needy and worthy artists "without any other consequences." But he claims to know better—for there are always other consequences, strings are always attached, there is always a catch. None of this is theoretically necessary; it could be avoided—if we were grown up and self-confident in our attitude toward the arts. Then help would be a boon. It is so sorely needed by impecunious painters that an artist can start out in response to our question about government support by exclaiming: "Any way an artist can get dough is okay with me. Why not? He's got to eat. It would make such a difference if he got a few thousand a year. There'd be red tape, all right. Filling out certain pages. Blah, blah, blah. It's a little boring to go through with, but I think it's a little boring to go look for a job every day." Then comes the kicker, the after-thought: "But damn it, they'd start telling you what to paint and how to paint it." Who are "they"? Why, the "narrow, phony, bigoted, unenlightened guys," a pack of ignorant administrators who come to control such situations. Concretely, "Look at the Fine Arts Commission we have in Washington. Everyone connected with it is old hat. They're so terrible I wouldn't *take* a subsidy from them. I know all about that outfit. The head of it used to be dean where I studied architecture. His tastes, his concepts, his terms belong to the 1920's, not the 1960's."

Disdain is the prevailing sentiment for current federal subsidies. All those asked (and several volunteered information without being asked) felt that these subsidies, without exception, go to the wrong kind of artist:

> *It's always some eager beaver who gets hold of everything. No artist wants to sit behind a desk running things. And as soon as you make a committee for writing, painting, or whatever, there's going to be some son of a bitch, who never did any writing or painting, sitting behind that desk telling the writers and painters what to do.*

Occasional rule by committee is disturbing enough. What would it be if a centralized government enmeshed art in the coils of a massive bureaucracy? An amiable man like August Heckscher, the late President Kennedy's arts adviser, might not dream of dictating to artists, but if a federal arts program really got going, he would be pushed aside, and "The man most likely to step forward and have his say, not permitting others to have theirs, the loud-mouth, you know, would be on all the committees, grab control of them, get his finger into that pie." It can happen anywhere: "It happened right here in the Artists' Club. We just had a terrific fight about it because this R. House wanted to have artistic activity there, and invited some of us down. It wasn't even a question of money: if you get any you're lucky. But what a squabble! Suppose the government got in on a scene like that."

As between support for every man who calls himself an artist (the number may be staggering) and support only for the artist of "proven accomplishment," one sculptor plumps for the latter—

on condition that such an artist is not now gaining the recognition he deserves, that he is not enjoying any kind of success, and "that he does not have enough to live on." The champion of this scheme admits it is utopian. After all, "the problem is one of quality and the nonrecognition of quality. Nothing is harder to promote and to sell. Real quality hardly ever gains immediate acceptance. It sells last." And what sells last is unlikely to interest a panel of judges who would be answerable to Congress for their expenditure of public funds.

The artists we interviewed are relatively much better off than any statistically accurate sample of people who would like to be full-time painters and sculptors. Yet quite a few of them live in poverty at this moment, and all of them know its conditions at first hand.

> *Most artists, even very good ones, earn less than $3,000 a year. The majority earn nothing. They develop an absolute sense of frustration about the amount of time left to them for their work. You sail on your ideas, literally live on them, along with false hopes and crazy illusions, but only for so long.*

Given this state, which is not far from desperation, what does an artist think he must have? Intangibly, he must have "the primary freedoms" which are not negotiable: he cannot exchange them for money from any source, however paternalistic it may be. Our respondents generally assume that no modern artist whose brothers have been *luftmenschen* for so long would willingly agree to the old subservience of pre-modern artists. No doubt there were great advantages, such as economic security and a commonality of taste, inherent in the traditional system of patronage. That system is, however, as extinct as the peasant society, the folk culture, and the feudal order of which it was an integral part. Ever since art was cut loose from its institutional moorings, artists have had to float, crawl, lurch, scramble, and otherwise navigate on their own. Eventually, they prized above all else the independence which was thrust upon them. Few of them would lightly dismiss it, none without reservations, qualms, and misgivings. At the same time they have material needs which, while defined as minimal, are still very real:

> *It's just too debilitating without any money. I'd settle for a few thousand. Some so-called top galleries in New York give contracts—and they're neither more nor less reprehensible than advances given by publishers. I think the artist needs that kind of advance. He needs a thousand or two thousand bucks in advance, but most galleries won't do it.*

For a few years in this country artists *were* directly subsidized by the federal government. They got their pittance from WPA, and it was enough. Everyone of a certain age recalls that experience—and has mixed feelings about it.

> *WPA did a lot for a whole bunch of artists who were able to paint and live because of the twenty bucks or so they got every week. Of course, that was a unique situation. I think that again, like art school, maybe out of all the thousands who were paid, maybe one was really helped and freed and came to life and painted, but probably that one would have done it anyway by himself.*

> *I knew painters like A. and G. who ate Cream of Wheat for a week at a time because that was all they had in the house. They were determined, they had talent, and they made it—which is what counts whether you're Kennedy's daughter or born in the gutter. . . . I don't think WPA hurt anything or improved anything. It made lots of people a little more comfortable. That was fine. But it didn't make artists.*

As many of these artists remember it, the WPA Arts Project was internally and externally politicized. Here is an old timer's graphic description:

> *When an artist went into WPA, he moved in under the control of the Arts Congress and said, "Buddy." I think that to some extent the situation since WPA has been influenced by that set-up. You see, under WPA the men in charge were able to determine who an artist was. If you were on an easel project, you were a real painter, but if you were one of the boys on a mural project, you weren't such a*

hot painter. And if you were on a teaching project, you weren't a painter at all. And they controlled it very tightly. I knew I couldn't function under that set-up. It went against my grain. So I went out and made a day's pay for an honest day's work—unlike most painters of my generation.

Disaffection also occurred early, when Communists achieved a measure of control in some sectors of the project. This alone made non-Communist artists uncomfortable. In addition it attracted the FBI, so artists felt harassed at both ends—by Communists trying to manipulate them from within and by police agents hunting Communists: "The FBI kept knocking at your door, asking if you knew so-and-so, and was he a Commie? It got so that somebody was coming, officially and officiously, to your door about every two days. They wanted spies to be planted all over. The whole thing was horrible—which is why quite a few of us got off the project."

Others did not measure up to the standard set by WPA administrators because they did completely abstract work at a time when social realism prevailed. A prominent sculptor ("prematurely" abstract in manner) first failed of acceptance for work on the project. For some years he was relegated to the role of technical supervisor, unable to contribute anything of his own. Finally, under a slightly different dispensation, "his stuff was deemed to be okay. So they allocated some things to a couple high schools in New York City, more or less shunting them out of sight. You could tell they didn't really want it. Well, then he cleared out."

An artist too young to have been on WPA himself personally interviewed "everyone" who was, to compile a catalogue on the subject. His impression is that in the thirties there was no other way: it was absolutely necessary. Nevertheless, he is convinced that WPA was a "sour experience." How so?

Well, there were many reasons. I think it was bad partly because the times were so bad. And the fact that whatever artists did nobody cared about. At the end there were tens of thousands of paintings sold at a penny a pound. People couldn't get back their own work. In other words, it was meaningless. That must have something to do with why

> *veterans of WPA art are so wary about subsidies. To do meaningless work is the worst possible punishment you can inflict on a man. That's what they used to do in Siberia.*

Another painter, in answer to the question, "Was WPA a good thing?" readily replies, "It wasn't bad when you needed it, and we all did." Yet in the next breath he adds, "The art that came out of it was not very good even though there were a lot of good artists around." And his verdict is not idiosyncratic. It makes most of his peers who use quality as their touchstone wonder about the desirability of any government sponsorship. They fear that even today art produced with official backing "would be terribly false and restricted." Indeed, they believe the art would be worse today than it was under WPA. Few among them blame government subsidies for mediocre and imitative social realism, which as Socialist Realism is still officially required of Soviet artists. They incline rather to the view that such work came as a natural by-product of the ideological situation throughout a prolonged economic slump, the whole Depression decade. At that time social art was the mainstream of all art. Many artists and sub-artists simply converted their art into political activity. They would have done so, it is argued, with or without government support; their social-mindedness coincided with WPA but was not ordered by it: "I don't think the social realists were constrained by their twenty-three bucks a week. They were constrained by each other, and also by the fact that during that period painters were much more socially conscious than they are now." Others dissent from this view, claiming that there was dictation, not so much through the government directly as through the opportunists and ideologues who, coming to power inside the Arts Project, staffed and operated it in a tendentious direction. Whether WPA evokes a touch of nostalgia or its opposite, artists generally do not care for any attempt to repeat the experiment which, at best, was appropriate only to "a moment in history."

A painter vividly recalls his WPA days, sandwiched in between union leadership and a private scholarship with which he was able to go abroad:

> *After I came back I got on the Adult Education and Recreation Project. Mainly I was put into Workmen's Circle groups.*

They sent me out to a lot of little places. I did that for about a year. About 1938 or '39, I got a job doing the New York Life Insurance display at the World's Fair in New York. Later I worked for an architect who hired me to do a lot of his coloring, designing displays, and whatever two-dimensional graphic work had to be done.

For such a man, WPA provided makeshift and unrewarding jobs like those available to him on a more profitable basis in the business world. Neither nurtured the artist in him that had to break away from both to achieve fulfillment. In retrospect, he is contemptuous of "those particular people who had the professional ability to become prize-winners or the professional ability to manipulate others." The prospect of a general subsidy does not thrill him, for he sees it as "just a gesture which reflects some narrow, selective idea." And then the clincher: "I'm afraid it might just sponsor bad art. I don't think bad art needs to be sponsored."

And in the same vein:

I think the disinterested artist ought to be subsidized much more than the interested one. But will he be? By whom? I'm thinking of the man who has a position which in science is occupied by the purely abstract research guy. He isn't on a project to build a better rocket or find a better germ or nerve gas or whatever the hell it is. He just wonders why, if you look through a crystal, the light does this, and if you look through a gallon of whiskey the light does that. This sort of guy will just go off and do what he feels like doing. That's what should be subsidized in science. In art, I think the man who works aimlessly at his easel should be supported over the man who does the monuments of the last great war.

The G.I. Bill comes in for more unqualified praise than WPA; its beneficiaries include many of the best artists between the ages of thirty-five and forty-five. "That was very good. Somebody wanted to study. So he was subsidized, and there was no control over where he should study, with whom he should study, or how he should study." Marvelous: "All you had to do to get your monthly check was to enroll and sign in every day." Notwithstanding all this, one remembers that: "Lots of people never finished up their entitlement from the G.I. Bill because they got bored, they got restless. They wanted to move on to bigger and better things and not to be hampered by their privilege."

One of our respondents, a naturalized American, worked for awhile in Fascist Italy where he experienced totalitarian oppression at first hand. Moving to Paris in the period of *l'art populaire,* he mingled with other sculptors and with painters, poets, and musicians who streamed into France from Germany and Italy where they and their work were vilified as "degenerate." That others remained and became darlings of the state only deepened their suspicion of such regimes and indeed of all regimes that are prepared to coddle and eviscerate them. Thus the feeling, deeply held and generally shared, that "government subsidy of art means government interference in art. I think it's better to be free."

After all, "True artists, without money and without subsidies, manage to survive and manage to work. It would be better if they had some money, but there are too many dangers inherent in government subsidies . . ." Already, we are told, a man of character has to fight "the big shots and the bums" in order to be received as an artist. But not even he feels adequate to the task of handling "those senators and distinguished saloon-keepers" who manage our political affairs.

Above and beyond their strictures on American political life, the nightmare of art in Soviet society haunts our artists and shapes their attitudes. They do not trust totalitarian leaders who now and then talk of "liberalization" and who now and then permit a "thaw" before resuming the usual freeze. Artists in Soviet Russia and her satellites (as well as those in such relatively autonomous countries as Poland and Yugoslavia) either serve the state and prosper with handsome commissions or defy the state and invite destitution. Marshal Tito, no less than the Soviet leaders, calls militantly for party purity, for "realities," as he recently called them, instead of "abstractions." All over Eastern Europe, political leaders demand heroic murals and take much time to denounce every "decadent, Western, modernist" tendency in painting and sculpture.

Toward the end of 1962, Moscow correspondent Theodore Shabad reported in the *New York Times:*

> *A campaign in the Soviet Union against unorthodox art spread today to the provinces. In Alma-Ata, capital of the the central Asian Republic of Kazakhstan, a meeting was called for Sunday in the city's art gallery to discuss allegedly objectionable paintings.*
>
> *At the same time* Pravda, *the Communist party newspaper, published a demand for the removal of some paintings in the Manege Exhibition Hall in Moscow. The newspaper carried excerpts from the visitors' books at the hall criticizing works of painters who had strayed from the officially approved style of Socialist Realism.*
>
> *Premier Khrushchev complained during a visit to Manege Hall last weekend that several artists were producing work that was alien to the ideas of Communism. This gave rise to a campaign against styles that, according to the Premier, do not "elevate man, inspire him, and lead him to noble deeds." . . . One result of the latest criticism of modern art forms is that a forty-year-old painting of a female nude has become the talk of much of Moscow. . . . Crowds milled all day in front of the controversial impressionistic painting by Robert Falk, a Soviet artist who died four years ago. The nude was one of several works assailed as "formalistic" by Premier Khrushchev and his entourage . . .*[1]

By January 31, 1963, after a visit to the Soviet Union, Marshal Tito came around to Khrushchev's position and echoed it on that day, bitterly berating painters who had "plunged into abstraction" and against whom "measures" would have to be taken. He railed particularly against "barren intellectuals in literature, painting, and films who are not on earth but floating somewhere in the air." And there, "somewhere in the air," the totalitarian state is as powerless to control them as it is effective in doing so when they are down here on earth and in uniform.

American society. squeezed and threatened from within though it may be, is not yet totalitarian. For the breathing space still ours that others have lost, we are indebted not least to our most cantankerous and unmanageable artists.

Speaking of the self-pity in which they wallow, Peter Drucker has indicted spokesmen for every "occupation, trade, or profession" in America.[2] He claims that *all* of them suffer from a martyr complex, feeling that they are misunderstood, neglected, underrated, unloved, rejected, slipping in popular esteem and in ability to attract the young. They complain of their "bad image" and set about to rectify it through articles, speeches, public relations campaigns, and resolutions. Drucker exempts no one. The military, science, medicine, the professoriate, business, and government are high among his "Martyrs Unlimited." Perhaps because they are not statistically significant, there is no mention of artists—who may in fact comprise the only occupational group of any importance not concerned about its "image." They still resist the general drift, clinging to the vestiges of their inner-direction in an other-directed society.

Appendix—
Creative Energy:
Sexuality and
Sublimation

Work is no less valuable for the opportunity it and the human relations connected with it provide for a very considerable discharge of libidinal component impulses, narcissistic, aggressive and even erotic, than because it is indispensable for subsistence and justifies existence in a society. The daily work of earning a livelihood affords particular satisfaction when it has been selected by free choice, i.e., when through sublimation it enables use of instinctual impulses that have retained their strength, or are more intense than usual for constitutional reasons.

—SIGMUND FREUD, 1930

TYPICALLY, artists are voluble about their motivations—without being able to account for them in an intellectually acceptable fashion. They find themselves "driven" or feel "impelled" to paint and sculpt. But the source, the "why" of their creative power exists as a continuing mystery to them.

When asked to assess the function of their art in society, however, they have so many well-articulated and diverse ideas that there is little overlap between the explanations offered by different respondents. Questions such as, "What's the purpose of your painting?" "What does the painter or sculptor accomplish through his work?" without further prompting evoke extended discussions of the historical and social role of art and the artist. Unexpectedly, the very same questions produce material from entirely different areas: specifically, those areas that touch the emotional and instinctual release which artists secure from their work. This became especially striking when so many responses pertained directly to matters of sexual excitation and discharge. These observations have been challenged so often by so many, including artists, that we did not anticipate such responses. In fact, we were so skeptical about this line of investigation that we initially intended to ignore it completely. But material appeared spontaneously and often enough to make us feel that it deserved further exploration and analysis, even though it meant a departure from the mainstream of our discussion.

PSYCHOANALYTIC THEORIES OF ART

Scientific theories linking sex and art were not propounded until the present century. Prior to that, and at least as far back as Plato,[1] occasional references to the matter can be found, but they are isolated statements and lack a common conceptual framework. Only with the advent of psychoanalysis was some effort made to treat the subject in detail. References to it are scattered throughout the psychoanalytic literature. While Freud himself initiated the work on this subject, he never treated it comprehensively in any one paper. Yet, here as elsewhere, his formulations were widely circulated in both analytic and non-analytic circles. Because of their pioneer position, Freud's ideas usually serve as the focus for all psychoanalytic discussions of art and artists.

Freud's major hypothesis—and he adhered to it without significant modification throughout his life—was based on the proposition that unacceptable libidinal impulses are "deinstinctualized" and then gain expression through more socially acceptable channels and through activities of a higher cultural order. Freud called this process *sublimation,* which has been defined more precisely as "the process by which an unconscious sexual wish is consciously gratified in work, play, or art, without sensual experience, without love of another person, and without contingent suffering." [2]

In reviewing the concept of sublimation, Edward Glover points out that historically it has passed through two phases of development: "Up to the year 1923 interest in sublimation was largely phenomenological. A few generalizations had been advanced concerning the mechanism of sublimation . . . From 1923 onwards interest became concentrated on the energies involved and the nature of their modification." [3] Glover summarizes Freud's views through 1923 as follows: "Sublimation is the term applied to a group of unconscious processes which have this in common, that as the result of inner or outer deprivation, the aim of object-libido undergoes a more or less complete deflection, modification, or inhibition. In the great majority of instances the new aim is one distinct or remote from sexual satisfaction, i.e., is an asexual or non-sexual aim." [4]

Looking at Freud's own writings, we find that although he alluded to sublimation several times before 1905, his first explicit contribution to the understanding of the relationship between sex and creativity was not published until that year, when he declared that: "The progressive concealment of the body which goes along with civilization keeps sexual curiosity awake. This curiosity seeks to complete the sexual object by revealing its hidden parts. It can, however, be diverted ('sublimated') in the direction of art, if its interest can be shifted away from the genital onto the shape of the body as a whole." [5]

In a subsequent statement of the repressive nature of Western civilization, Freud emphasized the degree of instinctual renunciation which each individual who wishes to survive in a highly civilized society must accept, since adjustments within the society are based on the suppression of instincts. He then noted that the sexual instinct is:

> *. . . probably more strongly developed in man than in most of the higher animals; it is certainly more constant, since it has almost entirely overcome the periodicity belonging to it in animals. It places an extraordinary amount of energy at the disposal of "cultural" activities; and this because of a particularly marked characteristic that it possesses, namely, the ability to displace its aim without materially losing its intensity. This ability to exchange the originally sexual aim for another which is no longer sexual, but is psychically related, is called the capacity for sublimation.*[6]

But while asserting the value of sublimation in providing substitute satisfactions, Freud assumed that those satisfactions would lose their sexual coloration: ". . . both object and aim are changed, so that what was originally a sexual instinct finds satisfaction in some achievement which is no longer sexual but has a higher social or ethical valuation." [7]

Freud thought that while sublimation of instinctual drives was necessary for the production of art, the individual artist also needed to enjoy a certain amount of direct sexual gratification. Otherwise, crippling emotional disturbances would develop and plague him in all of his endeavors:

> *The relation between possible sublimation and indispensable sexual activity naturally varies very much in different persons, and indeed with the various kinds of occupation. An abstinent artist is scarcely conceivable; an abstinent young intellectual is by no means a rarity. The young intellectual can by abstinence enhance his powers of concentration, whereas the production of the artist is powerfully stimulated by his sexual experience. On the whole I have not gained the impression that sexual abstinence helps to shape energetic, self-reliant men of action, nor original thinkers, bold pioneers*

*and reformers; far more often it produces "good" weaklings
who later became lost in the crowd that tends to follow pain-
fully the initiative of strong characters.*[8]

And further in the same vein:

*The behavior of a human being in sexual matters is often
a prototype for the whole of his other modes of reaction
to life. A man who has shown determination in possessing
himself of his love-object has our confidence in his success
in regard to other aims as well. On the other hand, a man
who abstains, for whatever reasons, from satisfying his
strong sexual instinct, will also assume a conciliatory and
resigned attitude in other paths of life.*[9]

In 1923, with the publication of *The Ego and the Id,* Freud
elaborated his previous fragmentary formulations of the concept of
sublimation by introducing a new supplementary concept, the transformation of instinctual energy: "I am only putting forward a hypothesis; I have no proof to offer. It seems a plausible view that this
displaceable and neutral energy, which is no doubt active both
in the ego and in the id, proceeds from the narcissistic store of
libido—that it is desexualized Eros. . . . If displaceable energy is
desexualized libido, it may also be described as *sublimated* energy.
. . . The transformation [of erotic libido] into ego-libido of course
involves an abandonment of sexual aims, a desexualization." [10]

By turning to his last major work, *An Outline of Psychoanalysis,*
we learn that Freud never drastically modified these views. There
he made what seems to have been his final statement on sublimation. After discussing prohibitions of infantile sexuality and their
influence on one's readiness for cultural growth, Freud stated:

*The instinctual demands, being forced aside from direct
satisfaction, are compelled to take new directions which lead
to substitute satisfaction, and in the course of these détours
they may become desexualized and their connection with
their original instinctual aims may become looser. And at
this point we can anticipate the idea that much of our most
highly valued cultural heritage has been acquired at the cost
of sexuality and by the restriction of sexual motive forces.*[11]

Freud believed that the capacity to "deinstinctualize" had physiological roots, and that its power varied from individual to individual. But though he clearly sensed the strong relationship between artistic creativity and free access to one's own sexuality, we do not know that he considered the possibility that undisguised sexual experience could be involved in sublimated activity, nor did he ever make explicit whether sexual gratification and sublimation or creativity are parallel or function in sequence within his conceptual scheme.

"OVERT" SEXUALITY IN ART

The reports of our respondents unequivocally substantiate Freud's basic hypothesis of the sexual roots of the energies involved in artistic creativity; at the same time they indicate that these energies often appear in a much less "transformed," "desexualized," or "neutralized" form than might have been expected from the hypothesis that Freud tentatively advanced in 1923. With minor variations, our painters reported having intense physical and emotional reactions *while working:*

> *Sometimes it's like a sexual experience. I mean sometimes there is actually a twinge. I've had it. Also, when I once went to a show of Cézanne, I had something like a contraction, you know, it was physical. I think that when you get very excited, and you do in painting, then there are certain physical feelings.*

One male artist reported even more specific sexual reactions while working: "You know, there are many times when I'm working out something on the canvas that I have an erection—I get excited, and you can tell that it isn't the content of my paintings that does it, just by looking at them." Others, as we shall see, told of feelings which ranged from those that were directly and unmistakably sexual through states of more or less diffuse excitation, to emotional reactions which could still be likened to sexual feelings, although they were consciously experienced at a point relatively remote from sexuality. Despite differences in the quality and intensity of their feelings, as well as in their reported frequency and duration, few respondents doubted their importance. Even the exceptional artist who was inclined to regard art as a completely intellectual activity still granted its power "to move":

> *There may be a sexual component in art, but I don't think it's an important one. You may be able to read in sexual images, or sexual content, or even sexuality into some art, just as you can read aggressiveness or lyrical qualities and so on. But I don't think they are really important factors. I don't think there is anything emotional about art. I don't think that art is emotional in the sense that we measure human emotions, such as under the headings of hate and love, anger, and so on. One is moved by art, real art, because one recognizes the great knowledge, skill, and perceptions of different kinds that go into the making of such great works. It may make you wonder or pause to wonder how it is possible for a man to have done such a thing. But it doesn't arouse emotional or, as far as I am concerned, sexual activity.*

More typical responses gave ready recognition to intense emotional experiences, however differently they were characterized. Even further, there were many direct references to sexuality. Some of the terminology was symbolic or derivative, that is, it pertained to matters of vigor, vitality, power, rebirth, the emergence of strength, second wind, and a new prowess. The rest referred to frank and undisguised sexuality:

> *It's the act of spending your life in a highly creative moment —it's almost a physical ecstasy that's very close to sexual excitement. I know it's not identified as such, but it is that kind.*

> *I've several times referred to vitality. That's important, and vitality doesn't always mean jumping around and looking vital. I can only speak for myself. I happen to have a lot of energy and am often very spontaneous. Physically I like to be on the go and my mind also races at times. There's an excitement and thrill in painting. I mean, if you are in the middle of a picture or if you stand back and look at a picture you made, you feel thrilled by it and your heart pounds. This is very real.*

Most of the time painting is not a pleasure. It's a kind of torment. Well, maybe it's pleasurable like the way you put your tongue in a cavity is pleasurable. You know, a sore spot in your mouth you keep going back to. But every now and then every artist has the feeling he's getting close to something and that is when it becomes quite intense. It starts out relatively calm and sort of builds up as you come nearer and nearer to completion.

It still is a thrilling thing to make something which is— which you feel works. When I'm making a thing, I'm very excited about it. I often have trouble in working it out, but in the end I always work it out to a point where I'm quite excited about it. I agree that afterwards, a few months later, or sometimes many months later, I've grown away from it and may be less convinced, but at the time I'm making it, it's all very exciting. In that way it's just like sex. It's hard to compare it with any other . . . with the last time you did it.

Oh, there's a big sexual component in everything. Haven't you ever read the book? I mean, really. I'm getting kind of funny now, but sure there is. Does anybody say no? But you have to be careful about language. After all, what do they mean when they say something? You see, people are complicated. Some people seem to be very vigorous and they are actually only manic. And other people seem to be quite calm and they are seething volcanos.

These quotations give a random picture of the varied feelings directly experienced by painters in their work. In light of what is known about creative artists, this richness and intensity of feeling should come as no surprise. The *sine qua non* for creative work in any field is a teeming inner life and an ability to allow its expression without being overwhelmed by it. Painters are given recognition for having rich fantasy lives, powerful emotional resources, and the ability to utilize these assets constructively. Of special interest here, however, is how frequently these artists suggest, either directly or indirectly, that many of the feelings they experience while painting are sexual in nature. Even those who deny libidinal elements still describe their feelings in such a way that sexual interpretations are almost inescapable.

One need not be a "Freudian" to feel the erotic content of such responses as: "The spread of art at any time is a real tender thing. You've got to be right on top of something, about to come down on it. And the thing is that art is a feminine thing, fresh and sensitive."

When confronted with the discrepancies between their reported feelings and those imputed to them by theoreticians who view painting as desexualized form of sublimation, our respondents simply reject the latter on the basis of their own experiences:

> *I think if you try to divorce sex from art, what would it be? I think it does have a big connection. I think any art has sexual implications.*

> *That's an interesting question. Well, I'm not going to answer you literally, and I don't think I even ought to answer you literally; I don't think I ought to answer it in any way because I have to use what Picasso said, that is, what the Spanish word for potency is. Cajones. [Is that important?] I think it is one of the most gracious things to have. Yes sir, yes sir; there is a sexual component in art. I'm not necessarily aware of it when I'm painting, but I do feel it.*

The responses of those artists who were inclined to dissociate art from sexuality have a surprisingly uncertain, groping, and querulous quality, which stands in sharp contrast to their usual firmness. This hesitancy no doubt reflects some quasi-conscious uncertainty about the stand they take:

> *Some things are obvious, that is, when you're doing a body and you're thinking about the parts, and this is a finger and this is another thing. You then have to think about sex; it's impossible to deny it, in that sense. I can get aroused doing that. But as far as when I put an orange there and I draw the shape, I would say that's a purely physical feeling. I wouldn't use the word sex for it. But there probably is a sexual aspect to anything physical. So when I make a line like that, it could possibly be related to something like sex. But that is what is horrible about a lot of people. That*

physical sensation that they have from painting is great because they are all through physically, you see?

The basic thing is that painting requires a greater concentration of energy and that's what makes anything good. This energy comes from the exertion, but it shouldn't ever be called sexual. It may coincide; it probably does coincide with a man's period of highest sexual prowess. I don't know what the charts say, but I suppose that a man in his twenties and early thirties is sexually more potent than in his fifties. But that doesn't mean that you should call painting sex.

When sex is eliminated by logic and fact, no alternate suggestion is easily found:

I don't think it's got anything to do with potency or virility or vigor. I mean, how can you explain some of the most revolutionary painting done, that is, painting which is in essence more revolutionary vis-à-vis its time than anything we've done in our time? It was done, for instance, by Monet, when he was in his eighties; Titian painted until he was ninety-six and did his most advanced work at the end; and Goya did his best work in his seventies. I mean this certainly can't be a sexual equivalent, at least in the usual sense. These men were more powerful pictorially and imaginatively and they were each in their old age.*

Some interesting questions may thus be raised about the specific relationship between sexuality and artistic productivity. The extraordinary output of some artists at very advanced ages, where there

---

* Kurt Eissler asks the same question:

There is something strange about the old-age achievements of some geniuses. When they reach an age at which others retrench their contact with a world that dwindlingly appeals and live in conformity with the gradual weakening of sense organs and memory, some geniuses burst forth with creations that sometimes overshadow everything they have created until then, as if impending death released them of an inhibition and they could say or express something that they had carried within themselves all their lives. This last impression, although not invalid, is one-sided, since a lifetime experience is synthesized in these last works. Such final-release works are Beethoven's last quartets, Titian's last paintings, Rembrandt's last self-portraits, Goethe's second part of *Faust* and *Wilhelm Meisters Wanderjahre,* and probably also Freud's book on *Moses.*[12]

is an apparent inverse relationship between increasing age and productivity, on the one hand, and the usual descending curve of sexual potency, on the other; the relationship between type of art produced and feelings associated with it; and the difference between the quality of sexual feelings experienced while painting and those experienced in direct sexual activity—the more we know about all this, the more light we can shed on the question of instinctual energy and artistic purpose.

THE LACK OF SUBLIMATION

Freud alone does not really clarify these matters. The cornerstone of his speculations, the concept of sublimation, as he left it, is not adequate to deal with such complex relationships. More recent work by Ernst Kris and Kurt Eissler, among others, may have opened new possibilities. Their formulations, based, as in the case of Freud, upon intensive investigations of small numbers of artists, are sufficiently disparate to dramatize how ambiguous is the concept of sublimation today. In time, however, these newer efforts may provide a conceptual framework within which questions like those posed above may be more fruitfully examined. In this connection, then, it is worth noting some of the significant modifications that have been introduced into the concept of sublimation * by these workers, especially since our painters' responses coincide better with some of their hypotheses.

Perhaps the most important reformulation was introduced by Heinz Hartmann, Ernst Kris, and Rudolph Loewenstein.† These

---

* Prior to these reformulations, certain theoretical modifications had been suggested by other psychoanalysts, such as S. Bernfeld, E. Glover, and R. Sterba, but none of them resulted in a basic recasting of the concept.

† Ernst Kris, himself a distinguished art historian and once curator of a museum in Vienna, briefly summarized their conclusions in 1952:

> Sublimation, listed also as one of the defense mechanisms of the ego, designated two processes so clearly related to each other that one might be tempted to speak of one and the same process: it refers to the displacement of energy discharge from a socially inacceptable goal to an acceptable one and to a transformation of the energy discharged; for this second process we here adopt the word "neutralization." The usefulness of the distinction between the two meanings becomes apparent when we realize that goal substitution and energy transformation need not be synchronous; the more acceptable, i.e., "higher," activity can be executed with energy that has retained or regained its original instinctual quality.[13]

psychoanalysts accepted Freud's hypothesis on the instinctual sources of energy channeled into creative activity, but they suggested *two* possible pathways for the use of this energy—each allowing expression of forbidden impulses at a higher and more socially acceptable level. The first route permits direct expression of *untransformed* energy through the "higher" activity, with the original instinctual quality of the energy unmodified, despite a shift in goals. The second pathway corresponds roughly with Freud's formulations: the instinctual energy itself is "neutralized" before being used for modified goals.[14] It is clear that the first pathway proposed by these writers comes closer to fitting our data than do Freud's constructs.

The new psychoanalytic view was supported by empirical observations made on creative persons during the so-called Gifted Adolescent Project. Annie Reich, one of the psychoanalysts who worked with Kris on this famous study, reported:

> *What impressed Kris and us all was that complex artistic and intellectual (i.e., mathematical) productions were mainly not expressions of neutralized energy and detached from areas of conflict, but to a large degree were accompanied by signs of openly sexual as well as aggressive excitement . . . made it tempting to conclude that talented people, especially those gifted in the field of art, are characterized by a particular nearness to instinctual life; that they are, one might say, "more alive" than other people. Such aliveness has to do with a special state of libidinal excitement . . . its sexual character is not always conscious . . . but it can be transformed into . . . background excitement that accompanies the so-called sublimated activity.*[15]

The similarity here to our own findings is self-evident. What surprised us was that, unlike the psychoanalytic material gathered by Kris and his associates, in every case ours came from a single and, by psychiatric standards, superficial interview.

All these observations clearly refer to instances where untransformed energy was used in the "sublimated" or displaced activity. While Kris and his associates still regarded energy transformation or neutralization as a precondition to normal psychological functioning in many areas, their empirical findings led them to propose the alternative and more direct route for expression of instinctual drives through creativity.* Kris contrasted the tone of the older formulations with more recent views of sublimation and instinctual gratification in the discussion of a sculptor studied during the Gifted Adolescent Project:

> *I have never learned so much about real creation. This case and another experience I have had show that we still have rather bookish ideas about sublimation, bookish in the sense that now we are inclined to think that sublimation is at a very great distance from instinctual life. . . . What you see here rather is how the instinctual gratification is omnipresent in the act itself, so that it is really the maximum gratification of the instinctual side. I think it is very impressive how the defensive and gratifying aspects in this man are constantly interwoven in his sublimation.*[17]

The usual criticism could be made of generalizing from psychoanalytic research: all subjects in the study were also analytic patients. Hence it is of great interest that our own respondents provide the same kind of material, even though they are actively functioning and highly successful painters, and all seemed to be making a reasonable personal adjustment.† Yet it must be admitted that when one of our first female respondents initially described her emotions while painting as involving a pattern of sexual arousal and

---

* It is worth noting that the use of "untransformed energy," in contradistinction to Freud's concept of sublimation, was found to apply to intellectual as well as artistic creativity. This was a direct challenge to Freud, who considered the intellect to be very far removed from instinctual life. The relevant observations were elaborated by Loomie, Rosen, and Stein in their description of a gifted young mathematician, a subject in the Gifted Adolescent Project. This man demonstrated:

> . . . a curious fluidity of fantasy. Although initially the mental content could directly represent intercourse, this could be replaced by the integral sign from calculus or by other mathematical symbols. It was his repeated experience when attempting to ward off nocturnal sexual feelings that a preoccupation with a mathematical problem would be accompanied by an erotic sensation and even the solution of the problem would often be attended by orgasm.[16]

Lest their material be construed to indicate very disturbed intellectual functioning, it should be said that the authors describe this man as an exceedingly successful mathematician who was regularly accorded professional honor and recognition.

† While personal adjustment is difficult to assess in a single interview, in any case our respondents could not be categorized as a "patient" population.

excitation, accompanied by several of their physical concomitants, and followed by a sense of release, fatigue, and finally a desire to sleep—we were somewhat dubious about the general nature of her experience. Indeed, we were inclined to dismiss it as a personal idosyncracy. Subsequent interviews convinced us that the phenomenon was not unusual. The comments of other artists clearly revealed undisguised sexual feelings that were aroused in painting:

X
> *I have a feeling that painting has a lot to do with sex; it really does. I mean, I'm sure you talked to a lot of artists. I often get sexually excited when I paint. A lot of artists do. They often get very excited and then start thinking about sex. There's something about the handling of the material that's very sexual. I don't know. I don't even want to get to the bottom of it; I just know it's there.*

> *Oh, listen. That stuff you never think of, you know. It comes from there to a great extent, from the balls. There is a direct sexual experience in the creating of an art work. In mine there is. When it comes, at a certain point, you will not even know when, it wells up. To me it is like a fountain . . . it spreads out like a huge orgasm.*

Our data thus lend support to reformulations introduced in recent psychoanalytic studies of creativity. At least for our sample of "normal" artists, it is clear that the act of painting provides opportunities for the displaced expression of untransformed instinctual drives, whether they be erotic or aggressive in nature. Thus Freud's concept of artistic sublimation, especially as it presupposed that sublimation and instinctual gratification were at a great distance from each other, appears definitely outdated.

ENERGY, CREATIVITY AND QUALITY

Kris made one other point concerning artistic creation, which in this context has at least tangential relevance. He saw the creative process as a reality that operates on two levels, each contributing to and being influenced by the other in a variety of ways. He labeled these levels *inspiration* and *elaboration,* and characterized them, in sequence, as ". . . the feeling of being driven, the experience of rapture, and the conviction that an outside agent acts through the creator" and ". . . the experience of purposeful organization, and the intent to solve a problem . . ." [18] The latter has to do with technical and intellectual aspects of creation. But for our more general discussion, inspiration must be seen as a phenomenon veined with erotic emotion. Kris's choice of words could not have been accidental and therefore their sexual connotations cannot be ignored. He later commented that not all artistic creation was inspirational in origin, "But whenever art reaches a certain level, inspiration is at work." [19] This suggests an additional avenue of exploration, that is, a study of the relationships between the quality (admittedly a very subjective matter) of an artistic creation and the intensity of instinctual energy available during its emergence. Our own painters offer a hint:

> *I thought you'd come to that. You find yourself involved in a certain magic of giving form to a material and feel its evocative power. There is a certain feeling of dealing with something that is secret and putting a finger on something that is exciting. There is a great deal of sensual feeling, but I don't believe in the sense of catharsis. It's another sense. It's a vitality of a certain kind, but not to do with will and power. Sometimes when we feel good, we feel more of it in order to get organized, and then the good picture comes. You obey your intentions easily. You can touch and pull things together that are more difficult when you don't feel vital.*

Kurt Eissler is even more definite about the relationship between unmodified instinctual energy and artistic creativity. As a result of his research he claims that "instinctual energy enters the creative process at its fullest whenever great art results." [20]

Eissler derives his conclusions from a detailed study of the lives of two creative geniuses, Leonardo da Vinci and Goethe. Since he puts particular stress upon the development of artistic creativity at its highest level, much that he has learned may apply only to the genius. Nevertheless, his schema is of considerable interest. It presents a new view of the questions we posed earlier in this chapter;

it revives older ideas that have been ignored far too long; and it may have greater applicability to mere talent than is now recognized.

Eissler distinguishes between genius and talent by using the ancient formula: "The talent *can create,* the genius *has to create."* * Beyond this, he observes that: "The genius and the talent have in common that both have talents, but the genius has the additional gift of creating out of his talents something that is not accessible to the talent." [22] He further emphasizes differences when he suggests: "What is correct for the talent is not necessarily valid for the genius, since in my estimation the genius is not to be looked upon as a quantitatively enhanced talent but as one different in quality—a view that does not deny that in the talent or in a patient some observations can be made that are valid also of the genius." [23] But for Eissler, the most telling distinction is that: "The difference between the genius and the talent may depend upon what biological source it is that supplies the energy for the sublimatory process . . ." [24] This turns on the theoretical assumption that the energy which powers the actions of an individual is derived from different sources at various stages in his development.† Many psychoanalysts hold that the energy utilized in the creative act derives from an early and less mature (pregenital) period in the individual's life. An occasional comment by our artists would support such a view:

> *I think there are intimate dimensions in painting. Much more than that, it's not like Freud's farfetched ideas. I think it has more to do with caressing, with touch, with certain types of scratching and biting. It's a very sensuous kind of*

---

* Ernest Jones quotes a variety of sources in his essay on *The Nature of Genius* [21] which utilize the same formula in attempting to make this differentiation. We have no way of making accurate comparisons of the urgency with which talent and genius create, but we have seen in our exceptionally talented group that their compulsion to create is very powerful; it is not likely that many of our respondents would be regarded as geniuses.

† Eissler believes that the source of sublimated energy for the genius is found in genital libido, whereas for most people it is the pregenital sexual components which are available for sublimation. He is in effect suggesting that for the genius ordinary relationships may be reversed, with pregenital pleasures often readily available to him as "a compensation for or an adjunct to keeping genitality free for sublimation." [25]

> *thing, you know, painting. You discover the brush and the*
> *canvas or the surface . . . the resistance of the surface. There*
> *are just so many levels; that's one of the levels.*

But the view that energies utilized in the creative act derive from mature (genital) sexual sources is more consistently supported by our painters. It is really not a new view. Adrian Stokes reminds us that as early as 1923 Melanie Klein had focused upon genital activity as an important determinant of artistic creativity. She had suggested that a certain amount of genital libido was deflected into sublimation. Stokes also quotes from a 1947 paper by Ella Sharpe:

> *It seems to me that the conception of a work of art in its*
> *total harmonious unity, is only possible when a unification*
> *of component trends under genital primacy has occurred.*
> *. . . This impulse may be foreshadowed in the pregenital*
> *impulses and is often expressed in their terms, but is neverthe-*
> *less dynamized by genital libido.*[26]

But Eissler, while generally limiting his conclusions to the creative genius, is the first writer to put this question into a systematic framework by relating the level of creativity to his own theoretical formulations about the sublimatory process.

Eissler rejects the concept of sublimation in its pure Freudian form,* but retains the term—applying it solely to changes of instinctual aim. The reader will recall that Kris accepted energy transformation as a possible pathway to creativity, simultaneously introducing the idea that untransformed energies could also be used within the "sublimated" activity. Eissler goes further by rejecting the concept of neutralized energy altogether. He holds that there is no alteration of instinctual drives when they are involved in a creative act; he believes that the energy preserves its instinctual quality throughout:

---

* Notwithstanding his deference to other psychoanalysts, Eissler clearly takes issue with them:
> It is always difficult to contend that an event observers assert they have witnessed did not take place at all; I therefore hesitate to dispute the existence of sublimation in terms of energy transformation or neutralization (as defined at present) and limit myself to the contention that, if it does exist, it is of minor importance in the total economy of the personality.[27]

> *. . . I feel certain that the energetic processes we are wont to denote under the term "sublimation" do not constitute a transformation of energy of instinctual quality into indifferent energy. Furthermore, the existence of such a thing as indifferent energy must be doubted quite generally.*[28]

Like Freud and Kris, then, Eissler accepts the intimate relationship between sexuality and creativity, but he excludes the possibility of an intermediate conversion process which makes the instinctual energy available in modified form. But this is not his only deviation from Freud and Kris; there are other matters on which he differs with equal vigor.

CREATIVITY AND SEXUAL INDULGENCE

Eissler departs radically from Freud's position when he suggests that artistic creativity and sexual indulgence are mutually incompatible, at least at the level of genius. He later tempers this position in a way which makes it seem less extreme and more plausible, but his basic view is still a departure:

> *Yet in view of the perfection of the few creations that have reached us from Leonardo, one could speculate on the possibility that without abstinence the quality of the few paintings would not have been so high. Moderate gratification of the instinctual demand might have resulted in increased production in quantitative terms, so it may be argued, but militated against the supreme quality Leonardo achieved. Only the genius totally deprived of the possibility of physical discharge because of an insuperable barrier could throw his total energy into the creative act. To be sure, one may continue to reason the price to pay may be the qualms and hesitations that beset the artist Leonardo, but this price is not too high in view of the excellence of the result.*[29]

This view runs directly counter to the theory propounded by Freud, who said that he could not conceive of a sexually abstinent artist. Eissler, on the other hand, contends that an artistic genius must be sexually abstinent to attain his highest creative potential.

Freud stated that direct sexual activity and experience provide the artist with inspiration, while Eissler feels that such inspiration will appear only when genital energies are dammed up, i.e., when they fail to be released in sexual exertion. Freud believed that the inhibitions and passivity implicit in sexual abstinence would be reflected in a lack of the forcefulness and confidence which are required for creative action. Eissler grants that qualms and hesitations may indeed befall the abstinent genius, but he believes that the quality of his creation reaches its peak in a state of sexual deprivation.

Eissler recognizes that his thesis is controversial, the more so since it does not pretend to fit the lives of many great artists. The same may be said of Freud when he argues that artists need sexual outlets for their work to flourish.* Eissler marshals some convincing evidence to support his position, for example, that in the sexual sphere Leonardo led an essentially monastic life. He also demonstrates how Goethe's level of productivity fluctuated inversely according to the degree of direct gratification he was experiencing in his love relationships. Eissler also reproduces a revealing excerpt from a Van Gogh letter (quoted by Meyer Schapiro in 1956) which indicates how negatively that artist felt about sexuality:

> *Personally, I feel that continence is good for me, that it is enough for our weak, impressionable artists' brains to give their essence to the creation of our pictures. For when we reflect, calculate, exhaust ourselves, we spend cerebral energy. Why exert ourselves to pour out all creative sap when the well-fed professional pimps and ordinary fools do better satisfying the genital organs of the whore, who is in this case more submissive than we ourselves?* [30]

(This excerpt also lends itself to other interpretations, especially if Van Gogh's known pathology is taken into consideration.) The lives of many other geniuses show the same degree of sexual disinclination. Richard and Editha Sterba, in discussing Beethoven's sexual life, comment that:

* Freud attributed Leonardo's relatively limited artistic output to his having avoided sexual activity throughout his life. Eissler takes the same evidence and uses it to support his contention that abstinence and the creativity of an artistic genius are strongly allied with each other.

> *Beethoven remained unmarried throughout his life. We*
> *know little—in fact, nothing concrete—of his love-life. Al-*
> *though the reports about it from different sources are some-*
> *what contradictory, they leave us with the general impression*
> *that his love-relationships were inhibited, cautious, and un-*
> *successful. We have no knowledge of any fully consummated*
> *love affair, although one document exists which expresses*
> *a deep feeling for a woman.*[31]

And in the three letters which make up this document,[32] there are numerous references to his sexual inhibitions and conflicts.

Despite this evidence about certain artistic titans of the Western world, there are of course other cases which contradict theirs. Eissler, in his effort to develop a general theory of artistic genius, deals with this problem by defining sexual abstinence in a very special sense. To Eissler, abstinence does not mean the absence of genital activity. Indeed, genital activity as such is almost irrelevant; it is the meaning and the psychic consequence of sexual behavior which are crucial:

> *It does not mean to suggest that the genius quality requires*
> *lack of genital activity. Frequency of genital activity is no*
> *indicator at all of the degree of genital sublimation; what*
> *counts is only such factors as actual pleasures gained or ex-*
> *haustion of the biological pleasure potential, and the mean-*
> *ing of the genital function in the conscious and unconscious*
> *systems.*[33]

Eissler maintains that, at least for the genius, it is the energy associated with genital sexuality which provides the driving power released in artistic expression, and he pictures its possible expenditure in direct sexual activity as erecting a great obstacle to any artist's fulfillment of his creative potential. But here he introduces so many reservations that in the end they cover all eventualities. For instance: "It is quite conceivable that a subject might be constitutionally endowed with a particularly great supply of genital libido, so that even extensive sublimation of genital libido would not interfere with a rich genital life." [34] This provides too much latitude; so qualified, Eissler's formulations cannot be empirically proved or disproved. It appears that the artistic genius should avoid direct genital satisfactions if he is to be lavishly creative; on the other hand, if he indulges in sex and continues to be effective, it may mean (1) that he is still achieving less than his ultimate artistic potential, (2) that he has been endowed with an excess of genital-libidinal energy, which makes it possible for him to engage in sustained sexual activity, and at the same time to expend maximum energy in creative work, or (3) that his sexual acts are psychically "meaningless" and do not drain the energies required for significant creation. Given this range, the role of sexuality could hardly be assessed at all in the creative artist, genius or not.

But Eissler carries his explanation beyond physical gratification into the realm of object-relationships.* He suggests that for the artistic genius, not only is it helpful if his available sexual outlets are blocked, but more importantly, severe limitations must be imposed on the quality and intensity of his object relations: "As soon as he achieves a satisfactory mode of object-relationship—and for the genius only an ideal mode is likely to be satisfactory—he simultaneously loses the capacity for creating great art." [35] Elsewhere Eissler makes essentially the same point:

> It is conceivable that we shall one day recognize that a normal vita sexualis *is incompatible with certain types of artistic geniushood . . . it does not seem possible that he would be capable of his extraordinary creations if his libido were gratified in an adequate object relation. The energy flow into the object relation would be diverted from the artistic process. Consequently, only the blockage of a permanent object attachment can produce that intense hunger for objects that results in the substitute formation of the perfect work of art.*[36]

And in *Goethe* he makes his most explicit statement on the matter:

> In general it may be said that objects are of importance to the genius only in so far as the experiences with them will serve the comprehensive goal of creating life in the form of art, that is to say, only those objects that are potential stimuli

---

* The term *object-relationship* in psychoanalytic language refers to the nature of enduring emotional ties to significant persons in the individual's life, which go beyond immediate gratification of instinctual needs.

> *of future works of art can become relevant in the genius's life. As soon as the longing for the objects themselves successfully competes with the urge to create, creativeness must lose in momentum. When the relation to the object provides real happiness and causes gratifications that reduce tensions to a normal level, again no momentum towards creation remains, and either no work of art will issue or only one of second quality. If, however, the longing for and the love of the object is experienced at maximum but the possession of the object is frustrated, then the full momentum towards the recreation of the object in the form of a work of art will be preserved. Thus maximum tension combined with maximum frustration is one of the constellations that may enable a genius to produce works in keeping with his innate talents.*[37]

According to Eissler, then, the artistic genius, if he is to be prodigiously creative, must live under the constant tension of unfulfilled longings; direct gratification of his instinctual and object needs would deplete his creative drive. Yet though they remain ungratified, his strong yearnings for the ideal object must persist. Otherwise, inner emotional pressures could not be maintained at the level of intensity which would result in the substitute creation of an extraordinary work of art.* These conclusions are consistent with those discussed in Chapter Four.

If such assumptions have even limited applicability to "ordinary" talent (and it seems to us that they do), then certain aspects of our artists' personal lives may be easier to interpret. We see more clearly why they so often seem detached and distant even in their most intimate relationships.† Regardless of whether it is justified as a deliberate choice or explained away as a psychic necessity outside the individual's control, artists do show a need to remain relatively

---

* Eissler is careful to point out these alternatives of object-relationships and genius creativity are not matters of will or conscious choice. He presumes that: "In the genius there are safety devices that come automatically into play and protect him against ever losing himself in the pleasures of a true object-relationship." [38]

† For an almost caricatured picture illustrating this point, see Diego Rivera's *My Art, My Life*.

uncommitted to everyone and everything except their work. This attitude is reflected also in their everyday affairs; where life draws them into involvements which go beyond a certain intensity, their work problems increase. Very likely, when they verbalize a need to protect themselves from debilitating encounters, to maintain a distance from personal and social involvements, and when they define themselves as "artists first," they express in volitional terms certain deeply rooted and partly unconscious attitudes. An insatiable search for the beautiful, the perfect, and the ideal probably represents a psychic necessity which all artists, those possessed of talent and genius alike, experience both consciously and unconsciously.

This theorizing may seem very remote from our painters, but similar views on the fate of creative artists have found expression elsewhere, even in purely literary representations, many of which predate psychoanalysis. In a recent volume, *The Double Image,* Victor Erlich traces varying attitudes toward that "fate" found in representatives of several literary movements. These attitudes vary from a consciously cultivated stance of "aloofness from, and superiority to, the common herd," [39] to regarding enforced artistic detachment as a curse. For example, in summarizing the attitudes expressed by the Russian symbolist poet Briusov: "It is his [the poet's] duty— and his destiny—to withdraw a part of himself from the maelstrom of emotion in order to keep it cool, and thus available for observation, introspection, recording, mental note-taking. Otherwise, it seems, the encounter might go to waste, the love affair might fail to produce a love poem." [40] In contrast to this, Thomas Mann's Tonio Kroeger regards his calling as a curse:

> *The artist must be inhuman, extra-human; he must stand in a queer aloof relationship to our humanity; . . . the very gift of style, of form and expression, is nothing else than this cool and fastidious attitude towards humanity. . . . For sound natural feeling, say what you like, has no taste. It is all up with the artist as soon as he becomes a man and begins to feel. . . . What a fate! That is, if you still have enough heart, enough warmth of affections, to feel how frightful it is!* [41]

Thus these somewhat speculative ideas on the relationship between an artist's instinctual life and his creativity find support in still another quarter—self-observation by poets.

The rather fragmentary way in which our data relate to the several hypotheses considered here reflects in part the incompleteness of our interviews. It also has to do with the present status of sublimation as an operational concept. There are so many conflicting views on the connection between instinctual energies and creative activity that Frederick Hacker scarcely exaggerates when he says that "the theory of sublimation, the mental mechanism presumably underlying artistic production, is in an almost hopeless state of confusion," [42] both as a psychoanalytic concept and as one which might further our understanding of the creative process. However, certain consistent trends we find both in the verbalizations of our artists and in the formulations of Kris, Eissler, and others lead us to hope that some of this confusion may yet be dispelled. Hartmann, Kris, and Loewenstein's specification of non-neutralized energy in the creative act has already been substantiated in large measure by a growing body of empirical evidence. Eissler's view which postulates an inverse relationship between object satisfaction and creative activity presents a provocative thesis for further research, relative to talent as well as genius. Phyllis Greenacre's writings on the creative artist's never-ending search for the "idealized father" (discussed in Chapter Four) are directly related to these views. Despite the confusions which now exist, data are accumulating on the subject—along with many interesting and suggestive hypotheses. One may hope that in time a more firmly validated, more fully unified concept of sublimation will emerge, and that it will do justice to the rich material now at hand.

NOTES

INTRODUCTION
(pages 1-9)

1. Randall Jarrell, *Poetry and the Age*, New York, 1953, pp. 21-22.
2. Robert N. Wilson, *The Arts in Society*, Englewood Cliffs, N. J., 1964, p. 8.

I

THE NEW YORK SCHOOL: EMERGENCE
AND TRIUMPH
(pages 11-38)

1. *Encounter*, October 1964, p. 44.
2. Hilton Kramer, "Art Chronicle," *The Hudson Review*, Vol. 15, No. 3 (Autumn 1962).
3. Lewis Mumford, "The Role of the Creative Arts in Contemporary Society," *The Virginia Quarterly Review*, Vol. 33, No. 4 (Autumn 1957), pp. 522-523.
4. John Rewald, *The History of Impressionism*, New York, 1961, p. 7.

2

GENERATIONAL CONFLICT
(pages 39-63)

1. Kingsley Davis, "The Sociology of Parent-Youth Conflict," *American Sociological Review*, Vol. 5 (1940), pp. 523-535.
2. Erving Goffman, *The Presentation of Self in Everyday Life*, New York, 1959.
3. *New York Times Book Review*, September 6, 1964.
4. Leo Tolstoy, "What Is Art?" in *The Art of the Essay*, Leslie Fiedler, ed., New York, 1958, p. 490.
5. Mark Harris, "Government as Patron of the Arts," *New York Times Magazine*, September 13, 1964.

3

SOCIAL AND PSYCHOLOGICAL
CHARACTERISTICS
(pages 65-99)

1. Miguel Prados, "Rorschach Studies on Artists and Painters," *Rorschach Research Exchange*, VIII (October 1944), pp. 178-183.
2. Anne Roe, "Artists and Their Work," *Journal of Personality*, Vol. 15 (1946), pp. 1-40.
3. Bernice T. Eiduson, "Artist and Nonartist: A Comparative Study," *Journal of Personality*, Vol. 26 (1958), pp. 13-14.

4. Alexander Eliot, *Sight and Insight,* New York, 1960, p. 30.
5. Clive Bell, *Art,* New York, 1958, p. 159.
6. Eiduson, pp. 25-26.
7. *Ibid.,* p. 22.
8. *Ibid.,* pp. 19-20.
9. Roe, p. 4.
10. Phyllis Greenacre, "The Childhood of the Artist," in *The Psychoanalytic Study of the Child,* XII, New York, 1957, p. 53.
11. Heinz Hartmann, "Notes on the Theory of Sublimation," in *The Psychoanalytic Study of the Child,* X, New York, 1955, p. 14.
12. R. G. Collingwood, *The Principles of Art,* New York, 1958, p. 6.
13. Greenacre, p. 47.
14. Morris and Natalie Haimowitz, "What Makes Them Creative?" in *Human Development,* Morris and Natalie Haimowitz, ed., New York, 1960, pp. 45-46.
15. Greenacre, p. 53.
16. André Malraux, *Voices of Silence,* New York, 1953, p. 493.
17. Eiduson, p. 22.
18. Greenacre, p. 58.
19. Prados, p. 183.
20. George Stoddard, *The Meaning of Intelligence,* New York, 1945, pp. 299-315.
21. Maurice Grosser, *The Painter's Eye,* New York, 1961, p. 101.
22. Malraux, p. 344.
23. Roe, p. 3.
24. Bruno Klopfer, as quoted in Anne Roe, "Painting and Personality," *Rorschach Research Exchange,* X (1946), p. 89.

4

ORIGINS: FAMILIAL AND CULTURAL

(pages 101-141)

1. Bernice T. Eiduson, "Artist and Nonartist: A Comparative Study," *Journal of Personality,* Vol. 26 (1958), p. 22.
2. André Malraux, *Voices of Silence,* New York, 1953, p. 281.
3. Anne Roe, "Artists and Their Work," *Journal of Personality,* Vol. 15 (1946), p. 5.
4. W. Lloyd Warner, Marcia Meeker, and Kenneth Eells, *Social Class in America,* Chicago, 1949.
5. Harold Rosenberg, *Arshile Gorky,* New York, 1962, p. 22.
6. Roe, p. 4.
7. Ernst Kris, *Psychoanalytic Explorations in Art,* New York, 1952, pp. 72-73; Phyllis Greenacre, *The Quest for the Father,* New York, 1963, pp. 18-19; Kurt Eissler, *Goethe,* Detroit, 1963, p. 1362.
8. Sigmund Freud, "Formulations Regarding the Two Principles in Mental Functioning," in *Collected Papers,* IV, London, 1948, p. 19.
9. Sigmund Freud, *Leonardo da Vinci,* New York, 1947, p. 62.
10. Ernst Kris, as quoted in "Ernst Kris and the Gifted Adolescent Project," in *The Psychoanalytic Study of the Child,* XIII, New York, 1958, p. 53.

11. Phyllis Greenacre, "The Childhood of the Artist," in *The Psychoanalytic Study of the Child*, XII, New York, 1957, p. 54.
12. *Ibid.*, p. 58.
13. Gardner Murphy, *Human Potentialities*, New York, 1958, p. 131.
14. *Ibid.*
15. Edward Hitschmann, *Great Men*, New York, 1956, p. 202.
16. *Ibid.*, p. 213.
17. Phyllis Greenacre, *Swift and Carroll*, New York, 1955, p. 122.
18. *Ibid.*, p. 127.
19. Kurt Eissler, *Leonardo da Vinci*, New York, 1961, p. 95.
20. Milton Miller, *Nostalgia*, London, 1957, pp. 3-9.
21. *Ibid.*, p. 279.
22. Erik Erikson, *Young Man Luther*, New York, 1958, p. 73.
23. David Beres, "The Family Romance of the Artist," in *The Psychoanalytic Study of the Child*, XIII, New York, 1958, p. 40.
24. Greenacre, 'The Childhood of the Artist," p. 58.
25. Greenacre, *The Quest for the Father*, p. 16.
26. Kurt Eissler, "Notes on the Environment of a Genius," in *The Psychoanalytic Study of the Child*, XIV, New York, 1959, p. 269.

5

ALIENATION AND INTEGRATION

(pages 143-178)

1. Jean-Paul Sartre, *Essays in Aesthetics*, New York, 1963, p. 61.
2. Quentin Bell, "Conformity and Nonconformity in the Fine Arts," in *Culture and Social Character*, S. M. Lipset and Leo Lowenthal, eds., New York, 1961, pp. 402-403.
3. *New York Post*, July 21, 1963.
4. Quoted by Alfred Kazin in *The Reporter*, January 31, 1963, p. 53.

6

THE ARTIST AND HIS PUBLICS:
THE AMBIGUITY OF SUCCESS

(pages 179-214)

1. *New York Times*, November 21, 1962.
2. *Philadelphia Inquirer*, February 2, 1963.
3. Alvin Shuster, "Stamps for Art's Sake," *New York Times Magazine*, September 20, 1964, p. 30.
4. *New York Times*, September 20, 1964.
5. José Ortega y Gasset, *The Dehumanization of Art*, Princeton, 1948, p. 5.
6. *New York Times*, November 21, 1962.
7. Virgil Thomson, *The State of Music*, New York, 1962, p. 36.
8. *Time*, December 8, 1961, p. 72.
9. John Canaday, *Embattled Critic*, New York, 1962, p. 187.

10. Thomson, *op. cit.*, p. 30.
11. Maurice Grosser, *The Painter's Eye,* New York, 1961, pp. 158-159.
12. Thomson, *op. cit.*, p. 19.
13. Canaday, *op. cit.*, pp. 187-188.

7

MUSEUMS AND DEALERS
(pages 215-250)

1. *New York Herald Tribune,* November 26, 1962.
2. Germain Seligman, *Oh! Fickle Taste,* New York, 1952, p. 1.
3. *Ibid.,* p. 21.
4. *The Art Market Guide and Forecaster,* 1963.
5. *Time,* January 25, 1963.
6. *A View of the Nation,* Henry M. Christman, ed., New York, 1960, pp. 72-76.
7. Patrick Heron, *The Changing Forms of Art,* New York, 1955, p. xiii.
8. Katherine Kuh, "The Fine Art of Art Dealing," *Saturday Review,* December 28, 1963, p. 31.

8

WOMEN ARTISTS: A NEW FORCE
(pages 251-278)

1. Cf. C. Wright Mills, *The Power Elite,* New York, 1956.
2. Havelock Ellis, *Man and Woman,* Boston, 1929, p. 366.
3. Ashley Montagu, *The Natural Superiority of Woman,* New York, 1954.
4. Rudi Blesh, *Modern Art USA,* New York, 1953, p. 291.
5. *Changing Times,* February 1964, p. 43.
6. Ellis, *op. cit.,* p. 368.
7. *Ibid.,* p. 376.
8. John Stuart Mill, *The Subjection of Women,* New York, 1911.
9. Sigmund Freud, " 'Civilized' Sexual Morality and Modern Nervousness," in *Collected Papers,* II, London, 1948, p. 93.
10. Montagu, *op. cit.,* p. 128.
11. Simone de Beauvoir, *The Second Sex,* New York, 1952, p. 699.

9

THE NEGRO ARTIST
(pages 279-304)

1. Margaret Butcher, *The Negro in American Culture,* New York, 1957, p. 169.
2. Richard Bardolph, *The Negro Vanguard,* New York, 1961, pp. 419-420.
3. Charles H. Thompson, "Problems in the Achievement of Adequate Educational Opportunity," in *Negro Education in America,* Virgil A. Clift and others, ed., New York, 1962, p. 177.

4. Ira De A. Reid, "The Relative Status of the Negro in the United States," *The Journal of Negro Education,* Vol. 22, No. 3 (1953), p. 446.
5. David Krech, Richard S. Crutchfield, and Egerton L. Ballachey, *Individual in Society,* New York, 1962, p. 314.
6. E. Franklin Frazier, *Black Bourgeoisie,* New York, 1962, p. 11.
7. Butcher, *op. cit.,* p. 165.
8. James Baldwin, "The Discovery of What It Means to Be an American," in *Nobody Knows My Name,* New York, 1961, p. 3.
9. James Baldwin, "A Fly in the Buttermilk," in *Nobody Knows My Name,* p. 83.
10. Erik Erikson, *Childhood and Society,* New York, 1950, pp. 213-214.
11. Charles E. Thompson, "The Thompson Modification of the Thematic Apperception Test," *Rorschach Research Exchange and Journal of Projective Techniques,* Vol. 13 (1949).
12. E. Franklin Frazier, *The Negro in the United States,* New York, 1949, p. 14.
13. *Ibid.,* pp. 328-329.
14. Erikson, *op. cit.,* p. 214.
15. Frazier, *The Negro in the United States,* p. 330.
16. Frazier, *Black Bourgeoisie,* p. 176.
17. Erikson, *op. cit.,* p. 214.
18. *Ibid.,* p. 216.
19. Quoted in Charles Childs, "Bearden: Identification and Identity," *Art News,* Vol. 63, No. 6 (1964), pp. 24-25, 54, 61-62.
20. *Ibid.,* p. 25.

I O

THE ARTIST: INSIDE OR OUTSIDE?

(pages 305-328)

1. *New York Times,* December 8, 1962.
2. *Harper's,* July 1964, p. 12.

APPENDIX

CREATIVE ENERGY: SEXUALITY
AND SUBLIMATION

pages (329-353)

1. Sigmund Freud, "The Resistances to Psychoanalysis," in *Collected Papers,* V, London, 1950, p. 169.
2. Ives Hendricks, *Facts and Theories of Psychoanalysis,* New York, 1948, pp. 364-365.
3. Edward Glover, *On the Early Development of Mind,* New York, 1956, p. 131.
4. *Ibid.*
5. Sigmund Freud, *Three Essays on the Theory of Sexuality,* New York, 1962, p. 22.

6. Sigmund Freud, " 'Civilized' Sexual Morality and Modern Nervousness," in *Collected Papers,* II, London, 1948, p. 82.
7. Sigmund Freud, "(B) The Libido Theory," in *Collected Papers,* V, London, 1950, pp. 132-133.
8. Freud, " 'Civilized' Sexual Morality and Modern Nervousness," pp. 91-92.
9. *Ibid.,* pp. 93-94.
10. Sigmund Freud, *The Ego and the Id,* New York, 1960, pp. 34-36.
11. Sigmund Freud, *An Outline of Psychoanalysis,* New York, 1949, p. 114.
12. Kurt Eissler, *Leonardo da Vinci,* New York, 1961, pp. 270-271.
13. Ernst Kris, *Psychoanalytic Explorations in Art,* New York, 1952, pp. 26-27.
14. Heinz Hartmann, Ernst Kris, and Rudolph M. Loewenstein, "Notes on the Theory of Aggression,'" in *The Psychoanalytic Study of the Child,* III/IV, New York, 1949, pp. 9-36.
15. Annie Reich in "Ernst Kris and the Gifted Adolescent Project," in *The Psychoanalytic Study of the Child,* XIII, New York, 1958, p. 60.
16. Leo S. Loomie, Victor H. Rosen, and Martin H. Stein in *ibid.,* p. 47.
17. *Ibid.,* pp. 50-51.
18. Kris, *op. cit.,* p. 59.
19. *Ibid.*
20. Kurt Eissler, *Goethe: A Psychoanalytic Study,* Detroit, 1963, p. 1387.
21. Ernest Jones, *Sigmund Freud: Four Centenary Addresses,* New York, 1956, p. 11.
22. Eissler, *Goethe,* pp. 1379, 1403.
23. Eissler, *Leonardo da Vinci,* p. 62.
24. *Ibid.,* p. 189.
25. *Ibid.*
26. Adrian Stokes, "Form in Art," in *New Directions in Psychoanalysis,* M. Klein and others, ed., New York, 1957, p. 413.
27. Eissler, *Goethe,* p. 1407.
28. *Ibid.,* p. 1406.
29. Eissler, *Leonardo da Vinci,* p. 63.
30. *Ibid.*
31. Richard and Editha Sterba, "Beethoven and His Nephew," *The International Journal of Psychoanalysis,* Vol. 33 (1952), pp. 2-3.
32. *Ibid.,* p. 3.
33. Eissler, *Goethe,* p. 1404.
34. *Ibid.,* p. 1415.
35. *Ibid.,* p. 1367.
36. Eissler, *Leonardo da Vinci,* p. 287.
37. Eissler, *Goethe,* p. 1365.
38. *Ibid.,* p. 1367.
39. Victor Erlich, *The Double Image,* Baltimore, 1964, p. 77.
40. *Ibid.,* p. 75.
41. Thomas Mann, *Death in Venice and Seven Other Stories,* New York, 1958, pp. 98-99.
42. Frederick J. Hacker, "On Artistic Production," in *Explorations in Psychoanalysis,* R. M. Lindner, ed., New York, 1953, p. 129.

Index

Abel, Lionel, 172

Abstract expressionism, 6, 21, 22, 27, 30, 31, 159, 160-161, 177, 205, 304

Abstracted model and offer of work, 137-141

Action painter, 62; action painting, 160-161

Affirmation of work, 151-153

Aldredge, John W., 52

Alienation, 7, 8-9, 29; and integration, 143-178; from society, 146, 148

Anomie in styles of art, 235-238

Applied art, rejection of, 153-158

Art: accessible to all in democracy, 3-4; combined with dentistry, 173-174; non-objective, 27; non-representational, 2, 29, 62, 159; organic part of premodern culture, 4; produced in every society, 103; representational, 62; revolution in American, 21; total involvement, 51; urban environment necessary, 18

Art Market Guide and Forecaster, 219

Art News, 58, 159, 209, 210, 237, 304

Art Students League, 121

Artist: as anarchist, 175; basic conflict, 69; compared with non-artist, 68-69, 92, 167; contradictory attitudes and ideas on self, 92; contrasted with beatnik, 112-113; disengagement, 148-151; personal qualities necessary, 70-78; as prophet, 175; self-image, 67-68; self-portrait, composite, 93-96

Artist and his publics: ambiguity of success, 181-214

Artist: inside or outside?, 307-328; making do, 308, 313; perils of subsidized art, 313-328

Arts Council, in England, 314, 316

Arts magazine, 58

Autonomy and perception, 165-170; early autonomy, 112

Baldwin, James, 293, 294, 302

Bardolph, Richard, 284-285

Barnes Foundation, 26

Barr, Alfred H., Jr., 165, 200, 210

Barthe, Richmond, 293

Bearden, Romare, 304

Beethoven, Ludwig von, 92, 339, 348-349

Bell, Quentin, 160, 161

Beres, David, 137

Berggruen Galleries, 220
Berlioz, Hector, 32
Bernfeld, S., 340
Bernier, Georg, 218
Black Bourgeoisie. See E. Franklin Frazier.
Blesh, Rudi, 254
Boas, Franz, 102
Bonheur, Rosa, 253, 254
Bouguereau, Adolphe William, 219
Bourdelle, Emile Antoine, 252
Brahms, Johannes, 135
Braque, Georges, 22, 45
Breakthrough to independence, 30-38
Breton, André, 22
Butcher, Margaret, 283, 289

Campbell, E. Simms, 293
Canaday, John, 48, 49, 195, 196, 209, 210
Carroll, Lewis, 135-136
Cassatt, Mary, 26, 253, 254
Cézanne, Paul, 26, 33, 34, 169
Childs, Charles, 304
Chirico, Giorgio di, 165
Cleveland Museum, 230
Collingwood, R. H., 73
Communists, 323
Confronting the "public," 191-193. *See also* Publics, four kinds.
Confronting success, 183-191
Cordier, Raymond, 218
Corot, J. B. C., 224
Courage, 87-89
Courbet, Gustave, 219
Creative arts, 31-32
Crosby, John, 218
Cubism, 25, 27, 29, 33
Cummings, E. E., 2

Dali, Salvador, 37
Dante Alighieri, 60
Davis, Kingsley, 42-43
Davis, Stuart, 48
Dawson, William L., 281
Dealer: acceptance of, 238-242; resentment of, 245-250; social and economic necessity of dealer, 242-245. *See also* Museums and dealers.
De Kooning, Elaine, 254; Willem, 13, 27, 28, 33, 37, 48, 49, 53, 54, 245, 269
Delacroix, Eugène, 315
De la Mare, Walter, 133
Derain, André, 165
Dewey, John, 74-75
Discipline and dedication, 85-87
Disenchantment with politics, 54
Donatello, 252
Drucker, Peter, 328
Dubuffet, Jean, 169
Duchamp, Marcel, 167

Eastman, Max, 314
"Ego" or confidence and conviction, 89-92
Eiduson, Bernice, 70, 84, 104-105
Eisenhower, Dwight D., 317, 318
Eissler, Kurt, 131, 140-141, 339, 340, 344-345, 346, 347, 348, 349-351, 353
Eliot, T. S., 60
Elkoff, Marvin, 13
Ellis, Havelock, 252, 253, 255-256
Ericson, Eric, 137, 294, 303
Erlich, Victor, 352
Ernst, Max, 22, 25

Falk, Robert, 327
Farrell, James T., 226

Faulkner, William, 226
Federal Bureau of Investigation, 323
Fine Arts Commission, 320
Fitzgerald, F. Scott, 226
Forge, Andrew, 20
Frankenthaler, Helen, 254
Frazier, E. Franklin, *Black Bourgeoisie,* 287, 299, 302
Freedom and independence, 81-82
Freud, Sigmund, 99, 130-131, 257, 329, 332-335, 339, 340, 341, 342, 343, 345, 346, 347, 348
Fulbright scholarship, 121

Galleries in New York, 158
Gauguin, Paul, 169
Generational conflict, 41-63; isolation of age groups, 42-45; resentment of "easy success," 48-49; resentment of market mentality of younger artists, 58; resentment of younger artists by elders, 45-48; resentment of younger artists' cynicism, 51. *See also* Love-hate syndrome.
G.I. Bill, 325-326
Gide, André, 227
Gifted Adolescent Project, 342
Glover, Edward, 332, 340
Goethe, Johann Wolfgang, 140-141, 339, 344, 348
Goffman, Erving, 51
Goodman, Paul, 159
Goodman, Walter, 221
Gorky, Arshile, 23, 44
Gorky, Bill, 44
Gottlieb, Adolph, 28
Goya, Francisco, 339
Grant, William, 281

Greenacre, Phyllis, 71, 76, 79-80, 84-85, 131-132, 134-135, 135-136, 137-138, 139, 353
Greenberg, Clement, 25, 209
Grosser, Maurice, 96
Guggenheim Foundation, 315; Museum, 230

Hacker, Frederick, 353
Hare, David, 28
Harper's, 57
Harper's Bazaar, 237
Harris, Mark, 59
Harrison, Ollie, 293
Hartigan, Grace, 254
Hartmann, Heinz, 71, 340, 353
Heckscher, August, 320
Hemingway, Ernest, 53, 226
Heron, Patrick, 234-235
Hess, Thomas, 209
Hirschorn collection, 230
Hitschmann, Edward, 135
Hofmann, Hans, 25, 37, 121, 122
Hudson, Derek, 136
Hughes, Langston, 280

Impressionists, 26, 29, 34, 35, 225
Income tax problems, 182
Ingres, J. A. Dominique, 315
Innocence, 92-93
Intelligence, 74-76

Jarrell, Randall, 3-4
Jean Santeuil. See Marcel Proust.
Jimson, Gulley, 172
Johns, Jasper, 6, 58
Johnson, William H., 293
Jones, Ernest, 345
Joyce, James, 227

Kafka, Franz, 319
Kandinsky, Wassily, 22
Kauffmann, Angelica, 253
Kennedy, John F., 317, 318, 320
Khrushchev, Nikita, 327
Klee, Paul, 22, 37
Klein, Melanie, 346
Kline, Franz, 44, 45, 48, 49, 53, 223, 230, 310
Klopfer, Bruno, 98-99
Kollwitz, Kaethe, 253
Kramer, Hilton, 21
Kretch, Crutchfield, and Ballachey, study of Negroes, 287
Kris, Ernst, 131, 132, 340, 341-342, 343-344, 346, 347, 348, 353
Kuh, Katherine, 240

Lascaux cave drawings, 33
Lassaw, Ibram, 28
Léger, Fernand, 22, 23-24, 25
Leonardo da Vinci, 131, 136, 223, 230, 266, 344, 347, 348
Levine, Jack, 47
Lewis, Sinclair, 226
Life magazine, 57, 58, 121, 209
Lincoln Center, 182
Lipchitz, 22
Lloyd, Frank, 240
Loewenstein, Rudolph, 340, 353
Louvre, 26, 117
Love-hate syndrome, 46
Luther, Martin, 137

Mailer, Norman, 159
Malraux, André, 84, 98, 116
Mann, Thomas, 227, 352
Market: growth of, 219-221; influence on styles, 222-224
Marlborough-Gerson Gallery, 240

Marx, Karl, 148
Matisse, Henri, 26, 45, 90
Matisse, Pierre, American dealer, 312
Meissonier, Jean Louis Ernest, 219
Metropolitan Museum of Art, 115, 133, 181, 233, 237
Michelangelo Buonarrati, 230, 252
Middle class life, rejection of, 170-175
Mill, John Stuart, 256
Mills, C. Wright, 159
Miró, Joan, 22, 25
Mitchell, Joan, 254
Mobius, P. J., 256, 257
"Mona Lisa," 181, 230
Mondrian, Piet, 22, 25, 154
Monet, Claude, 34, 92, 224, 339
Montagu, Ashley, 253, 257
Morisot, Berthe, 34
Motherwell, Robert, 28, 37, 44
Mumford, Lewis, 31-32
Murphy, Gardner, 133
Museum of Modern Art, 117, 163, 165, 182, 200, 229, 233, 237
Museums and dealers, 217-250; irrelevancy of taste in museum, 230-235; museum as purveyor of novelty, 224-230. *See also* Dealers.

"Nation of Art Collectors," 181
Negro artist, 281-304; burden of personality, 297-303; economic and socio-cultural poverty, 286-289; influence of history, 289-291; Negro's dilemma, 284-286; psychological problems, 291-296
Negro Vanguard, The, 285
Nevelson, Louise, 254
Newman, Barney, 44

New York: reasons for preference, 13-21; world art center, 13-14

New York School, 6, 11-38, 172; compared with Impressionists, 34-35

New York Times, 209, 210, 232, 327

New Yorker, 209, 232

Norman, Charles, 2

L'Oeil Gallery, 218

O'Keeffe, Georgia, 253

Origins: familial and cultural, 103-141; early appearance of talent, 104-105; early exposure to culture, 113-116; early freedom and model stimulus, 125-137; environment and education, 116-122; money as principal focus, 109-110; parental opposition, 108-116; parental recognition and acceptance, 106-108; resistance hardened during adolescence, 108

Ortega y Gasset, José, 181

Pederson, Carl-Henning, 185

Phidias, 252

Picasso, Pablo, 26, 33, 45, 60, 90, 117, 169, 223, 338

Pissaro, Camille, 34

Plato, 331

Pollock, Jackson, 27, 30, 35, 37, 53, 54, 62

Pop art, 49, 188, 228, 248

Prados, Miguel, 68, 94-95

Pravda, 327

Price, Vincent, 219-221, 239

Proust, Marcel, *Jean Santeuil,* 136-137

Psychoanalytic theories of art, 331-335

Publics, four kinds: buyers and collectors, 194-203; critics, 208-214; friends, 193-194; viewers, 203-208

Rauschenberg, Robert, 6

Reinhardt, Ad, 144, 159-160

Rembrandt van Rijn, 114, 181, 266, 339

Renoir, Pierre Auguste, 34

Rewald, John, 34

Rexroth, Kenneth, 60

Riesman, David, 160

Rivera, Diego, 351

Rockefeller, David, 200

Roe, Anne, 68, 70-71, 95, 98, 121, 124-125

Rorschach study, 94-95, 98-99

Rosenberg, Harold, 123-124, 209

Rothko, Mark, 28

Royal Academy, 95

Saint-Evrémond, 216

Sartre, Jean-Paul, 160

Schapiro, Meyer, 209, 348

Sears, Roebuck & Co., 219-221

Seligman, Germain, 218

Sense of responsibility and capacity for work, 73-74

Sensitivity, 79-80

Seurat, Georges, 26

Sexuality, "overt," in art, 335-353

Sharpe, Ella, 346

Sloan, John, 190

Smith, Logan Pearsall, 41

Social and psychological characteristics, 67-99

Socio-economic backgrounds, 122-125; mostly from lower-middle class, 122

Solitude and privacy, 82-85

Sterba, Richard, 340; Richard and Editha, 348
Stoddard, George, 96
Stokes, Adrian, 346
Subsidized art, perils of, 313-328
Success and its dangers, 158-165
Suffering, 76-78
Surrealism, 25

Talent, creativity, and genius, 96-99
Tallmer, Jerry, 164-165
Tanner, Henry, 293
Tate Gallery, 20
Taubman, Howard, 181-182
Thompson, Charles E., 294
Thompson, Virgil, 66, 183, 192
Time magazine, 58, 209, 210, 220
Tinguely, Jean Charles, 229
Titian, 120, 339
Tito, Marshall, 327
Tobey, Mark, 224-225
Tolstoy, Leo, 56
Toynbee, Arnold, 148
Troyon, Constant, 218

Valéry, Paul, 231
Van den Haag, Ernest, 221
Van Gogh, Vincent, 348
Vermeer, Johannes, 114
Vogue magazine, 274

Warner, Lloyd, 122
Weber, Max, 48
Whitney Museum, 172
Wilson, Robert N., 4
Wind, Edgar, 306
Witkin, Herman, 133
Wolfe, Thomas, 226
Women artists: male chauvinism, 258-261; a new force, 253-278; prejudice against female artists, 261-266; reasons for "female inferiority," 255-257; role conflict of the female artist, 267-272; costs of role conflicts, 272-278
WPA Arts Project, 21, 23, 24, 33, 159, 313, 322, 325
Wright, Richard, 302

Yunkers, Adja, 230

A Note on the Authors

BERNARD ROSENBERG was born in Detroit, Michigan, studied at the University of Michigan, and received his Ph.D. from the New School for Social Research. He is now Associate Professor of Sociology at the City University of New York and a member of the graduate faculty of the New School. He has been a Fulbright Professor at the University of Buenos Aires, a consultant to presidential committees on juvenile delinquency and youth mobilization, and a co-director of the Institute for the Social Study of the Arts. His books include *Values of Veblen; Mass Culture* (with David Manning White); *Sociological Theory; Mass, Class and Bureaucracy* (with Joseph Bensman); *Thorstein Veblen;* and *Mass Society in Crisis* (with Israel Gerver and F. William Howton).

NORRIS FLIEGEL was born in Beverly, Massachusetts, studied at Boston University and Harvard University, and received his Ed.D. from New York University. He is now Assistant Professor of Education at Hunter College and maintains a private practice of psychotherapy in New York City.